"*Radical Acceptance* offers us an invitation to embrace ourselves with all our pain, fear, and anxieties, and to step lightly yet firmly on the path of understanding and compassion."

—Thich Nhat Hanh

"*Radical Acceptance* offers gentle wisdom and tender healing, a most excellent medicine for our unworthiness and longing. Breathe, soften, and let these compassionate teachings bless your heart."

—Jack Kornfield, author of *A Path with Heart* and *After the Ecstasy, the Laundry*

"Tara Brach reminds us that no matter how wounded we are, we can choose to belong to life. *Radical Acceptance* is an invitation to heal our pain by accepting our heart."

—Rachel Naomi Remen, M.D., author of *Kitchen Table Wisdom* and *My Grandfather's Blessings*

"Tara Brach slillfully weaves together some of the most important new insights in contemporary psychotherapy with one of the central psychological insights of the Buddha: There is no part of ourselves that we need to exile from our awareness and our love. *Radical Acceptance* is a book, and a practice, that we all need."

—Stephen Cope, author of *Yoga and the Quest for the True Self*

"*Radical Acceptance* is an insightful, warmhearted, and important contribution to the emerging field of therapeutic mindfulness."

—Tara Bennett-Goleman, author of *Emotional Alchemy*

"If you are struggling with the feeling that you are not good enough, lovely enough, smart enough, or deserving enough, *Radical Acceptance* should be at the top of your reading list."

—Larry Dossey, M.D., author of *Healing Beyond the Body, Reinventing Medicine,* and *Healing Words*

"*Radical Acceptance* is one of the best guides to real meditation practice I've seen. Taking our bodies, our emotions and our whole human situations along, Tara shows us an awakened intelligence and kindness that are a radical freedom in themselves."

—Richard Freeman, internationally known Ashtanga yoga teacher

"Most of us react to suffering by mindlessly trying to avoid or escape the experience. This groundbreaking book provides an alternative pathway, one that enables us to accept ourselves and others with love and understanding."

**—G. Alan Marlatt, Ph.D., Director,
Addictive Behaviors Research Center, University of Washington**

RADICAL ACCEPTANCE

Embracing Your Life with the Heart of a Buddha

TARA BRACH, PH.D.

BANTAM BOOKS

NEW YORK TORONTO LONDON SYDNEY AUCKLAND

RADICAL ACCEPTANCE
A Bantam Book

PUBLISHING HISTORY
Bantam hardcover edition published June 2003
Bantam trade paperback edition / December 2004

Published by Bantam Dell
A Division of Random House, Inc.
New York, New York

Book design by Joseph Rutt

Library of Congress Catalog Card Number: 2002043794

ISBN 0-553-38099-0

Printed in the United States of America
Published simultaneously in Canada

BVG 20 19 18 17 16 15 14 13 12

To my parents, who have graced my life
with their generous, loving hearts.

CONTENTS

GUIDED REFLECTIONS AND MEDITATIONS

Out beyond ideas of wrongdoing and rightdoing,
there is a field. I'll meet you there.

When the soul lies down in that grass,
the world is too full to talk about.
Ideas, language, even the phrase each other
doesn't make any sense.

—Rumi

FOREWORD

You hold in your hands a beautiful invitation: to remember that it is possible to live your life with the wise and tender heart of a Buddha. In *Radical Acceptance,* Tara Brach graciously offers both healing words and transformative understanding, the fruits of her many years as a beloved meditation teacher and psychotherapist. Because she has immersed herself in the day-to-day work of reclaiming human dignity with heartfelt compassion and forgiveness, Tara's teachings are immediate and tangible; they melt the barriers that keep us from being fully alive.

In a stressful and competitive modern society that has fostered unworthiness, self-judgment and loss of the sacred for so many, the principles of Radical Acceptance articulated here are essential for reclaiming a joyful and liberated life. Through her rich stories and accounts of students and clients, through Tara's own personal journey and through the clear, systematic practices she offers, *Radical Acceptance* shows us wise ways to nurture ourselves, transform our sorrows and reclaim our wholeness.

Most importantly, *Radical Acceptance* reawakens us to our Buddha nature, the fundamental happiness and freedom that are the birthright of every human being. Read these pages slowly. Take their words and practices to heart. Let them guide you and bless your path.

Jack Kornfield
Spirit Rock Center
February 2003

RADICAL ACCEPTANCE

PROLOGUE

"SOMETHING IS WRONG WITH ME"

When I was in college, I went off to the mountains for a weekend of hiking with an older, wiser friend of twenty-two. After we set up our tent, we sat by a stream, watching the water swirl around rocks and talking about our lives. At one point she described how she was learning to be "her own best friend." A huge wave of sadness came over me, and I broke down sobbing. I was the furthest thing from my own best friend. I was continually harassed by an inner judge who was merciless, relentless, nit-picking, driving, often invisible but always on the job. I knew I would never treat a friend the way I treated myself, without mercy or kindness.

My guiding assumption was "Something is fundamentally wrong with me," and I struggled to control and fix what felt like a basically flawed self. I drove myself in academics, was a fervent political activist and devoted myself to a very full social life. I avoided pain (and created more) with an addiction to food and a preoccupation with achievement. My pursuit of pleasure was sometimes wholesome—in nature, with friends—but it also included an impulsive kind of thrill-seeking through recreational drugs, sex, and other adventures. In the eyes of the world, I was highly functional. Internally, I was anxious, driven and often depressed. I didn't feel at peace with any part of my life.

Feeling not okay went hand in hand with deep loneliness. In my early teens I sometimes imagined that I was living inside a transparent orb that separated me from the people and life around me. When I felt good about myself and at ease with others, the bubble thinned until it was like an invisible wisp of gas. When I felt bad about myself, the walls got so thick it seemed others must be able to see them. Imprisoned within, I felt hollow and achingly alone. The fantasy faded somewhat as I got older, but I lived with the fear of letting someone down or being rejected myself.

With my college friend it was different—I trusted her enough to be completely open. Over the next two days of hiking on high mountain ridges, sometimes talking with her, sometimes sitting in silence, I began to realize that beneath all my mood swings, depression, loneliness and addictive behavior lurked that feeling of deep personal deficiency. I was getting my first clear glimpse into a core of suffering that I would revisit again and again in my life. While I felt exposed and raw, I intuitively knew that by facing this pain I was entering a path of healing.

As we drove down from the mountains that Sunday night, my heart was lighter but still aching. I longed to be kinder to myself. I longed to befriend my inner experience and to feel more intimacy and ease with the people in my life.

When some years later these longings drew me to the Buddhist path, I found there the teachings and practices that enabled me to directly face my feelings of unworthiness and insecurity. They gave me a way of seeing clearly what I was experiencing and showed me how to relate to my life with compassion. The teachings of the Buddha also helped undo my painful and mistaken notion that I was alone in my suffering, that it was a personal problem and somehow my fault.

Over the past twenty years, as a psychologist and Buddhist teacher, I've worked with thousands of clients and students who have revealed how painfully burdened they feel by a sense of not being good enough. Whether our conversation takes place in the middle of a ten-day meditation retreat or during a weekly therapy session, the suffering—the fear of being flawed and unworthy—is basically the same.

For so many of us, feelings of deficiency are right around the corner. It doesn't take much—just hearing of someone else's accomplishments, being criticized, getting into an argument, making a mistake at work—to make us feel that we are not okay.

As a friend of mine put it, "Feeling that something is wrong with me is the invisible and toxic gas I am always breathing." When we experience our lives through this lens of personal insufficiency, we are imprisoned in what I call the trance of unworthiness. Trapped in this trance, we are unable to perceive the truth of who we really are.

A meditation student at a retreat I was teaching told me about an experience that brought home to her the tragedy of living in trance. Marilyn had spent many hours sitting at the bedside of her dying mother—reading to her, meditating next to her late at night, holding her hand and telling her over and over that she loved her. Most of the time Marilyn's mother remained unconscious, her breath labored and erratic. One morning before dawn, she suddenly opened her eyes and looked clearly and intently at her daughter. "You know," she whispered softly, "all my life I thought something was wrong with me." Shaking her head slightly, as if to say, "What a waste," she closed her eyes and drifted back into a coma. Several hours later she passed away.

We don't have to wait until we are on our deathbed to realize what a waste of our precious lives it is to carry the belief that something is wrong with us. Yet because our habits of feeling insufficient are so strong, awakening from the trance involves not only inner resolve, but also an active training of the heart and mind. Through

Buddhist awareness practices, we free ourselves from the suffering of trance by learning to recognize what is true in the present moment, and by embracing whatever we see with an open heart. This cultivation of mindfulness and compassion is what I call Radical Acceptance.

Radical Acceptance reverses our habit of living at war with experiences that are unfamiliar, frightening or intense. It is the necessary antidote to years of neglecting ourselves, years of judging and treating ourselves harshly, years of rejecting this moment's experience. Radical Acceptance is the willingness to experience ourselves and our life as it is. A moment of Radical Acceptance is a moment of genuine freedom.

The twentieth-century Indian meditation master Sri Nisargadatta encourages us to wholeheartedly enter this path of freedom: ". . . all I plead with you is this: *make love of your self perfect.*" For Marilyn, the final words of her dying mother awakened her to this possibility. As she put it, "It was her parting gift. I realized I didn't have to lose my life in that same way that she did. Out of love—for my mother, for life—I resolved to hold myself with more acceptance and kindness." We can each choose the same.

When we practice Radical Acceptance, we begin with the fears and wounds of our own life and discover that our heart of compassion widens endlessly. In holding ourselves with compassion, we become free to love this living world. This is the blessing of Radical Acceptance: As we free ourselves from the suffering of "something is wrong with me," we trust and express the fullness of who we are.

My prayer is that the teachings offered in this book may serve us as we awaken together. May we each discover the pure awareness and love that are our deepest nature. May our loving awareness embrace all beings everywhere.

ONE

THE TRANCE OF UNWORTHINESS

You will be walking some night . . .
It will be clear to you suddenly
that you were about to escape,
and that you are guilty: you misread
the complex instructions, you are not
a member, you lost your card
or never had one . . .

Wendell Berry

For years I've had a recurring dream in which I am caught in a futile struggle to get somewhere. Sometimes I'm running up a hill; sometimes I am climbing over boulders or swimming against a current. Often a loved one is in trouble or something bad is about to happen. My mind is speeding frantically, but my body feels heavy and exhausted; I move as if through molasses. I know I should be able to handle the problem, but no matter how hard I try, I can't get where I need to go. Completely alone and shadowed by the fear of failure, I am trapped in my dilemma. Nothing else in the world exists but that.

This dream captures the essence of the trance of unworthiness. In our dreams we often seem to be the protagonist in a pre-scripted drama, fated to react to our circumstances in a given way. We seem unaware that choices and options might exist. When we are in the trance and caught up in our stories and fears about how we might fail, we are in much the same state. We are living in a waking dream that completely defines and delimits our experience of life. The rest of the world is merely a backdrop as we struggle to get somewhere, to be a better person, to accomplish, to avoid making mistakes. As in a dream, we take our stories to be the truth—a compelling reality—and they consume most of our attention. While we eat lunch or drive home from work, while we talk to our partners or read to our children at night, we continue to replay our worries and plans. Inherent in the trance is the belief that no matter how hard we try, we are always, in some way, falling short.

Feeling unworthy goes hand in hand with feeling separate from others, separate from life. If we are defective, how can we possibly belong? It's a vicious cycle: The more deficient we feel, the more separate and vulnerable we feel. Underneath our fear of being flawed is a more primal fear that something is wrong with life, that something bad is going to happen. Our reaction to this fear is to feel blame, even hatred, toward whatever we consider the source of the problem: ourselves, others, life itself. But even when we have directed our aversion outward, deep down we still feel vulnerable.

Our feelings of unworthiness and alienation from others give rise to various forms of suffering. For some, the most glaring expression is addiction. It may be to alcohol, food or drugs. Others feel addicted to a relationship, dependent on a particular person or people in order to feel they are complete and that life is worth living. Some try to feel important through long hours of grueling work—an addiction that our culture often applauds. Some create outer enemies and are always at war with the world.

The belief that we are deficient and unworthy makes it difficult to trust that we are truly loved. Many of us live with an undercurrent of depression or hopelessness about ever feeling close to other people. We fear that if they realize we are boring or stupid, selfish or insecure, they'll reject us. If we're not attractive enough, we may never be loved in an intimate, romantic way. We yearn for an unquestioned experience of belonging, to feel at home with ourselves and others, at ease and fully accepted. But the trance of unworthiness keeps the sweetness of belonging out of reach.

The trance of unworthiness intensifies when our lives feel painful and out of control. We may assume that our physical sickness or emotional depression is our own fault—the result of our bad genes or our lack of discipline and willpower. We may feel that the loss of a job or a painful divorce is a reflection of our personal flaws. If we had only done better, if we were somehow different, things would have gone right. While we might place the blame on someone else, we still tacitly blame ourselves for getting into the situation in the first place.

Even if we ourselves are not suffering or in pain, if someone close to us—a partner or a child—is, we can take this as further proof of our inadequacy. One of my psychotherapy clients has a thirteen-year-old son who was diagnosed with attention deficit disorder. She has tried everything she can to help—doctors, diet, acupuncture, drugs, love. Yet still he suffers from academic setbacks and feels socially isolated. He is convinced that he is a "loser" and, out of pain and frustration, frequently lashes out in rage. Regardless of her loving efforts, she lives in anguish, feeling that she is failing her son and should be doing more.

The trance of unworthiness doesn't always show up as overt feelings of shame and deficiency. When I told a good friend that I was writing about unworthiness and how pervasive it is, she took issue. "My main challenge isn't shame, it's pride," she insisted. This woman, a successful writer and teacher, told me how easily she gets caught up in feeling superior to others. She finds many people mentally slow and boring. Because so many people admire her, she often rides surges of feeling special and important. "I'm embarrassed to admit it," she said, "and maybe *this* is where shame fits in. But I like having people look up to me . . . that's when I feel good about myself." My friend is playing out the flip side of the trance. She went on to acknowledge that during dry periods, times when she isn't feeling productive or useful or admired, she does slip into feeling unworthy. Rather than simply recognizing her talents and enjoying her strengths, she needs the reassurance of feeling special or superior.

Convinced that we are not good enough, we can never relax. We stay on guard, monitoring ourselves for shortcomings. When we inevitably find them, we feel even more insecure and undeserving. We have to try even harder. The irony of all of this is . . . where do we think we are going anyway? One meditation student told me that he felt as if he were steamrolling through his days, driven by the feeling that he needed to do more. In a wistful tone he added, "I'm skimming over life and racing to the finish line—death."

When I talk about the suffering of unworthiness in my meditation classes, I frequently notice students nodding their heads, some of them in tears. They may be realizing for the first time that the shame they feel is not their own personal burden, that it is felt by many. Afterward some of them stay to talk. They confide that feeling undeserving has made it impossible for them to ask for help or to let themselves feel held by another's love. Some recognize that their sense of unworthiness and insecurity has kept them from realizing their dreams. Often students tell me that their habit of feeling chronically deficient has made them continually doubt that they are meditating correctly and mistrust that they are growing spiritually.

A number of them have told me that, in their early days on the spiritual path, they assumed their feelings of inadequacy would be transcended through a dedicated practice of meditation. Yet even though meditation has helped them in important ways, they find that deep pockets of shame and insecurity have a stubborn way of persisting—sometimes despite decades of practice. Perhaps they have pursued a style of meditation that wasn't well suited for their emotional temperament, or perhaps they needed the additional support of psychotherapy to uncover and heal deep wounds. Whatever the reasons, the failure to relieve this suffering through spiritual practice can bring up a basic doubt about whether we can ever be truly happy and free.

BRINGING AN UNWORTHY SELF INTO SPIRITUAL LIFE

In their comments, I hear echoes of my own story. After graduating from college, I moved into an ashram, a spiritual community, and enthusiastically devoted myself to the lifestyle for almost twelve years. I felt I had found a path through which I could purify myself and transcend the imperfections of my ego—the self and its strategies. We were required to awaken every day at 3:30 A.M., take a cold shower, and then from four until six-thirty do a *sadhana* (spiritual discipline) of yoga, meditation, chanting and prayer. By breakfast time I often felt as if I were floating in a glowing, loving, blissful state. I was at one with the loving awareness I call the Beloved and experienced this to be my own deepest essence. I didn't feel bad or good *about* myself, I just felt good.

By the end of breakfast, or a bit later in the morning, my habitual thoughts and behaviors would start creeping in again. Just as they had in college, those ever-recurring feelings of insecurity and selfishness would let me know I was falling short. Unless I found the time for more yoga and meditation, I would often find myself feeling once again like my familiar small-minded, not-okay self. Then I'd go to bed, wake up and start over again.

While I touched genuine peace and openheartedness, my inner

critic continued to assess my level of purity. I mistrusted myself for the ways I would pretend to be positive when underneath I felt lonely or afraid. While I loved the yoga and meditation practices, I was embarrassed by my need to impress others with the strength of my practice. I wanted others to see me as a deep meditator and devoted yogi, a person who served her world with care and generosity. Meanwhile, I judged other people for being slack in their discipline, and judged myself for being so judgmental. Even in the midst of community, I often felt lonely and alone.

I had the idea that if I really applied myself, it would take eight to ten years to release all my self-absorption and be wise and free. Periodically I would consult teachers I admired from various other spiritual traditions: "So, how am I doing? What else can I do?" Invariably, they would respond, "Just relax." I wasn't exactly sure what they meant, but I certainly didn't think it could be "just relax." How could they mean that? I wasn't "there" yet.

Chögyam Trungpa, a contemporary Tibetan Buddhist teacher, writes, "The problem is that ego can convert anything to its own use, even spirituality." What I brought to my spiritual path included all my needs to be admired, all my insecurities about not being good enough, all my tendencies to judge my inner and outer world. The playing field was larger than my earlier pursuits, but the game was still the same: striving to be a different and better person.

In retrospect, it is no surprise that my self-doubts were transferred intact into my spiritual life. Those who feel plagued by not being good enough are often drawn to idealistic worldviews that offer the possibility of purifying and transcending a flawed nature. This quest for perfection is based in the assumption that we must change ourselves to belong. We may listen longingly to the message that wholeness and goodness have always been our essence, yet still feel like outsiders, uninvited guests at the feast of life.

A CULTURE THAT BREEDS SEPARATION AND SHAME

Several years ago a small group of Buddhist teachers and psychologists from the United States and Europe invited the Dalai Lama to join them in a dialogue about emotions and health. During one of their sessions, an American vipassana teacher asked him to talk about the suffering of self-hatred. A look of confusion came over the Dalai Lama's face. "What is self-hatred?" he asked. As the therapists and teachers in the room tried to explain, he looked increasingly bewildered. Was this mental state a nervous disorder? he asked them. When those gathered confirmed that self-hatred was not unusual but rather a common experience for their students and clients, the Dalai Lama was astonished. How could they feel that way about themselves, he wondered, when "everybody has Buddha nature."

While all humans feel ashamed of weakness and afraid of rejection, our Western culture is a breeding ground for the kind of shame and self-hatred the Dalai Lama couldn't comprehend. Because so many of us grew up without a cohesive and nourishing sense of family, neighborhood, community or "tribe," it is not surprising that we feel like outsiders, on our own and disconnected. We learn early in life that any affiliation—with family and friends, at school or in the workplace—requires proving that we are worthy. We are under pressure to compete with each other, to get ahead, to stand out as intelligent, attractive, capable, powerful, wealthy. Someone is always keeping score.

After a lifetime of working with the poor and the sick, Mother Teresa's surprising insight was: "The biggest disease today is not leprosy or tuberculosis but rather the feeling of not belonging." In our own society, this disease has reached epidemic proportions. We long to belong and feel as if we don't deserve to.

Buddhism offers a basic challenge to this cultural worldview. The Buddha taught that this human birth is a precious gift because it gives us the opportunity to realize the love and awareness that are our true nature. As the Dalai Lama pointed out so poignantly, *we all have Buddha nature.* Spiritual awakening is the process of recognizing our essential goodness, our natural wisdom and compassion.

In stark contrast to this trust in our inherent worth, our culture's guiding myth is the story of Adam and Eve's exile from the Garden of Eden. We may forget its power because it seems so worn and familiar, but this story shapes and reflects the deep psyche of the West. The message of "original sin" is unequivocal: Because of our basically flawed nature, we do not deserve to be happy, loved by others, at ease with life. We are outcasts, and if we are to reenter the garden, we must redeem our sinful selves. We must overcome our flaws by controlling our bodies, controlling our emotions, controlling our natural surroundings, controlling other people. And we must strive tirelessly—working, acquiring, consuming, achieving, e-mailing, overcommitting and rushing—in a never-ending quest to prove ourselves once and for all.

GROWING UP UNWORTHY

In their book *Stories of the Spirit,* Jack Kornfield and Christina Feldman tell this story: A family went out to a restaurant for dinner. When the waitress arrived, the parents gave their orders. Immediately, their five-year-old daughter piped up with her own: "I'll have a hot dog, french fries and a Coke." "Oh no you won't," interjected the dad, and turning to the waitress he said, "She'll have meat loaf, mashed potatoes, milk." Looking at the child with a smile, the waitress said, "So, hon, what do you want on that hot dog?" When she left, the family sat stunned and silent. A few moments later the little girl, eyes shining, said, "She thinks I'm real."

My own mother was visiting when I told this story at my weekly meditation group in Washington, D.C. As we drove home from the class together, she turned to me and in a teary voice said, "That little girl in the restaurant was me." She had never felt real in the eyes of her parents, she went on. Being an only child, she felt as if she was on the planet to be the person her parents wanted her to be. Her value rested solely on how well she represented them, and whether or not she made them proud. She was their object to manage and control, to show off or reprimand. Her opinions and feelings didn't matter because, as she said, they didn't see her as "her own person." Her identity was based on pleasing others and the fear of not being liked if she didn't. In her experience, she was not a real person who deserved respect and who, without any fabrication or effort, was lovable.

Most of the clients that come to see me are very aware of the qualities of an ideal parent. They know that when parents are genuinely present and loving, they offer their child a mirror for his or her goodness. Through this clear mirroring a child develops a sense of security and trust early in life, as well as the capacity for spontaneity and intimacy with others. When my clients examine their wounds, they recognize how, as children, they did not receive the love and understanding they yearned for. Furthermore, they are able to see in their relationships with their own children the ways they too fall short of the ideal—how they can be inattentive, judgmental, angry and self-centered.

Our imperfect parents had imperfect parents of their own. Fears, insecurities and desires get passed along for generations. Parents want to see their offspring make it in ways that are important to them. Or they want their children to be special, which in our competitive culture means more intelligent, accomplished and attractive than other people. They see their children through filters of fear (they might not get into a good college and be successful) and filters of desire (will they reflect well on us?).

As messengers of our culture, parents usually convey to their children that anger and fear are bad, that their natural ways of expressing their wants and frustrations are unacceptable. In abusive situations the message is "You are bad, you are in the way, you are worthless." But even in less extreme situations, most of us learn that our desires, fears and views don't carry much weight, and that we need to be different and better if we are to belong.

At a meditation retreat, one of my students, Jeff, told me about a memory that had suddenly arisen during his last sitting. When he was about seven years old he got hurt while playing with his big brother. Crying, Jeff ran to his mother, who was working in the kitchen. Following her around, he pleaded with her to set his brother straight. Suddenly she stopped and turned, hands on her hips, a look of irritation and disdain written all over her face. Jeff didn't remember what she actually said, but her whole expression told him, "Don't be so needy."

As an adult, Jeff came to understand that because his mother had grown up in a large and chaotic family, she had been taught that kids need to fend for themselves. When Jeff whined or acted clingy, she felt irritated by his "weakness." Our culture, with its emphasis on self-reliance and independence—qualities deemed especially important for men—had reinforced the message. Despite his understanding, Jeff still felt that having needs made him unappealing, undesirable, even bad. As is the case for so many of us, any feeling of need brought up shame. Even the word *needy* made him cringe.

By teaching us that something is fundamentally wrong with us, our parents and culture carry forth the message of Eden. As we internalize this view of our nature, we become ensnared in the trance of unworthiness. We can spend years and decades of our life trying to be who they wanted us to be, trying to be good enough to reenter the garden.

STRATEGIES TO MANAGE THE PAIN OF INADEQUACY

We do whatever we can to avoid the raw pain of feeling unworthy. Each time our deficiencies are exposed—to ourselves or others—we react, anxiously trying to cover our nakedness, like Adam and Eve after the fall. Over the years we each develop a particular blend of strategies designed to hide our flaws and compensate for what we believe is wrong with us.

We embark on one self-improvement project after another. We strive to meet the media standards for the perfect body and looks by coloring out the gray, lifting our face, being on a perpetual diet. We push ourselves to get a better position at work. We exercise, take enriching courses of study, meditate, make lists, volunteer, take workshops. Certainly any of these activities can be undertaken in a wholesome way, but so often they are driven by anxious undercurrents of "not good enough." Rather than relaxing and enjoying who we are and what we're doing, we are comparing ourselves with an ideal and trying to make up for the difference.

We hold back and play it safe rather than risking failure. When my son, Narayan, was around ten he went through a stage of being very reluctant to try new things. He wanted to be instantly good at everything, and if he sensed that an activity would take practice he felt intimidated. I would try talking about how all the most wonderful parts of living involve some risk and that mistakes are inevitable. My suggestions that he expand his horizons with tennis lessons or by participating in a music recital were always met with resistance. After one of my futile attempts to get him engaged in something new, Narayan's response was to quote Homer (Homer Simpson, that is): "Trying is the first step to failure."

Playing it safe requires that we avoid risky situations—which covers pretty much all of life. We might not take on leadership or responsibility at work, we might not risk being really intimate with others, we might hold back from expressing our creativity, from saying what we really mean, from being playful or affectionate.

We withdraw from our experience of the present moment. We pull away from the raw feelings of fear and shame by incessantly telling ourselves stories about what is happening in our life. We keep certain key themes going: what we have to do, what has not worked out, what trouble might lie ahead, how others are viewing us, how others are (or are not) meeting our needs, how others are interfering or letting us down. There's an old joke about a Jewish mother who sends a telegram to her son: "Start worrying, details to follow." Because we live in a free-floating state of anxiety, we don't even need a problem to set off a stream of disaster scenarios. Living in the future creates the illusion that we are managing our life and steels us against personal failure.

We keep busy. Staying occupied is a socially sanctioned way of remaining distant from our pain. How often do we hear that someone who has just lost a dear one is "doing a good job at keeping busy"? If we stop we run the risk of plunging into the unbearable feeling that we are alone and utterly worthless. So we scramble to fill ourselves—our time, our body, our mind. We might buy something new or lose ourselves in mindless small talk. As soon as we have a gap, we go on-line to check our e-mail, we turn on music, we get a snack, watch television—anything to help us bury the feelings of vulnerability and deficiency lurking in our psyche.

We become our own worst critics. The running commentary in our mind reminds us over and over that we always screw up, that others are managing their lives so much more efficiently and successfully. Often we take over where our parents left off, pointedly reminding ourselves of our flaws. As cartoonist Jules Feiffer puts it: "I grew up to have my father's looks, my father's speech patterns, my father's posture, my father's walk, my father's opinions and my mother's contempt for my father." Staying on top of what is wrong with us gives us the sense that we are controlling our impulses, disguising our weaknesses and possibly improving our character.

We focus on other people's faults. There is a saying that the world is divided into people who think they are right. The more inadequate we feel, the more uncomfortable it is to admit our faults. Blaming others temporarily relieves us from the weight of failure.

The painful truth is that all of these strategies simply reinforce the very insecurities that sustain the trance of unworthiness. The more we anxiously tell ourselves stories about how we might fail or what is wrong with us or with others, the more we deepen the grooves—the neural pathways—that generate feelings of deficiency. Every time we hide a defeat we reinforce the fear that we are insufficient. When we strive to impress or outdo others, we strengthen the underlying belief that we are not good enough as we are. This doesn't mean that we can't compete in a healthy way, put wholehearted effort into work or acknowledge and take pleasure in our own competence. But when our efforts are driven by the fear that we are flawed, we deepen the trance of unworthiness.

TURNING OTHERS INTO THE ENEMY

In most of this chapter we've focused on how, out of fear, we turn on ourselves and make ourselves the enemy, the source of the problem. We also project these feelings outward and make others the enemy. The greater the fear, the more intense our hostility. Our enemy becomes the parent who never really respected us, the boss who is preventing us from being successful, a political group that is taking away our power or a nation that threatens our lives. In this "us versus them" world, the unworthiness, the evil, is "out there."

Whether it is a family schism or a generations-long war between ethnic groups, creating an enemy imparts a sense of control—we feel superior, we feel right, we believe we are doing something about the problem. Directing anger at an enemy temporarily reduces our feelings of fear and vulnerability.

This is not to say that real threats don't exist. We can be a danger to ourselves; others can harm us. Yet if we lash out with hatred and violence, if we make war on ourselves or each other, we generate more fear, reactivity and suffering. Freeing ourselves from this trance of fear and alienation becomes possible only as we respond to our vulnerability with a wise heart.

THE ROOTS OF TRANCE—TAKING OURSELVES TO BE A SEPARATE SELF

More than twenty-five hundred years ago in northern India, the Buddha became fully enlightened after meditating through the night under the now-famous bodhi tree. He knew he had found the "Great Way" because his heart was open and free. Several days later, in his first sermon, he gave the teachings that were to set in motion a new era of human spiritual unfolding. At this pivotal moment in history, the Buddha taught that going to the root of our suffering and seeing it clearly was the beginning of freedom. This was his first noble truth: Suffering or discontent is universal, and fully recognizing its existence is the first step on the path of awakening.

During his all-night vigil, the Buddha looked deeply into his own suffering. His amazing insight was that *all suffering or dissatisfaction arises from a mistaken understanding that we are a separate and distinct self.* This perception of "selfness" imprisons us in endless rounds of craving and aversion. When our sense of being is confined in this way, we have forgotten the loving awareness that is our essence and that connects us with all of life.

What we experience as the "self" is an aggregate of familiar thoughts, emotions and patterns of behavior. The mind binds these together, creating a story about a personal, individual entity that has continuity through time. Everything we experience is subsumed into this story of self and becomes *my* experience. *I* am afraid. This is *my* desire. The contemporary Thai Buddhist meditation master and writer Ajahn Buddhadasa refers to this habit of attaching a sense of self to our experience as "I-ing" and "my-ing." We interpret everything we think and feel, and everything that happens to us, as in some way belonging to or caused by a self.

Our most habitual and compelling feelings and thoughts define the core of who we think we are. If we are caught in the trance of unworthiness, we experience that core as flawed. When we take life personally by I-ing and my-ing, the universal sense that "something is wrong" easily solidifies into "something is wrong with me."

When I look into my own feelings of unworthiness, sometimes I can't point to any significant way I'm actually falling short. Yet just this feeling of being a self, separate from others, brings up a fundamental assumption that I am not okay. This might be a background whisper that keeps me anxious and on the move. Or it might be a deep loneliness, as if being an "I" tears me away from belonging and wholeness.

Believing that we are separate, incomplete and at risk is not some malfunction of nature. Rather, this perception is an intrinsic part of our human experience—indeed of all life. Zen biologist and writer David Darling points out that even the earliest single-celled creatures "had established barriers, definite, sustainable boundaries, between themselves and the outside world . . . Thus, the foundations for dualism—the belief in the separation of self and the rest of the world—were laid." This existential sense of separation is the theme song of our amazingly diverse and mysterious world. One-celled entities push away what is threatening and go toward what will enhance them. We humans have these same basic reflexes, but our grasping and aversion play out through a dauntingly complex array of physical, mental and emotional activities, many of them outside our ordinary awareness.

Wanting and fearing are natural energies, part of evolution's design to protect us and help us to thrive. But when they become the core of our identity, we lose sight of the fullness of our being. We become identified with, at best, only a sliver of our natural being—a sliver that perceives itself as incomplete, at risk and separate from the rest of the world. If our sense of who we are is defined by feelings of neediness and insecurity, we forget that we are also curious, humorous and caring. We forget about the breath that is nourishing us, the love that unites us, the enormous beauty and fragility that is our shared experience in being alive. Most basically, we forget the pure awareness, the radiant wakefulness that is our Buddha nature.

"WITHOUT ANXIETY ABOUT IMPERFECTION"

Many people have told me that when they finally are able to see how long their life has been imprisoned by self-hatred and shame, they feel not only grief but also a sense of life-giving hope. Like waking up from a bad dream, when we can see our prison, we also see our potential.

The renowned seventh-century Zen master Seng-tsan taught that true freedom is being "without anxiety about imperfection." This means accepting our human existence and all of life as it is. Imperfection is not our personal problem—it is a natural part of existing. We all get caught in wants and fears, we all act unconsciously, we all get diseased and deteriorate. When we relax about imperfection, we no longer lose our life moments in the pursuit of being different and in the fear of what is wrong.

D. H. Lawrence described our Western culture as being like a great uprooted tree with its roots in the air. "We are perishing for lack of fulfillment of our greater needs," he wrote, "we are cut off from the great sources of our inward nourishment and renewal." We come alive as we rediscover the truth of our goodness and our natural connectedness to all of life. Our "greater needs" are met in relating lovingly with each other, relating with full presence to each moment, relating to the beauty and pain that is within and around us. As Lawrence said, "We must plant ourselves again in the universe."

Although the trance of feeling separate and unworthy is an inherent part of our conditioning as humans, so too is our capacity to awaken. We free ourselves from the prison of trance as we stop the war against ourselves and, instead, learn to relate to our lives with a wise and compassionate heart. This book is about the process of embracing our lives. When we learn to cultivate Radical Acceptance, we begin to rediscover the garden—a forgotten but cherished sense of wholeness, wakefulness and love.

Guided Reflection: Recognizing the Trance of Unworthiness

Recognizing the beliefs and fears that sustain the trance of unworthiness is the beginning of freedom. You might find it useful to pause for a few minutes to consider the parts of yourself that you habitually reject and push away.

Do I accept my body as it is?

Do I blame myself when I get sick?

Do I feel I am not attractive enough?

Am I dissatisfied with how my hair looks?

Am I embarrassed about how my face and body are aging?

Do I judge myself for being too heavy? Underweight? Not physically fit?

Do I accept my mind as it is?

Do I judge myself for not being intelligent enough? Humorous? Interesting?

Am I critical of myself for having obsessive thoughts? For having a repetitive, boring mind?

Am I ashamed of myself for having bad thoughts—mean, judgmental or lusty thoughts?

Do I consider myself a bad meditator because my mind is so busy?

Do I accept my emotions and moods as they are?

Is it okay for me to cry? To feel insecure and vulnerable?

Do I condemn myself for getting depressed?

Am I ashamed of feeling jealous?

Am I critical of myself for being impatient? Irritable? Intolerant?

Do I feel that my anger or anxiety is a sign that I am not progressing on the spiritual path?

Do I feel I'm a bad person because of ways I behave?

Do I hate myself when I act in a self-centered or hurtful way?

Am I ashamed of my outbursts of anger?

Do I feel disgusted with myself when I eat compulsively? When I smoke cigarettes or drink too much alcohol?

Do I feel that because I am selfish and often do not put others first, I am not spiritually evolved?

Do I feel as if I am always falling short in how I relate to my family and friends?

Do I feel something is wrong with me because I am not capable of intimacy?

Am I down on myself for not accomplishing enough—for not standing out or being special in my work?

Often we perceive the trance most clearly by recognizing how we want others to see us—and what we *don't* want them to see. Bring to mind someone you've spent time with recently—someone you like and respect but don't know well.

What do you most want this person to see about you (e.g., that you are loving, generous, attractive)?

What do you not *want this person to perceive about you (e.g., that you are selfish, insecure, jealous)?*

As you go through your day, pause occasionally to ask yourself, "This moment, do I accept myself just as I am?" Without judging yourself, simply become aware of how you are relating to your body, emotions, thoughts and behaviors. As the trance of unworthiness becomes conscious, it begins to lose its power over our lives.

TWO

AWAKENING FROM THE TRANCE: THE PATH OF RADICAL ACCEPTANCE

Last night, as I was sleeping,
I dreamt—marvelous error!—
that I had a beehive
here inside my heart.
And the golden bees
were making white combs
and sweet honey
from my old failures

Antonio Machado,
translated by Robert Bly

The curious paradox is that when I accept myself
just as I am, then I can change.

Carl Rogers

Mohini was a regal white tiger who lived for many years at the Washington, D.C. National Zoo. For most of those years her home was in the old lion house—a typical twelve-by-twelve-foot cage with iron bars and a cement floor. Mohini spent her days pacing restlessly back and forth in her cramped quarters. Eventually, biologists and staff worked together to create a natural habitat for her. Covering several acres, it had hills, trees, a pond and a variety of vegetation. With excitement and anticipation they released Mohini into her new and expansive environment. But it was too late. The tiger immediately sought refuge in a corner of the compound, where she lived for the remainder of her life. Mohini paced and paced in that corner until an area twelve by twelve feet was worn bare of grass.

Perhaps the biggest tragedy in our lives is that freedom is possible, yet we can pass our years trapped in the same old patterns. Entangled in the trance of unworthiness, we grow accustomed to caging ourselves in with self-judgment and anxiety, with restlessness and dissatisfaction. Like Mohini, we grow incapable of accessing the freedom and peace that are our birthright. We may want to love other people without holding back, to feel authentic, to breathe in the beauty around us, to dance and sing. Yet each day we listen to inner voices that keep our life small. Even if we were to win millions of dollars in the lottery or marry the perfect person, as long as we feel not good enough, we won't be able to enjoy the possibilities before us. Unlike Mohini, however, we can learn to recognize when we are keeping ourselves trapped by our own beliefs and fears. We can see how we are wasting our precious lives.

The way out of our cage begins with *accepting absolutely everything* about ourselves and our lives, by embracing with wakefulness and care our moment-to-moment experience. By accepting absolutely everything, what I mean is that we are aware of what is happening within our body and mind in any given moment, without trying to control or judge or pull away. I do not mean that we are putting up with harmful behavior—our own or another's. *This is an inner process of accepting our actual, present-moment experience.* It means feeling sorrow and pain without resisting. It means feeling desire or dislike for someone or something without judging ourselves for the feeling or being driven to act on it.

Clearly recognizing what is happening inside us, and regarding what we see with an open, kind and loving heart, is what I call Radical Acceptance. If we are holding back from any part of our experience, if our heart shuts out any part of who we are and what we feel, we are fueling the fears and feelings of separation that sustain the trance of unworthiness. Radical Acceptance directly dismantles the very foundations of this trance.

Radical Acceptance flies in the face of our conditioned reactions. When physical or emotional pain arises, our reflex is to resist it not only by stiffening our body and contracting our muscles, but also by contracting our mind. We lose ourselves in thoughts about what is wrong, how long it will last, what we should do about it and how the pain reflects our unworthiness. A physical pain, such as a backache or a migraine, might turn into a commentary on how we don't know how to take care of ourselves, how we don't eat well or exercise enough. The pain might make us feel like a victim; it might tell us we can't count on our body, that things will always go wrong. In the same way, we amplify emotional pain with our judgments and stories. Feeling fear or anger or jealousy means something is wrong with us, that we are weak or bad.

When we get lost in our stories, we lose touch with our actual experience. Leaning into the future, or rehashing the past, we leave the living experience of the immediate moment. Our trance deepens as we move through the day driven by "I have to do more to be okay" or "I am incomplete; I need more to be happy." These "mantras" reinforce the trance-belief that our life should be different from what it is.

When things are going well, we question whether we deserve it, or fear that now something bad is bound to happen. No sooner do we take a bite of our favorite flavor of ice cream than we start calculating how much more we can eat without feeling too guilty or piling on the pounds. We stand in a beautiful landscape and worry because we have run out of film or start thinking that we really should move to the country. When we are meditating, we experience a delicious stretch of tranquility and peace, and then immediately begin wondering how to keep it going. Our enjoyment is tainted by anxiety about keeping what we have and our compulsion to reach out and get more.

UNFOLDING THE WINGS OF ACCEPTANCE

When we are caught in the trance of unworthiness, we do not clearly recognize what is happening inside us, nor do we feel kind. Our view of who we are is contorted and narrowed and our heart feels hardened against life. As we lean into the experience of the moment—releasing our stories and gently holding our pain or desire—Radical Acceptance begins to unfold. The two parts of genuine acceptance—seeing clearly and holding our experience with compassion—are as interdependent as the two wings of a great bird. Together, they enable us to fly and be free.

The wing of clear seeing is often described in Buddhist practice as mindfulness. This is the quality of awareness that recognizes exactly what is happening in our moment-to-moment experience. When we are mindful of fear, for instance, we are aware that our thoughts are racing, that our body feels tight and shaky, that we feel compelled to flee—and we recognize all this without trying to manage our experience in any way, without pulling away. Our attentive presence is unconditional and open—we are willing to be with whatever arises, even if we wish the pain would end or that we could be doing something else. That wish and that thought become part of what we are accepting. Because we are not tampering with our experience, mindfulness allows us to see life "as it is." This recognition of the truth of our experience is intrinsic to Radical Acceptance: *We can't honestly accept an experience unless we see clearly what we are accepting.*

The second wing of Radical Acceptance, compassion, is our capacity to relate in a tender and sympathetic way to what we perceive. Instead of resisting our feelings of fear or grief, we embrace our pain with the kindness of a mother holding her child. Rather than judging or indulging our desire for attention or chocolate or sex, we regard our grasping with gentleness and care. Compassion honors our experience; it allows us to be intimate with the life of this moment *as it is.* Compassion makes our acceptance wholehearted and complete.

The two wings of clear seeing and compassion are inseparable; both are essential in liberating us from the trance. They work together, mutually reinforcing each other. If we are rejected by someone we love, the trance of unworthiness may ensnare us in obsessive thinking, blaming the one who hurt us and at the same time believing that we were jilted because we are defective. We may feel caught in a relentless swing between explosive anger and wrenching grief and shame. The two wings of Radical Acceptance free us from this swirling vortex of reaction. They help us find the balance and clarity that can guide us in choosing what we say or do.

If we were to bring only the wing of mindfulness to our process of Radical Acceptance, we might be clearly aware of the aching in our heart, the flush of rage in our face; we might clearly see the stories we are telling ourselves—that we are a victim, that we will always be alone and without love. But we might also compound our suffering by feeling angry with ourselves for getting into the situation in the first place. This is where the wing of compassion joins with mindfulness to create a genuinely healing presence. Instead of pushing away or judging our anger or despondency, compassion enables us to be softly and kindly present with our open wounds.

In the same way, mindfulness balances compassion. If our heartfelt caring begins to bleed over into self-pity, giving rise to another story line—we tried so hard but didn't get what we so dearly wanted—mindfulness enables us to see the trap we're falling into.

Both wings together help us remain in the experience of the moment, just as it is. When we do this, something begins to happen—we feel freer, options open before us, we see with more clarity how we want to proceed. Radical Acceptance helps us to heal and move on, free from unconscious habits of self-hatred and blame.

While the ground of Radical Acceptance is our moment-to-moment experience, we can bring the same clear and kind attention to the patterns of thoughts and feelings, behaviors and events that shape our life experience. We become more aware of the intentions that motivate our behavior. We also become aware of the consequences of our actions, as they affect both ourselves and others. In Buddhist psychology, including this larger view in an accepting awareness is called "clear comprehension."

Suppose that we become aware that we are regularly losing our temper and treating our children in a disrespectful, disparaging way. We can begin examining our intentions, opening with acceptance to the thoughts and feelings that arise as we do so. Perhaps we realize that we want to push our children away because we feel too stressed to handle their needs: "I'm sinking and trying to save my own life." Along with this thought we might feel a tightness in our belly that spreads like a wave and grips at our throat. We might also look and see the actual effect of our behavior on our children. Have they withdrawn from us? As we notice that our children are becoming secretive and fearful around us, we might feel in our chest a rising sense of sorrow. We also notice the effect our angry behavior has on our own body and mind, how isolated or bad we feel after we impulsively lash out.

The larger view offered by clear comprehension invariably leads us back to our deepest intention. *We don't want to suffer or cause suffering.* We might recognize that, more than anything, we want our children to know how much we love them. This longing too is met with clear seeing and kindness. In this way, by regarding the entire context of our circumstances with Radical Acceptance, we become increasingly able to align our actions with our heart.

Since nonacceptance is the very nature of the trance, we might wonder how, when we feel most stuck, we take the first step toward Radical Acceptance. It can give us confidence to remember that the Buddha nature that is our essence remains intact, no matter how lost we may be. *The very nature of our awareness is to know what is happening. The very nature of our heart is to care.* Like a boundless sea, we have the capacity to embrace the waves of life as they move through us. Even when the sea is stirred up by the winds of self-doubt, we can find our way home. We can discover, in the midst of the waves, our spacious and wakeful awareness.

We lay the foundations of Radical Acceptance by recognizing when we are caught in the habit of judging, resisting and grasping, and how we constantly try to control our levels of pain and pleasure. We lay the foundations of Radical Acceptance by seeing how we create suffering when we turn harshly against ourselves, and by remembering our intention to love life. As we let go of our stories of what is wrong with us, we begin to touch what is actually happening with a clear and kind attention. We release our plans or fantasies and arrive openhanded in the experience of this moment.

Whether we feel pleasure or pain, the wings of acceptance allow us to honor and cherish this ever-changing life, as it is.

FACING THE ANGUISH OF TRANCE

When I first started practicing yoga and meditation I didn't realize that acceptance was at the heart of spiritual life. I was only partly aware of how my feelings of never being good enough were keeping me from the peace and freedom I longed for. In the end, it took an experience that broke me apart emotionally to awaken from the habits and conditioning of years. Although the outer circumstances of my personal story were unusual, many people have told me they recognize the inner drama as their own.

By the time I was in my late twenties, I had lived for eight years in the spiritual community I joined after college. In addition to teaching regular classes in yoga and meditation, I was going to school to get a doctorate in clinical psychology and seeing clients in a full-time counseling practice. This meant I was often stressfully stretched between my life in the "outside world" and life in the ashram. I was sometimes chastised by my teacher for not giving more energy to the community, and I often felt guilty that I was spread so thin. But I valued both worlds and couldn't imagine giving up either.

At the suggestion of our teacher, I had married a man from our spiritual community several years before. From our first days together we longed to have a child. Although my life was pulled in so many directions, when I finally got pregnant, we were thrilled that our dream was coming true. We agreed that it would be a good time for me to take a month off from my therapy practice for some rest and spiritual nourishment. I decided to spend the time at a yoga and meditation retreat being led by our teacher in the desert of Southern California.

Two weeks into the retreat I started bleeding heavily. My friends took me to a nearby hospital where my dream of motherhood ended in miscarriage. I was filled with grief over losing the baby. As I lay in the hospital bed I struggled to make sense of what had gone wrong. Could the strenuous yoga and intense summer heat have been too much for me? When I got back to our retreat site, I left a phone message for my teacher telling him what had happened and mentioning my concerns. I didn't hear back from him.

I spent the next two days in bed, recovering, grieving, praying. On the third day I decided to attend the daily gathering where the teacher would be giving a talk. I felt I could use the inspiration, and I knew I would feel comforted being with my spiritual family.

It was a hot desert evening and several hundred of us sat under a huge open tent, quietly meditating, waiting for our teacher to arrive. When we saw his car pull up, we all stood and began chanting a song of devotion. Trailed by his entourage of robed yogis, he entered the tent and settled in front on cushions that matched the orange and pink of the setting sun. Our chant ended and we sat down, watching quietly as he ate a cookie and some grapes from a carefully prepared tray of food. His gaze swept the sea of upturned faces, each eagerly awaiting his inspiration. With a sudden start, I realized he was staring directly at me. Breaking the silence, he called out my name, the Sanskrit name he had given me years before when I committed myself to following his teachings. The sound of his voice rang in my ears as he asked me to stand up.

Sometimes in such gatherings he would publicly address a particular student, so I thought he might be checking to see how I was doing. Instead, without any prelude, he declared in a harsh tone that I had caused my baby's death by being so professionally ambitious and ego centered. I felt as if I had been kicked in the stomach—the shock of pain twisted my insides. I stood frozen and numb as he continued, telling me in crude language that I had been willing to have sex but did not really want a child. This must be a bad dream. Certainly he had criticized me privately for my life outside the ashram, but never viciously, never with such rage and contempt.

I sat down burning with shame. While my doubts about him had grown over the past few years, my trust was now fully betrayed. A raw and deep hole of pain began to swallow up everything in me. Trembling, I listened without comprehension as his voice droned on somewhere in the background.

When the talk was over and his car drove off several friends embraced me, awkwardly searching for the right words. I could see the confusion in their eyes: His teaching must have been given in this way to serve a spiritual purpose; our teacher couldn't be wrong . . . yet something didn't seem right. I was grateful for their comfort, but mostly I just wanted to disappear. Years before I had read a story about a young, injured soldier who, after returning from battle, was rumored to be a traitor and banished from his village. He could feel everyone watching, even pitying him, as he limped away with his small bag of clothes and food. That's what I felt like now. Humiliated and unreachable, I tried to avoid the eyes of fellow yogis as I made my way to the edge of the crowd. I felt as if all 150 of them either sat in judgment or pitied me. I desperately wanted to be alone—feeling this wretched, how could I be with anyone?

Through tears, I found my way to a small sanctuary nestled in a circle of Joshua trees. Sitting on the hard, bare floor, I sobbed aloud for hours. How could this have happened? My baby was gone and my teacher had condemned me. Was he right? My whole body told me he was wrong about the baby. But what was it about me that made him lash out so angrily when I was clearly so vulnerable? Maybe he had been offended by the phone message I left and believed I was challenging the wisdom of his program and teachings.

Maybe he knew I harbored doubts about him, that I didn't fully trust him. But why so venomous, so hateful? Was I really as bad as he said?

My heart breaking with fear and grief, I felt severed from my world and estranged from my own being. Was I on the right spiritual path? How could I continue to belong to a community so unquestioningly devoted to such a teacher? What would happen to my marriage if I could no longer follow this path? Could I bear to lose my spiritual family, a whole way of life, by leaving?

As the world closed in around me, an old and familiar despair took hold. Not only had his words flung me into a pit of my own ugliness, now the voices inside me were confirming that I was fundamentally flawed. For as long as I could remember I had been trying to prove my worth. I remembered myself as a teenager, debating with my lawyer father at the dinner table, feeling so proud—and relieved—when he was impressed by a persuasive argument. My heart sank as I recalled how I had played out this same routine with my teachers or others in authority. When images of my mother arose—her lying in bed reading a mystery novel, gin and tonic by her side—I felt flooded by memories of her struggle with depression and anxiety. Maybe my compulsion to appear strong and together was a way of avoiding those same currents in myself. Was I even a caring person? Maybe helping clients or friends was merely a way of getting appreciation or recognition. All my striving—to get my doctorate, to be a good yogi, to be *good*—all fit into this story of an insecure and defective person. Nothing about me felt pure or trustworthy.

In anguish and desperation, I reached out as I had many times before to the presence I call the Beloved. This unconditionally loving and wakeful awareness had always been a refuge for me. As I whispered "Beloved" and felt my yearning to belong to this loving awareness, something began to happen. It was subtle at first, just a feeling that I wasn't so lost and alone. Instead of being entirely immersed in a cauldron of suffering, I was beginning to sense an openness and tenderness within and around me. My world was becoming more spacious.

Through the long hours of the night I moved between the pain of my wounds and this growing openness. Each time one of those condemning voices tried to take over, when I could remember that caring presence, I found I could hear the judgments without believing them. When stories arose of times when I had acted selfishly or pretended to be something I wasn't, I could release the thoughts and simply feel the aching bruise in my heart. As I opened to pain without resisting it, everything in my experience softened and became more fluid.

In my mind a new voice arose: *I want to accept myself completely,* even if I am as flawed as my teacher claimed. Even if my striving and insecurity meant I was "caught up in my ego," I wanted to hold myself warmly, honor myself, not condemn myself. Even if I was selfish and critical, I wanted to accept those aspects of myself unconditionally. I wanted to stop the ceaseless monitoring and criticizing.

I found myself praying: "May I love and accept myself just as I am." I began to feel as if I were gently cradling myself. Every wave of life moving through me belonged and was acceptable. Even the voice of fear, the one that told me "something is wrong with me," was acceptable and could not taint this deep and genuine caring.

THE SUFFERING THAT OPENS US TO RADICAL ACCEPTANCE

My mother was one of several alumnae selected on the basis of life achievement to address a class of graduating seniors at Barnard College. One day, just before her seventy-fifth birthday, she received a call from the student assigned to interview her. The young reporter began by complimenting my mother for her work in heading the large nonprofit organization that was doing so much to serve people suffering from alcoholism. "When she asked how I got into this fascinating field," my mother later wryly commented to me, "I said to this earnest undergrad, 'Barbara, dear, I *drank* my way in.'"

During my childhood my mother had used alcohol to numb her emotional pain. Increasingly anxious and miserable, she found meaning and purpose only in her love for her family. Yet by the time I was sixteen, she could no longer avoid the fact that those of us closest to her were in distress over her drinking. None of her well-worn modes of denial, of being secretive or trying to please others worked anymore. Her life was fully out of control. My mother was hitting bottom.

The twelve-step program of Alcoholics Anonymous (AA) talks about "hitting bottom" as the turning point where genuine recovery from addiction becomes possible. With the support of AA, my mother was able to acknowledge and respond to her disease. By facing her suffering directly, by accepting and opening to her insecurity and shame, she reconnected with meaning in her life. Through her years of recovery she began to move beyond her identity as that little girl who was unreal and undeserving of attention. She learned that belonging didn't depend on her efforts to please others. Now her work and way of relating to others arise from a deep and genuine well of caring. But to awaken from her trance, my mother had to stop running and accept her pain.

The poet Rumi saw clearly the relationship between our wounds and our awakening. He counseled, "Don't turn away. Keep your gaze on the bandaged place. That's where the light enters you." When we look directly at the bandaged place without denying or avoiding it, we become tender toward our human vulnerability. Our attention allows the light of wisdom and compassion to enter.

In this way, times of great suffering can become times of profound spiritual insight and opening. Nearly all of us have faced seasons in our life where everything seemed to be falling apart. At these times, all the beliefs upon which we based our life are torn from their moorings; we thought we understood how to live life but now we feel lost in a stormy sea. As the storm quiets, we begin to see our life with freshness and a striking clarity.

Over the years, I've come to see my experience at the desert retreat less as a betrayal by my teacher than as a window into how much I had betrayed myself. In the face of his attack, my habitual defensive strategies crumbled, and I hit bottom. While I was plunged into excruciating pain, it served to reveal the pain of unworthiness I had been living with for years. Fear of being a flawed person lay at the root of my trance, and I had sacrificed many moments over the years in trying to prove my worth. Like the tiger Mohini, I inhabited a self-made prison that stopped me from living fully. Radical Acceptance of all my feelings and fears of imperfection was the only way I could free myself. By attending to the bandaged place—embracing the pain I had been running from—I began to trust myself and my life.

COMMON MISUNDERSTANDINGS ABOUT RADICAL ACCEPTANCE

The practice of Radical Acceptance runs at such crosscurrents to our culture of nonacceptance that it can be difficult to understand. It may sound as if I'm talking about resignation or self-indulgence, or excusing bad behavior: "I am practicing Radical Acceptance, so don't judge me for not taking responsibility at work or being unpleasant and insensitive at home." Because Radical Acceptance is such a powerful practice, I'd like to examine these areas of potential confusion in more detail.

Radical Acceptance is not resignation. The greatest misunderstanding about Radical Acceptance is that if we simply accept ourselves as we are, we will lose our motivation to change and grow. Acceptance can be misconstrued as an excuse for persisting in bad habits: "That's just the way I am. Take it or leave it." Or we might want to change in positive ways, but conclude: "I am the way I am, I'll never change anyway." Acceptance might suggest that we resign ourselves to being exactly as we are, which often enough means "not good enough." However, as psychologist Carl Rogers's seminal insight proclaims: "The curious paradox is that when I accept myself just as I am, then I can change." Our deepest nature is to awaken and flower. I have discovered again and again that bringing Radical Acceptance to any part of our experience is the fundamental shift that opens the way to genuine, lasting change. This book offers many examples of how such change unfolds when a seemingly intractable situation or deeply entrenched habit is met with Radical Acceptance.

Radical Acceptance does not mean defining ourselves by our limitations. It is not an excuse for withdrawal. Maybe we tell ourselves, for instance, that we don't have the credentials or experience to suit a job we really want, so we're not even going to apply. Maybe we conclude that, based on our past history, we're not cut out for intimate relationships, and so we're just staying single. While there may be some truth in our assessments, Radical Acceptance means bringing a clear, kind attention to our capacities and limitations without giving our fear-based stories the power to shut down our lives.

The same applies to physical challenges. What if we were to get into a car accident and end up paralyzed from the waist down? If we're told that we may never walk again, does acceptance mean that we hopelessly resign ourselves to our fate? Do we give up on the possibility of having a full and happy life? Radical Acceptance wouldn't mean denying our enormous grief about losing the freedom to move on our own. We would fully honor our feelings and responses. We would honestly assess the immediate effect our new limitations would have on our work, our sexuality, our parenting, our household tasks. But Radical Acceptance also means not overlooking another important truth: the endless creativity and possibility that exist in living. By accepting the truth of change, accepting that we don't know how our life will unfold, we open ourselves to hope so that we can move forward with vitality and will. As so beautifully modeled by actor Christopher Reeve after he was paralyzed in a riding accident, we can throw our full spirit into recovery—we can "go for it" in physical therapy, in sustaining rich relationships with others, in growing and learning from whatever we experience. In fact, through his efforts Mr. Reeve has discovered a level of recovery formerly deemed impossible. By meeting our actual experience with the clarity and kindness of Radical Acceptance, we discover that whatever our circumstances, we remain free to live creatively, to love fully.

Radical Acceptance is not self-indulgence. It does not say, "I accept that I have this lust or craving, and therefore I'll act on it." While it's important not to deny or suppress our desires, it's also important to be aware of what motivates us and the effects of our behavior. If we are addicted to nicotine, for example, Radical Acceptance doesn't mean that each time we feel like having a cigarette, we go ahead and light up. Rather, we bring clear seeing and compassion to the craving and tension we feel when we "have to have another smoke." We notice the stories that convince us we need a break from the stress we're under. We feel the agitation in our body and taste the memory of tobacco in our mouth. We read the warning label without denying the truth that smoking harms us. If we do have the next cigarette, we don't indulge our justifications or our guilt; we notice them arise and accept them mindfully. Meeting the entire process of smoking with the wakefulness and kindness of Radical Acceptance can move us toward wiser choices.

Radical Acceptance does not make us passive. A friend of mine, who is an environmental activist, recently told me if she *accepted* the degradation of our environment, she would no longer be an active agent for change. An abused woman I saw in therapy told me if she *accepted* the way her husband was treating her, she would lose her capacity to take care of herself. Students often challenge me: Wouldn't Radical Acceptance mean accepting Hitler's mass extermination of people, or simply allowing racism, war and famine to exist in the world? Does Radical Acceptance mean we don't respond to suffering in the world?

When we feel outrage at human atrocities or despair over the degradation of our environment, we are powerfully and rightfully moved to do something about them. When we see how our own behavior or that of others causes suffering, we are naturally compelled to initiate change. Throughout our lives, these strong responses guide us to pursue spiritual practices and healing therapies, to choose political affiliations, to decide whom we spend time with, what projects to undertake and how to raise our children. Yet there is a difference between actions and decisions that arise from Radical Acceptance and those that reflexively spring from our grasping after certain outcomes and our fear of certain consequences.

Radical Acceptance acknowledges our own experience in this moment as the first step in wise action. Before acting or reacting, we allow ourselves to feel and accept our grief for how the earth has been polluted, our anger about the destruction of wildlife, our shame about how we have been mistreated, our fear about what others may think about us, our guilt about our own insensitivity. No matter what the situation, our immediate personal experience is the fundamental domain of Radical Acceptance. This is where we cultivate the genuine wakefulness and kindness that underlie effective action.

Some of the most revered social activists in the world based their work in Radical Acceptance. Gandhi in India, Aung San Suu Kyi in Burma, Nelson Mandela in Africa—all underwent the suffering of imprisonment and faced the powerlessness, loneliness and discomfort of their oppression. With clear comprehension they saw the potential suffering of angry reactivity, and remained mindful of their intention to benefit others. By accepting rather than denying or reacting to their own suffering, they freed themselves to work without bitterness or self-pity for peace and justice. These and many others model the power of placing Radical Acceptance at the heart of the effort to alleviate suffering.

Radical Acceptance doesn't mean accepting a "self." Sometimes when I talk to students of Buddhism about accepting and loving ourselves, they ask me how this fits with the Buddhist teaching of "anatta," or no-self. Doesn't the very idea of self-acceptance affirm a mistaken notion of self? As the Buddha taught, our habitual perception of self is a mental construct—the idea of an entity who causes things to happen, who is victimized, who controls the show. When we say, "I accept myself as I am," we are not accepting a story about a good or bad self. Rather, we are accepting the immediate mental and sensory experiences we interpret as self. We are seeing the familiar wants and fears, the judging and planning thoughts as a part of the flow of life. Accepting them in this way actually enables us to recognize that experience is impersonal and frees us from the trap of identifying ourselves as a deficient and limited self.

I like to remind students that *radical* is derived from the Latin word *radix,* meaning "going to the root or origin." Radical Acceptance enables us to return to the root or origin of who we are, to the source of our being. When we are unconditionally kind and present, we directly dissolve the trance of unworthiness and separation. In accepting the waves of thought and feeling that arise and pass away, we realize our deepest nature, our original nature, as a boundless sea of wakefulness and love.

ON THE PATH OF THE BUDDHA: DISCOVERING THE FREEDOM OF RADICAL ACCEPTANCE

In contrast to orthodox notions of climbing up a ladder seeking *perfection,* psychologist Carl Jung describes the spiritual path as an unfolding into *wholeness.* Rather than trying to vanquish waves of emotion and rid ourselves of an inherently impure self, we turn around and embrace this life in all its realness—broken, messy, mysterious and vibrantly alive. By cultivating an unconditional and accepting presence, we are no longer battling against ourselves, keeping our wild and imperfect self in a cage of judgment and mistrust. Instead, we are discovering the freedom of becoming authentic and fully alive.

While the acceptance I touched in the desert sanctuary dramatically deepened my trust in myself, integrating this experience was a gradual process. Back in my "home" ashram on the East Coast, I felt as if I were looking at life through clearer eyes, but it would still take almost two years before I would finally be ready to leave. These men, women and children were my spiritual family; giving up the community would be a tremendous loss.

As I gradually pulled back from my involvement with the ashram, I began to see with increasing clarity how my life there had reinforced my tendencies to climb the ladder of perfection and hide my deficiencies. Also, because now I wasn't doubting or second-guessing myself as much, I could no longer deny the underlying problems in the community I hadn't wanted to confront. My husband had already become disenchanted with life in the ashram, and together we finally agreed it was time to go. When I formally took leave of the teacher, he warned me that if I turned away from him and left this spiritual path I would be barren for the rest of my life. As fate would have it, within days of announcing our decision and giving up our robes, I got pregnant again. While I anticipated Narayan's birth with great happiness and never questioned our decision to leave, still the pain of so much loss stayed with me for years.

Looking back, it makes complete sense that the teachings of the Buddha would guide me through this wrenching transition. As I felt myself withdrawing from the ashram, I had begun reading books about other spiritual traditions. I felt particularly drawn to Buddhism and began to experiment with a Buddhist mindfulness meditation called *vipassana,* which means "to see clearly" in Pali, the language of the Buddha. It is a practice based on teachings that explicitly acknowledged the suffering I was feeling and offered a way to awaken from it.

In the ashram our meditation had been geared toward cultivating a state of peacefulness, energy or rapture. We would quiet the mind by concentrating on the breath or a sacred Sanskrit phrase. It was a valuable training, but I found that when I was in emotional turmoil, these meditations at best only temporarily covered over my distress. I was manipulating my inner experience rather than being with what was actually happening. The Buddhist mindfulness practices, on the other hand, taught me to simply open and allow the changing stream of experience to move through me. When a harsh self-judgment appeared, I could recognize it simply as a passing thought.

It might be a tenacious and regular visitor, but *realizing it wasn't truth was wonderfully liberating.* When I got lost in feelings of insecurity or loneliness, I found that the lovingkindness and compassion meditations could guide me back to that tenderness I had felt in the desert sanctuary. I was no longer striving to rid myself of pain, rather I was learning to relate to the suffering I felt with care. From the very start, these practices carried me to a loving, open and accepting awareness that felt like my true nature.

After several years of meditating on my own I attended my first silent retreat at the Insight Meditation Society in Massachusetts. I knew I had come home. At the end of one of the evening talks, something the teacher said struck me profoundly; it addressed the core suffering I had been struggling with for so long. The words I remember were: *The boundary to what we can accept is the boundary to our freedom.* During the silence that followed, memories flashed through my mind revealing how much of my life experience I had been defended against. I could feel the walls I had erected to keep out those people who were different from me, those who intimidated me or demanded too much from me. I recognized my aversion to physical discomfort, to feeling fear and loneliness. I realized how unforgiving I felt toward myself for hurting others, for being judging, obsessive, selfish.

When the teacher and most of the students left the hall, I remained in the quiet and stillness. I wanted to know what it would be like if all boundaries dissolved and I just let life live through me. As I relaxed open, my heart and mind filled with tenderness toward everything that felt so painful in me and seemed so wrong. I realized that any argument I had with life—from a slight self-criticism to the utter anguish of shame—separated me from the love and awareness that are my true home.

Many times since then, especially when I've been caught up in tension or self-judgment, I have stopped and asked myself, *"What would it be like if I could accept life—accept this moment—exactly as it is?"* Regardless of which particular mental movie has been playing, just the intention to accept my experience begins to deepen my attention and soften my heart. As I grow more intimate with the actual waves of experience moving through me, the running commentary in my mind releases its grip, and the tension in my body begins to dissolve. Each time I begin again, wakefully allowing life to be as it is, I experience that vivid sense of *arriving*, of reentering the changing flow of experience. This "letting be" is the gateway to being filled with wonder and fully alive. As author Storm Jameson puts it:

> There is only one world, the world pressing against you at this minute. There is only one minute in which you are alive, this minute here and now. The only way to live is by accepting each minute as an unrepeatable miracle.

We are all capable of learning Radical Acceptance—the two wings of clear recognition and compassionate presence are expressions of who we intrinsically are. Yet because we quite naturally get lost in trance, we need both a sincere resolve and effective practices in order to awaken our heart and mind. The teachings and meditations offered in this book belong to a rich spiritual heritage that has, for centuries, guided those who seek genuine peace and freedom. On this sacred path of Radical Acceptance, rather than striving for perfection, we discover how to love ourselves into wholeness.

Guided Meditation:
The Practice of Vipassana (Mindfulness)

The Buddhist practice for developing mindfulness is called *vipassana,* which means "to see clearly" or "insight" in Pali, the language of the Buddha. What follows is a simple introduction to this practice. You might tape it or have someone read it to you until it becomes familiar.

Find a sitting position that allows you to be alert—spine erect but not rigid—and also relaxed. Close your eyes and rest your hands in an easy, effortless way. Allow your awareness to scan through your body and, wherever possible, soften and release obvious areas of physical tension.

Because we so easily get lost in thoughts, vipassana begins with attention to the breath. Using the breath as a primary anchor of mindfulness helps quiet the mind so that you can be awake to the changing stream of life that moves through you.

Take a few very full breaths, and then allow your breath to be natural. Notice where you most easily detect the breath. You might feel it as it flows in and out of your nose; you might feel the touch of the breath around your nostrils or on your upper lip; or perhaps you feel the movement of your chest or the rising and falling of your abdomen. Bring your attention to the sensations of breathing in one of these areas, perhaps wherever you feel them most distinctly.

There is no need to control the breath, to grasp or fixate on it. There is no "right" way of breathing. With a relaxed awareness, discover what the breath is really like as a changing experience of sensations.

You will find that the mind naturally drifts off in thoughts. Thoughts are not the enemy, and you do not need to clear your mind of thoughts. Rather, you are developing the capacity to recognize when thoughts are happening without getting lost in the story line. When you become aware of thinking, you might use a soft and friendly mental note: "Thinking, thinking." Then, without any judgment, gently return to the immediacy of the breath. Let the breath be home base, a place of full presence. While you might notice other experiences—the sounds of passing cars, feelings of being warm or cool, sensations of hunger—they can be in the background without drawing you away.

If any particular sensations become strong and call your attention, allow those sensations, instead of the breath, to become the primary subject of mindfulness. You might feel heat or chills, tingling, aching, twisting, stabbing, vibrating. With a soft, open awareness just feel the sensations as they are. Are they pleasant or unpleasant? As you fully attend to them, do they become more intense or dissipate? Notice how they change. When the sensations are no longer a strong experience, return to mindfulness of breathing. Or if the sensations are so unpleasant that you are unable to regard them with any balance or equanimity, feel free to rest your attention again in the breath.

In a similar way, you can bring mindfulness to strong emotions—fear, sadness, happiness, excitement, grief. Meet each experience with a kind and clear presence, neither clinging to nor resisting what is happening. What does this emotion feel like as sensations in your body? Where do you feel it most strongly? Is it static or moving? How big is it? Are your thoughts agitated and vivid? Are they repetitive and dull? Does your mind feel contracted or open? As you pay attention, notice how the emotion changes. Does it become more intense or weaken? Does it change into a different state? Anger to grief? Happiness to peace? When the emotion is no longer compelling, turn your attention back to the breath. If the emotion feels overwhelming for you, or if you are confused about where to place your attention, relax and come home to your breath.

The particular sensations, emotions or thoughts that arise when we practice mindfulness are not so important. It is our willingness to become still and pay attention to our experience, whatever it may be, that plants the seeds of Radical Acceptance. With time we develop the capacity to relate to our passing experience, whether in meditation or daily life, with deep clarity and kindness.

THREE

THE SACRED PAUSE: RESTING UNDER THE BODHI TREE

Enough. These few words are enough.
If not these words, this breath.
If not this breath, this sitting here.

This opening to the life
we have refused
again and again
until now.

Until now.

David Whyte

In the 1950s a few highly trained pilots in the U.S. Air Force were set a life-or-death task—to fly at altitudes higher than ever before attempted. Going beyond the earth's denser atmosphere, they found, much to their horror, that the ordinary laws of aerodynamics no longer existed. As Tom Wolfe describes it in *The Right Stuff*: ". . . a plane could skid into a flat spin, like a cereal bowl on a waxed Formica counter, and then start tumbling—not spinning and diving but tumbling end over end."

The first pilots to face this challenge responded by frantically trying to stabilize their planes, applying correction after correction. The more furiously they manipulated the controls, the wilder the ride became. Screaming helplessly to ground control, "What do I do next?" they would plunge to their deaths.

This tragic drama occurred several times until one of the pilots, Chuck Yeager, inadvertently struck upon a solution. When his plane began tumbling, Yeager was thrown violently around the cockpit and knocked out. Unconscious, he plummeted toward earth. Seven miles later, the plane reentered the planet's denser atmosphere, where standard navigation strategies could be implemented. Yeager came to, steadied the craft and landed safely. He had discovered the only lifesaving response that was possible in this desperate situation: Don't *do* anything. You take your hands off the controls. This solution, as Wolfe puts it, was "the only choice you had." It countered all training and even basic survival instincts, but it worked.

In our lives we often find ourselves in situations we can't control, circumstances in which none of our strategies work. Helpless and distraught, we frantically try to manage what is happening. Our child takes a downward turn in academics, and we issue one threat after another to get him in line. Someone says something hurtful to us, and we strike back quickly or retreat. We make a mistake at work, and we scramble to cover it up or go out of our way to make up for it. We head into emotionally charged confrontations nervously rehearsing and strategizing. The more we fear failure the more frenetically our bodies and minds work. We fill our days with continual movement: mental planning and worrying, habitual talking, fixing, scratching, adjusting, phoning, snacking, discarding, buying, looking in the mirror.

What would it be like if, right in the midst of this busyness, we were to consciously take our hands off the controls? Chuck Yeager had to go unconscious to interrupt the compulsion to control. What if we were to intentionally stop our mental computations and our rushing around and, for a minute or two, simply pause and notice our inner experience?

Learning to pause is the first step in the practice of Radical Acceptance. A pause is a suspension of activity, a time of temporary disengagement when we are no longer moving toward any goal. Unlike the frantic pilots, we stop asking, "What do I do next?" The pause can occur in the midst of almost any activity and can last for an instant, for hours or for seasons of our life. We may take a pause from our ongoing responsibilities by sitting down to meditate. We may pause in the midst of meditation to let go of thoughts and reawaken our attention to the breath. We may pause by stepping out of daily life to go on a retreat or to spend time in nature or to take a sabbatical. We may pause in a conversation, letting go of what we're about to say, in order to genuinely listen and be with the other person. We may pause when we feel suddenly moved or delighted or saddened, allowing the feelings to play through our heart. In a pause we simply discontinue whatever we are doing—thinking, talking, walking, writing, planning, worrying, eating—and become wholeheartedly present, attentive and, often, physically still. You might try it now: Stop reading and sit there, doing "no thing," and simply notice what you are experiencing.

A pause is, by nature, time limited. We resume our activities, but we do so with increased presence and more ability to make choices. In the pause before sinking our teeth into a chocolate bar, for instance, we might recognize the excited tingle of anticipation, and perhaps a background cloud of guilt and self-judgment. We may then choose to eat the chocolate, fully savoring the taste sensations, or we might decide to skip the chocolate and instead go out for a run. When we pause, we don't know what will happen next. But by disrupting our habitual behaviors, we open to the possibility of new and creative ways of responding to our wants and fears.

Of course there are times when it is not appropriate to pause. If our child is running toward a busy street, we don't pause. If someone is about to strike us, we don't just stand there, resting in the moment—rather, we quickly find a way to defend ourselves. If we are about to miss a flight, we race toward the gate. But much of our driven pace and habitual controlling in daily life does not serve surviving, and certainly not thriving. It arises from a free-floating anxiety about something being wrong or not enough. Even when our fear arises in the face of actual failure, loss or—like the military pilots—death, our instinctive tensing and striving are often ineffectual and unwise.

Taking our hands off the controls and pausing is an opportunity to clearly see the wants and fears that are driving us. During the moments of a pause, we become conscious of how the feeling that something is missing or wrong keeps us leaning into the future, on our way somewhere else. This gives us a fundamental choice in how we respond: We can continue our futile attempts at managing our experience, or we can meet our vulnerability with the wisdom of Radical Acceptance.

During my pause in the desert sanctuary, I began to see how utterly stuck I was in the stories and suffering of trance. By staying put and not occupying myself with other activities, I faced the shame and fears that I had been running from for years. In fact, pausing and accepting the intensity of my suffering was the only way I could have released the grip of trance.

Often the moment when we most need to pause is exactly when it feels most intolerable to do so. Pausing in a fit of anger, or when overwhelmed by sorrow or filled with desire, may be the last thing we want to do. Like the high-altitude pilots, letting go of the controls seems to run counter to our basic and instinctual ways of getting what we want. Pausing can feel like falling helplessly through space—we have no idea of what will happen. We fear we might be engulfed by the rawness of our rage or grief or desire. Yet without opening to the actual experience of the moment, Radical Acceptance is not possible.

Charlotte Joko Beck, Zen teacher and author, teaches that the "secret" of spiritual life is the capacity to ". . . return to that which we have spent a lifetime hiding from, to rest in the bodily experience of the present moment—even if it is a feeling of being humiliated, of failing, of abandonment, of unfairness." *Through the sacred art of pausing, we develop the capacity to stop hiding, to stop running away from our experience.* We begin to trust in our natural intelligence, in our naturally wise heart, in our capacity to open to whatever arises. Like awakening from a dream, in the moment of pausing our trance recedes and Radical Acceptance becomes possible.

RUNNING AWAY DEEPENS THE TRANCE

A traditional folktale tells the story of a man who becomes so frightened by his own shadow that he tries to run away from it. He believes that if only he could leave it behind, he would then be happy. The man grows increasingly distressed as he sees that no matter how fast he runs, his shadow never once falls behind. Not about to give up, he runs faster and faster until finally he drops dead of exhaustion. If only he had stepped into the shade and sat down to rest, his shadow would have vanished.

Our own personal shadow is made up of those parts of our being that we experience as unacceptable. Our families and culture let us know early on which qualities of human nature are valued and which are frowned upon. Because we want to be accepted and loved, we try to fashion and present a self that will attract others and secure our belonging. But we inevitably express our natural aggression or neediness or fear—parts of our emotional makeup that frequently are taboo—and the significant people in our life react to us. Whether we are mildly scolded, ignored or traumatically rejected, on some level we are hurt and pushed away.

The shadow becomes a force in our psyche as we regularly exile the emotions that could elicit rejection from others. We might bury and forget our childlike excitement; ignore our anger until it becomes knots of tension in our body; cover our fears with endless self-judgment and blame. Our shadow is rooted in shame, bound by our sense of being basically defective.

The more deeply we feel flawed and unlovable, the more desperately we run from the clutches of the shadow. *Yet by running from what we fear, we feed the inner darkness.* Whenever we reject a part of our being, we are confirming to ourselves our fundamental unworthiness. Underneath "I shouldn't get so angry" lies "There's something wrong with me if I do." Like being stuck in quicksand, our frantic efforts to get away from our badness sink us deeper. As we strive to avoid the shadow, we solidify our identity as a fearful, deficient self.

When Laura came to me for psychotherapy, her way of hiding from the shadow had nearly destroyed her marriage. She had turned into what her husband, Phil, called "a land mine rigged to blow at my slightest misstep." When they first started dating, her sensitivity and dramatic flair had appealed to him. Laura was a nurse, and Phil, much like her patients, loved her soothing touch and concern for his well-being. Laura had fun with Phil, and she enjoyed Phil's intelligence and quick wit. But after a few months of marriage, his sharp mind and caustic humor began to feel like a weapon directed at her. When Phil would comment on the way she was driving or putting away the dishes, she would feel wounded and humiliated. Everything inside her would begin collapsing into the sense that she was totally incompetent. Often her anger at being judged would boil up, and without warning she would explode at him in rage. Lashing out was Laura's primary strategy for running away from her shadow of shame.

On all levels the intimacy in their marriage had nearly vanished—they scarcely even talked. An attorney by profession, Phil was so good with words that he could make everything seem her fault. When this happened Laura would end up screaming at him and then storming away. By the time she came to me for therapy she had concluded, "It's not even worth trying to talk. He's Mr. Rational, and I always get creamed."

In fact, something had happened the night before our first session that was typical of their dynamic. Laura had had a heated argument that day with her supervisor at the hospital, and she had quit on the spot. At dinner when she was telling Phil what had happened, he seemed impatient. When the phone rang, he answered it and headed for his office. Laura had followed him and stood in the doorway, waiting for him to finish. Immediately after hanging up Phil turned on the TV. Laura called out in a sarcastic voice, "You're interested in any news but *my* news." Phil shot back with irritation: "That was Nathan, and he said I had to catch something on Fox Five. Why do you have to interpret my every behavior as a personal slight? If this is what you've been doing with your supervisor, she was probably glad to see you go." Her face hot and eyes glaring, Laura shouted back, "I know what you're thinking . . . why not just say it, Phil. *You'd* be glad to see me go. Right? That's it, isn't it?" Grabbing a law book from one of the shelves, she hurled it toward the television, screaming, "You just want to get rid of me! Maybe you'll get what you want!" The next book flew even closer to his head. That night, they again slept in separate rooms.

While she was growing up, Laura learned to shield herself from her volatile and critical mother. One minute they'd be happily together, the next her mother would light into her about how she never cleaned her room or that she looked terrible with her bangs in her face. When Laura became a teenager, the dramatic shift in her hormones and body chemistry made it impossible for her to keep a lid on her hurt and anger. When her mother would berate her for the way she dressed, for her slumping posture, for choosing losers as friends, for being too stupid to get into a decent four-year college, Laura would scream back, call her names and spend the night at a friend's house. Actually she spent as much time as she could elsewhere to avoid her mother's constant accusation that she "couldn't do anything right." When she was around and they argued, Laura was surprised by the intensity of her own rage. She felt as if there were a demon inside her who, given the chance, could slash and kill. By the time Laura left home, lashing out had become a way of life.

During our first few therapy sessions, Laura told me that she felt defensive and easily injured in most of her relationships—with friends, with family, at work. There was always a drama going on somewhere. If she felt someone was critical of her, she would avoid them or unleash an angry attack that put the relationship on ice, sometimes for good. When her supervisor had called her in and asked pointed questions about the tension between Laura and another nurse at her station, Laura had defended herself with open hostility. When her supervisor suggested she calm down so they could have a real conversation, Laura had announced her resignation and walked out.

No matter what situation she was in, when the raw feelings of not being "good enough" were triggered, Laura was thrown back to her childhood, where she had been powerless to do anything but defend herself. Any of us, when our particular place of insecurity or woundedness is touched, easily regress into the fullness of trance. At these times there seems to be no choice as to what we feel, think, say or do. Rather, we "go on automatic," reacting in our most habitual way to defend ourselves, to cover over the rawness of our hurt.

As happens in any addiction, the behaviors we use to keep us from pain only fuel our suffering. Not only do our escape strategies amplify the feeling that something is wrong with us, they stop us from attending to the very parts of ourselves that most need our attention to heal. As Carl Jung states in one of his key insights, *the unfaced and unfelt parts of our psyche are the source of all neurosis and suffering.* Laura's lashing out kept her from feeling how ashamed and hurt she really felt. Yet this "defense" only made her feel even more ashamed for being so out of control. Caught in a vicious cycle, the more ashamed she felt, the more driven she was to attack others to protect herself and hide her shame. When we learn to face and feel the fear and shame we habitually avoid, we begin to awaken from trance. We free ourselves to respond to our circumstances in ways that bring genuine peace and happiness.

WHEN WE STOP RUNNING: BECOMING AVAILABLE TO THE LIFE OF THE MOMENT

Siddhartha Gautama, the Buddha-to-be, was the son of a wealthy king who ruled over a beautiful kingdom in the foothills of the Himalayas. At his birth, the king's advisors predicted that either he would forgo the world and become a holy man or he would be a great king and ruler. Siddhartha's father was determined to have his son follow in his own footsteps. Knowing that seeing the pain of the world would turn the prince toward spiritual pursuits, he surrounded him with physical beauty, wealth and continuous entertainment. Only kind and beautiful people were allowed to care for him.

Of course the king's project to protect his son from the suffering of life failed. As the traditional story tells it, when Siddhartha was twenty-nine, he insisted on taking several excursions outside the palace walls with his charioteer, Channa. Realizing his son's intent, the king ordered his subjects to prepare for the prince by cleaning and beautifying the streets, and hiding the sick and poor. But the gods, seeing this as the opportunity to awaken Siddhartha, had other plans. They appeared to him in the guise of a sick person, an old person and a corpse. When Siddhartha realized that such suffering was an intrinsic part of being alive, his comfortable view of life was shattered. Determined to discover how human beings could find happiness and freedom in the face of such suffering, he left the luxurious palaces, his parents, his wife and son. Setting forth in the dark of the night, Siddhartha began his search for the truths that would liberate his heart and spirit.

Most of us spend years trying to cloister ourselves inside the palace walls. We chase after the pleasure and security we hope will give us lasting happiness. Yet no matter how happy we may be, life inevitably delivers up a crisis—divorce, death of a loved one, a critical illness. Seeking to avoid the pain and control our experience, we pull away from the intensity of our feelings, often ignoring or denying our genuine physical and emotional needs.

Because Siddhartha had been so entranced by pleasure, the path of denial at first looked like the way to freedom. He joined a group of ascetics and began practicing severe austerities, depriving himself of food and sleep, and following rigorous yogic disciplines. After several years Siddhartha found himself emaciated and sick, but no closer to the spiritual liberation he yearned for. He left the ascetics and made his way to the banks of a nearby river. Lying there nearly dead, Siddhartha cried out, "Surely there must be another way to enlightenment!" As he closed his eyes, a dreamlike memory arose.

It was the annual celebration of the spring plowing, and his nurses had left him resting under a rose apple tree at the edge of the fields. Sitting in the cool shade of the tree, the child watched the men at work, sweat pouring down their faces; he saw the oxen straining to pull the plow. In the cut grasses and the freshly overturned soil, he could see insects dying, their eggs scattered. Sorrow arose in Siddhartha for the suffering that all living beings experience. In the tenderness of this compassion, Siddhartha felt deeply opened. Looking up he was struck by how brilliantly blue the sky was. Birds were dipping and soaring freely and gracefully. The air was thick with the sweet fragrance of apple blossoms. In the flow and sacred mystery of life, there was room for the immensity of joy and sorrow. He felt completely at peace.

Remembering this experience gave Siddhartha a profoundly different understanding of the path to liberation. If a young, untrained child could taste freedom in this effortless and spontaneous way, then such a state must be a natural part of being human. Perhaps he could awaken by stopping the struggle and, as he had done as a child, meeting all of life with a tender and open presence.

What conditions had made this childhood experience of profound presence possible? If we look at our own life, we see that such moments of presence often occur in times of stillness or solitude. We have stepped outside the normal rush and into the openness and clarity of a "time out of time." Had Siddhartha been around the distracting chatter of the nurses or playing games with the other children, he would not have been so attentive and open to his deeper experience. In the moments of pausing and resting under the rose apple tree, he was neither pursuing pleasure nor was he pushing away the suffering of the world. By pausing, he had relaxed into a natural wakefulness and inner freedom.

Inspired by his childhood experience, Siddhartha began his final search for lasting freedom. After bathing himself in the river, he accepted the sweet rice offered to him by a village maiden, and then slept a sleep with wondrous dreams. When he awoke, refreshed and strengthened, he once again sought solitude under a pipal tree—known now as the bodhi tree—and resolved to remain in stillness there until he experienced full liberation.

The image of the Buddha seated under the bodhi tree is one of the great mythic symbols depicting the power of the pause. Siddhartha was no longer clinging to pleasure or running away from any part of his experience. He was making himself absolutely available to the changing stream of life. This attitude of neither grasping nor pushing away any experience has come to be known as the Middle Way, and it characterizes the engaged presence we awaken in pausing. In the pause, we, like Siddhartha, become available to whatever life brings us, including the unfaced, unfelt parts of our psyche.

When the Buddha-to-be resolved to pause under the bodhi tree, he came fully face-to-face with the shadow-side of human nature, represented as the god Mara. In Sanskrit, *mara* means "delusion," the dreamlike ignorance that entangles us in craving and fear and obscures our enlightened nature. Traditional stories speak of Mara as appearing in many forms—violent storms, temptingly beautiful women, raging demons, massive armies. When the temptress appeared, Siddhartha could most certainly recognize the enormous lure of seduction, yet he sat unmoving, neither grasping after nor pushing away the longing arising in his body and mind. When Mara transformed into a gigantic clawed and fanged demon that swooped through the air to attack him, Siddhartha bravely and mindfully opened to the fear he felt, without fleeing or trying to fight back. By paying attention instead of reacting, he saw beyond the delusion of separate self that imprisons us in suffering.

Throughout the night, Siddhartha was assaulted by the armies of Mara, and showered with arrows of greed and hatred. As he met each with an open and tender heart, it was transformed into a flower blossom that drifted gently to his feet. With the passing hours, the mound of fragrant petals grew, and Siddhartha became increasingly peaceful and clear.

As dawn approached Mara issued his greatest challenge, demanding that Siddhartha defend his right to occupy the seat of freedom. In response, the Buddha-to-be touched the ground, calling on the earth to bear witness to his thousands of lifetimes of compassion. The earth shook in violent affirmation, and darkness and thunder filled the skies. Terrified, Mara fled and along with him the final traces of delusion vanished. In this way, as the morning star appeared like a sparkling diamond on the horizon, Siddhartha won his freedom. He realized his pure nature—loving, radiant awareness—and became the Buddha, the Awakened One.

The practice of Radical Acceptance begins with our own pause under the bodhi tree. Just as the Buddha willingly opened himself to an encounter with Mara, we too can pause and make ourselves available to whatever life is offering us in each moment. In this way, as the Vietnamese Buddhist monk Thich Nhat Hanh puts it, we "keep our appointment with life."

PAUSING IN THE FACE OF MARA

During our therapy sessions, Laura began referring to her mother as "the dragon" because of the incinerating burn of her words. At one meeting, after talking about her mother, we did a guided visualization. In her imagery Laura found herself involved in a struggle with a real dragon. She saw herself crawling on the ground, dodging behind boulders, climbing and hiding in tree branches. Reptilian and ferocious, the dragon found her everywhere she hid. Avoiding its eyes, Laura continually struggled to escape from its fiery breath. Immersed in this drama, she told me she felt weak and exhausted from her efforts to escape, and much too small to fight back. I asked her what she wanted to do.

"Give up, stop running."

"What happens if you do?"

"I don't know, maybe die, it will hurt too much."

"What will hurt so much?"

Laura sat quietly for a minute or two and then responded, "I'll see that I don't have a mother anymore, that it's true—she really is a dragon. There is no one who loves me . . . I'm too awful to be loved." Realizing she had been holding on to the hope that the dragon would be replaced by her real mother, the mother who cared for her, Laura began to sob. It had been better to run than to get burned by the truth, better to run than to feel that she was bad and unloved. But now with hope stripped away, Laura was returning to the feelings she had spent a lifetime hiding from.

Until we stop our mental busyness, stop our endless activities, we have no way of knowing our actual experience. Like Laura, we primarily know how to avoid it. But stopping can be terrifying—to sit under the bodhi tree and face the arrows of Mara takes courage and resolve. Laura would need both in order to get herself out of the patterns that were ruining her life. I ended the session by asking her if she knew what the dragon really looked like. Instead of fighting or fleeing, had she ever looked into the dragon's eyes when she felt under attack?

During our next session I told Laura that she could learn to face the dragon from a place of inner strength through what I called the art of pausing. When fear or rage surged up in her, she could stop all outward activity and simply pay attention to what she was experiencing inside her. I let her know that if she could pause instead of shouting or storming out of painful encounters, she would, in time, find inner resources to guide her in responding wisely. We began by practicing the pause in our therapy sessions.

I asked Laura to close her eyes and bring to mind the recent confrontation at the hospital, recalling as vividly as possible how she felt when her supervisor implied she was at fault. When I suggested she imagine what it would be like to pause right in the midst of those intense feelings and not do or say anything, her mouth tightened and her chin began quivering. Noticing how her body had stiffened, I whispered softly that it was fine to take a few long full breaths. "What thoughts are going on in your mind, Laura?" Without hesitation, Laura said, "She's a bitch. Why did she have to assume I was the one causing the problem? She didn't even know what had happened!" She was quiet for a few moments and then added bitterly, "She made me feel like I was screwing up, just like my mother . . . I was wrong again."

When I asked what she was now aware of in her body, she responded, "My face is burning . . . there's a huge swelling pressure in my chest that feels like it's going to explode." I asked her if she could continue to pause and experience those feelings. Suddenly she burst out, "This just isn't right. What am I supposed to do . . . be a sitting duck and just let people humiliate me?" Laura opened her eyes, and tears began welling up. "Tara, when someone criticizes me, I can't handle it. I lose it . . . I feel as if I *have* to fight with them. If I pause I'm afraid I'll fall apart." Sobbing, Laura put her face in her hands and said, "I feel so ashamed of myself. I'm just not the person I want to be."

When we first practice pausing, we can easily be swept away into the raw feelings that have been dictating our behavior for so many years. It is important to ease in gradually, and if possible, with the support of others. As Laura was doing in our session, practicing by imagining a recent or likely situation is useful. Yet if we get caught in a charged situation, a good way to begin is to take a "time-out" and find a quiet, safe place to practice the pause. It always helps to start with a few deep breaths, consciously relaxing the body and mind.

In our sessions, Laura started with pauses that lasted no more than a minute. Over time she learned to remain present with waves of intense feeling as the insecurity she had been avoiding for years came to the surface. Yet it would take Laura a number of sessions before the pause could begin to feel like a real refuge—a place where she could be aware of her pain without feeling possessed or overwhelmed by it. Eventually the pause would allow her to come home to herself in an intimate and honest way.

In bullfighting there is an interesting parallel to the pause as a place of refuge and renewal. It is believed that in the midst of a fight, a bull can find his own particular area of safety in the arena. There he can reclaim his strength and power. This place and inner state are called his *querencia.* As long as the bull remains enraged and reactive, the matador is in charge. Yet when he finds *querencia,* he gathers his strength and loses his fear. From the matador's perspective, at this point the bull is truly dangerous, for he has tapped into his power. Each time Laura felt provoked and charged madly against the enemy, she became more off balance, further ensnared in her fear and shame. The forces of Mara, Laura's matador, remained in control. As she learned to find *querencia* by pausing, she could respond to her circumstances in a more balanced and effective way.

One day Laura came in and told me that something had genuinely shifted. At a birthday dinner with her brother's family, her mother had started in on her once again, demanding to know when she was going to start looking for a new nursing position. Before

Laura had a chance to respond, her mother leaned forward, her voice sharp and derisive. "Don't tell me. I know. You're just waiting for it to drop into your lap . . . like manna from heaven." As if Laura's silence were a green light to continue, her mother broadened the attack: "So, are you planning to have Phil support you all your life?"

Heart pounding loudly, Laura paused and took a few deep breaths. She felt searing heat in her chest, as if she had been stabbed, and everything in her wanted to scream out in rage. But instead, she simply said, "I don't know, Mom," and sat back in her chair. "Right," her mother retorted, perhaps surprised to receive so little fuel for her fire, and turned away to talk with Laura's brother.

Laura didn't know what would happen next. As she continued in the pause, she felt her body trembling and shaking. Her chest felt like it was about to burst open. She noticed the confusion of stories swirling through her mind: "Laura the one who screws up," "Laura the raging maniac." In the midst of this turmoil she heard an inner voice whisper, "This feels horrible . . . and I can handle it." She had felt this agitation many times in our therapy sessions, and knew it was bearable and wouldn't last. As Laura relaxed she felt a spaciousness slowly opening in her chest and throat. The sharp hurt began dissolving, and in its place a profound sense of sorrow arose. As she allowed all these feelings to unfold, she felt as if she were gently caring for the wounded places inside her.

No longer trapped inside the trance, Laura could now imagine some choices. She could stay for the rest of the evening or go home. She could confront her mother and tell her why she hadn't found a job, or she could let the incident slide. Whatever her response to her mother, it would now arise from a fresh way of responding to her own self. Pausing had enabled Laura to accept everything she was feeling, and she was left with a surprising warmth and kindness. When she looked over at her mother, Laura felt an upsurge of tenderness. She saw a woman ensnared in her own insecurity, words tumbling out of control, hands tightened into fists. By the time they parted later that evening, she was actually able to look her mother in the eye, touch her arm, smile.

Laura had faced the dragon, both in her mother and in herself. Underneath her mother's fiery exterior she had found a wounded person. Similarly, Laura's dragon had been guarding her own vulnerability, her fear of being bad, her shame. Under the layers of sharp scales she had found her own soft and kind heart. Poet Rainer Maria Rilke expresses a deep understanding of the dragons all of us face: "How could we forget those ancient myths that stand at the beginning of all races—the myths about dragons that at the last moment are transformed into princesses. Perhaps all the dragons in our lives are only princesses waiting for us to act, just once, with beauty and courage. Perhaps everything that frightens us is, in its deepest essence, something helpless that wants our love."

THE SACRED PAUSE—FERTILE GROUND FOR WISE ACTION

Having learned to pause, Laura was ready to explore what sorts of strategies might follow pausing to help heal her marriage. While we knew it would take a while for her to break the habit of reacting, in our sessions we explored various scenarios that might emerge when she felt criticized by Phil. If she felt she was going to explode, she could pause, tell him she needed a time-out and suggest they could talk later. Then she might go into another room and notice what story she was trapped in and how she was feeling. If she did react and they began arguing, she could choose to interrupt the fight with a pause and, after a few moments, try to tell Phil what she was experiencing. She might ask him what he was feeling as well. We even imagined a time when she might be comfortable enough after a pause to take his hand in hers and simply be silent for a few moments.

The first time she tried after a pause to tell Phil what she was feeling, he wasn't ready for it. Used to her communications erupting into stormy tirades, he stopped her midsentence: "Laura, I'm tired of your eternal dramas. Do we have to go through this again?" Not waiting for an answer, he had grabbed the newspaper and left the room. That week Laura asked me, "Tara, how can this work if I'm the only one doing it?" Of course changing the patterns in the marriage wouldn't all be up to Laura, but it could start with her.

Even if only one person in a relationship practices pausing and opening with Radical Acceptance, this has the potential of freeing both from a painful impasse. Pausing interrupts entrenched patterns of interaction. When the downward spiral of judging and misunderstanding is stopped, even for a brief time, it becomes possible to recognize the unconscious beliefs and feelings that lie behind the problem. Such insight naturally leads to making wiser choices. When one partner chooses to avoid making hurtful comments or to listen more carefully, the other may become more relaxed, less defensive. While pausing might not necessarily salvage a crippled relationship, it invariably helps move it toward some resolution.

For Laura, pausing opened the door to real communication with her husband. The turning point happened one evening when Phil told her he couldn't take a full week off for their vacation together. They immediately launched into one of their typical arguments. In the midst of it Laura remembered to pause. Speaking in a slow, quiet voice, she said, "I'm feeling that same fear again—that you don't really want to be around me. When I feel this way, I just need some sign that you really do care."

At first Phil was annoyed: "You know, Laura, I feel like if I don't bend over backward to treat your fragile self 'just so,' you'll blow up. I don't want to be held hostage by your anger." His words just hung in the air, and when Laura didn't jump in to defend herself, something seemed to shift in Phil. After a few moments, with a softer voice he added, "It's hard for me to be affectionate on demand. When you need me to reassure you, to take back a critical comment, well . . . I feel manipulated. But, honest to God, Laura, I just hate myself for being so mean to you." This last part was not something Laura had even imagined. She managed to tell him how humiliated she felt when she exploded at him. After a long silence she added, "Phil, I can't believe how hard this has been . . . being so far apart." By the end of the evening they had decided together that seeing a marriage counselor might help them.

Over time Phil and Laura were able to recapture a warm and playful affection. Freed from the constricting bonds of her anger toward Phil, Laura felt her sensuality reawaken, and they once again shared a vibrant intimacy. Laura attributed this renewal of their marriage to the power of the pause. The atmosphere of pausing was inviting—as Phil also slowed down his reactions, he began to notice and accept what he was really feeling. For both of them, the words and actions that emerged from the openness of pausing revealed a growing tenderness and trust.

PRECIOUS MOMENTS OF FREEDOM

We learn Radical Acceptance by practicing pausing again and again. At the very moment when we're about to lash out in verbal outrage, we don't. When we feel anxious, instead of turning on the TV or making a phone call or mentally obsessing, we sit still and feel our discomfort or restlessness. In this pause we let go of thinking and doing, and we become intimate with what is happening in our body, heart and mind.

Pausing as a technique may feel unfamiliar, awkward or at odds with our usual way of living. But actually there are many moments—showering, walking, driving—when we release our preoccupations and are simply aware and letting life be. We may pause at seeing the new green in spring; or in the supermarket we may pause to gaze at the freshness of an infant's face. When we finally understand a problem we've been grappling with, our pause may be a sigh as our body and mind relax. At the end of a long day, we may experience a natural pause when we lie down in bed and let everything go.

We can also purposefully pause during regular activities. I often pause before getting out of my car and simply feel what is going on inside me. Sometimes after I hang up the phone, I'll just sit at my desk, breathing, listening, not doing the next thing. Or I might stop cleaning the house for a moment and simply listen to the music I'd put on to keep myself company. We can choose to pause on the top of a mountain or in a subway, while we are with others or meditating alone.

Ajahn Buddhadasa calls these interludes of natural or purposeful pausing "temporary nirvana." We touch the freedom that is possible in any moment when we are not grasping after our experience or resisting it. He writes that without such moments of pausing, ". . . living things would either die or become insane. Instead, we survive because there are natural periods of coolness, of wholeness and ease. In fact, they last longer than the fires of our grasping and fear. It is this that sustains us."

The pauses in our life make our experience full and meaningful. The well-known pianist Arthur Rubinstein was once asked, "How do you handle the notes as well as you do?" His response was immediate and passionate, "I handle notes no better than many others, but the pauses—ah! That is where the art resides." Like a rest note in a musical score, the pure stillness of a pause forms the background that lets the foreground take shape with clarity and freshness. The moment that arises out of the pause can, like the well-sounded note, reflect the genuineness, the wholeness, the truth of who we are.

Pausing is the gateway to Radical Acceptance. In the midst of a pause, we are giving room and attention to the life that is always streaming through us, the life that is habitually overlooked. It is in this rest under the bodhi tree that we realize the natural freedom of our heart and awareness. Like the Buddha, rather than running away, we need only commit ourselves to arriving, here and now, with wholehearted presence.

Guided Reflection: The Sacred Pause

The sacred pause helps us reconnect with the present moment. Especially when we are caught up in striving and obsessing and leaning into the future, pausing enables us to reenter the mystery and vitality only found here and now.

Choose a time when you are involved in a goal-oriented activity—reading, working on the computer, cleaning, eating—and explore pausing for a moment or two. Begin by discontinuing what you are doing, sitting comfortably and allowing your eyes to close. Take a few deep breaths and with each exhale let go of any worries or thoughts about what you are going to do next; let go of any tightness in the body.

Now, notice what you are experiencing as you inhabit the pause. What sensations are you aware of in your body? Do you feel anxious or restless as you try to step out of your mental stories? Do you feel pulled to resume your activity? Can you simply allow, for this moment, whatever is happening inside you?

You can weave the sacred pause into your daily life by pausing for a few moments each hour or as you begin and end activities. You can pause while sitting, standing or lying down. Even in motion—going for a walk or driving—you can pause internally, eyes open and senses awake. Whenever you find you are stuck or disconnected, you can begin your life fresh in that moment by pausing, relaxing and paying attention to your immediate experience.

Experiment by choosing one thing you do daily and make a weeklong commitment to pause before beginning this activity. It might be brushing your teeth, making a phone call, getting out of the car, taking a sip of tea, turning on your computer. Each time, take a few moments to pause, relax and bring awareness to what is happening within you. After you have completed the pause, notice if anything has changed when you return to doing.

FOUR

UNCONDITIONAL FRIENDLINESS: THE SPIRIT OF RADICAL ACCEPTANCE

This being human is a guest house.
Every morning a new arrival.

A joy, a depression, a meanness,
Some momentary awareness
comes as an unexpected visitor.

Welcome and entertain them all! . . .

The dark thought, the shame, the malice,
meet them at the door laughing,
and invite them in.

Be grateful for whoever comes,
because each has been sent
as a guide from beyond.

Rumi

Jacob, almost seventy, was in the midstages of Alzheimer's disease. A clinical psychologist by profession and a meditator for more than twenty years, he was well aware that his faculties were deteriorating. On occasion his mind would go totally blank; he would have no access to words for several minutes and become completely disoriented. He often forgot what he was doing and usually needed assistance with basic tasks—cutting his food, putting on clothes, bathing, getting from place to place.

With his wife's help, Jacob attended a ten-day meditation retreat I was leading. A couple of days into the course Jacob had his first interview with me. These meetings, which students have regularly with a teacher, are an opportunity to check in and receive personal guidance in the practice. During our time together Jacob and I talked about how things were going both on retreat and at home. His attitude toward his disease was interested, sad, grateful, even good-humored. Intrigued by his resilience, I asked him what allowed him to be so accepting. He responded, "*It doesn't feel like anything is wrong.* I feel grief and some fear about it all going, but it feels like real life." Then he told me about an experience he'd had in an earlier stage of the disease.

Jacob had occasionally given talks about Buddhism to local groups and had accepted an invitation to address a gathering of over a hundred meditation students. He arrived at the event feeling alert and eager to share the teachings he loved. Taking his seat in front of the hall, Jacob looked out at the expectant faces before him . . . and suddenly he didn't know what he was supposed to say or do. He didn't know where he was or why he was there. All he knew was that his heart was pounding furiously and his mind was spinning in confusion. Putting his palms together at his heart, Jacob started naming out loud what was happening: "Afraid, embarrassed, confused, feeling like I'm failing, powerless, shaking, sense of dying, sinking, lost." For several more minutes he sat, head slightly bowed, continuing to name his experience. As his body began to relax and his mind grew calmer, he also noted that aloud. At last Jacob lifted his head, looked slowly around at those gathered, and apologized.

Many of the students were in tears. As one put it, "No one has ever taught us like this. Your presence has been the deepest teaching." Rather than pushing away his experience and deepening his agitation, Jacob had the courage and training simply to name what he was aware of, and, most significantly, to bow to his experience. In some fundamental way he didn't create an adversary out of feelings of fear and confusion. *He didn't make anything wrong.*

We practice Radical Acceptance by pausing and then meeting whatever is happening inside us with this kind of unconditional friendliness. Instead of turning our jealous thoughts or angry feelings into the enemy, we pay attention in a way that enables us to recognize and touch any experience with care. Nothing is wrong—whatever is happening is just "real life." Such unconditional friendliness is the spirit of Radical Acceptance.

One of my favorite stories of the Buddha shows the power of a wakeful and friendly heart. While Mara fled in disarray on the morning of the Buddha's enlightenment, it seems that he was only temporarily discouraged. Even after the Buddha had become deeply revered throughout India, Mara continued to make unexpected appearances. The Buddha's loyal attendant, Ananda, always on the lookout for any harm that might come to his teacher, would report with dismay that the "Evil One" had again returned. Instead of ignoring Mara or driving him away, the Buddha would calmly acknowledge his presence, saying, "I see you, Mara." He would then invite him for tea and serve him as an honored guest. Offering Mara a cushion so that he could sit comfortably, the Buddha would fill two earthen cups with tea, place them on the low table between them, and only then take his own seat. Mara would stay for a while and then go, but throughout the Buddha remained free and undisturbed.

When Mara visits us, in the form of troubling emotions or fearsome stories, we can say, "I see you, Mara," and clearly recognize the reality of craving and fear that lives in each human heart. By accepting these experiences with the warmth of compassion, we offer Mara tea rather than fearfully driving him away. *Seeing what is true, we hold what is seen with kindness.* This is the unconditional friendliness that Jacob bravely offered when he bowed to his confusion. We express such wakefulness of heart each time we recognize and embrace our hurts and fears.

Our habit of being a fair-weather friend to ourselves—of pushing away or ignoring whatever darkness we can—is deeply entrenched. But just as a relationship with a good friend is marked by understanding and compassion, we can learn to bring these same qualities to our own inner life. Pema Chödrön, an American nun who is a highly respected teacher of Tibetan Buddhism, says that through spiritual practice "We are learning to make friends with ourselves, our life, at the most profound level possible." We befriend ourselves when, rather than resisting our experience, we open our hearts and willingly invite Mara to tea.

"I SEE YOU, MARA": THE PRACTICES OF INQUIRY AND NAMING

Carl, a good friend of mine, had eight months of bruising encounters with Mara after his business failed. An Ivy League graduate with an MBA, he had put years of hard work into building a successful computer software business. When two longtime associates presented him with an opportunity that promised a lucrative niche in the exploding on-line world, Carl converted his business assets and equity and jumped in. In the first three years of running their retail Web site, the partners netted over $20 million. During their fourth year the stock market took a plunge and the business collapsed. At the age of forty-five, married, with two young children and a major mortgage to pay off, Carl found himself filing for bankruptcy.

Although he was aware that many others were also foundering due to market fluctuations, Carl felt personally responsible for the disastrous loss. Others had realized that the economy was going to crash and that dot-com enterprises were risky business. Why hadn't he? Had greed gotten in the way of perspective? How could anyone possibly respect him now? At his lowest moments, Carl had a hard time imagining that even his wife and friends still loved him.

When our own carefully constructed lives fall apart, we, like Carl, torture and berate ourselves with stories about how we are failures, what we could have done better, how no one cares about us. This response of course only digs us deeper into trance. Distracted by our judgments, we are not even able to recognize the raw pain of our emotions. In order to begin the process of waking up, we need to deepen our attention and touch our real experience.

One tool of mindfulness that can cut through our numbing trance is inquiry. As we ask ourselves questions about our experience, our attention gets engaged. We might begin by scanning our body, noticing what we are feeling, especially in the throat, chest, abdomen and stomach, and then asking, "What is happening?" We might also ask, "What wants my attention right now?" or, "What is asking for acceptance?" Then we attend, with genuine interest and care, listening to our heart, body and mind.

Inquiry is not a kind of analytic digging—we are not trying to figure out, "Why do I feel this sadness?" This would only stir up more thoughts. In contrast to the approach of Western psychology, in which we might delve into further stories in order to understand what caused a current situation, the intention of inquiry is to awaken to our experience exactly as it is in this present moment. While inquiry may expose judgments and thoughts about what we feel is wrong, it focuses on our immediate feelings and sensations.

I might be feeling like a bad mother because I lashed out at Narayan for repeated interruptions while I was working. When I pause and ask myself what wants to be accepted, I drop below the self-judgment to tiredness and anxiety. I can feel my stomach contract, my face tighten. This is a familiar feeling—fear. As I sit with it, I become aware that I'm afraid of not having the energy to get everything done, afraid of failing. This fear that has hardened my heart is what now needs my attention. The moment I recognize Mara, some of the power of that fear lessens, and with it, the self-judgment. I am not so caught in my assumed identity as a stressed, striving and potentially deficient person. While my worries might not go away, if Narayan does dare to appear again, I am more likely to meet him with affection than with irritation.

It is important to approach inquiry with a genuine attitude of unconditional friendliness. If I were to ask myself what wants attention with even the slightest aversion, I would only deepen my self-judgment. It may take some practice to learn how to question ourselves with the same kindness and care we would show to a troubled friend.

One day I went over to Carl's house to see how he was doing. His thin frame was slumped in a chair and he spoke with a weary cynicism. I listened for a while, and then seeing how trapped he was in bitterness about the past and fear for the future, I gently asked, "Carl, what's happening right now? What inside you most needs attention?" He glanced up at me, perhaps a bit surprised, but then said simply and clearly, "I feel like an absolute failure." He went on to describe the anxiety that was taking over his body and mind—the racing thoughts, cold sweats, the sudden gripping around his heart. "It won't back off, Tara. It wakes me up every night. I'm completely tied up in knots . . . my guts are in knots right now." After a few minutes of talking he thanked me for being interested. "It just helps to say this out loud."

Naming or noting is another tool of traditional mindfulness practice that we can apply, as Carl did, when we're lost. Mental noting, like inquiry, helps us recognize with care and gentleness the passing flow of thoughts, feelings and sensations. If I am feeling anxious and disconnected before giving a talk, for example, I often pause and ask myself what is happening or what wants my attention. With a soft mental whisper I'll name what I am aware of: "afraid, afraid, tight, tight." If I notice myself anxiously assuming that my talk will be boring and fall flat, I simply continue naming: "story about blowing it, fear of rejection," then, "judging, judging." If instead of noting I try to ignore this undercurrent of fear, I carry it into my talk and end up speaking in an unnatural and insincere way. The simple action of having named the anxiety building before my talk opens my awareness. Anxiety may still be present, but the care and wakefulness I cultivate through noting allows me to feel more at home with myself.

Like inquiry, noting is an opportunity to communicate unconditional friendliness to our inner life. If fear arises and we pounce on it with a name, "Fear! Gotcha!" we're only creating more tension. Naming an experience is not an attempt to nail an unpleasant experience or make it go away. Rather, it is a soft and gentle way of saying, "I see you, Mara." This attitude of Radical Acceptance makes it safe for the frightened and vulnerable parts of our being to let themselves be known.

In traditional cultures, naming plays a significant role in the healing process. It is believed that no matter how powerful the spirits causing the illness may be, if the shaman can name them, they are subdued. They can no longer control their victim, so healing takes place. In the same vein, Western psychology holds that aspects of our psyche that are not seen and consciously named exert control over our life. By naming the forces of Mara when they arise, we are no longer possessed or driven by them. Even the very act of relating to them with friendliness rather than fear diminishes their power.

The practices of inquiry and noting are actually ways to wake us up to the fact that we are suffering. Caught up in our stories, we can effectively deny the truth of our experience. I sometimes spend days being impatient and judgmental toward myself before I stop and pay attention to the feelings and beliefs that have been disconnecting me from my heart. When I do pause and look at what's happening, I realize that I've been caught up in the suffering of anxiety and self-doubt.

I have worked with many clients and students who reach a critical gateway when they finally register just how much pain they are in. This juncture is very different from feeling self-pity or complaining about our lives. It is different from focusing on how many problems we have. Rather, seeing and feeling the degree of suffering we are living with reconnects us to our heart.

I could see this happen with Carl the day we visited. After he described the iron grip of his anxiety, I let him know what I saw: "Carl, the pain you are experiencing would be hard for me . . . for anybody. Your body is gripped by anxiety. You're filled with failure and shame, so much so that you can't even find comfort with your family. This pain is huge . . . I can see how much this hurts." Tears filled his eyes as he began to let himself acknowledge the depth of his pain. "It's true," he said quietly. "I'm hurting. Badly." Then, for the first time in months, Carl let himself weep.

Recognizing that we are suffering is freeing—self-judgment falls away and we can regard ourselves with kindness. When Carl stopped crying, his face was soft and his body relaxed. All the bitterness had left his voice. "I've been so angry about failing . . . I completely ignored how much it meant to me to be successful and how hard it's been to lose."

When we offer to ourselves the same quality of unconditional friendliness that we would offer to a friend, we stop denying our suffering. As we figuratively sit beside ourselves and inquire, listen and name our experience, we see Mara clearly and open our heart in tenderness for the suffering before us.

INVITING MARA TO TEA: THE PRACTICE OF SAYING YES

Some years ago in the middle of a weeklong vipassana retreat I found myself swamped in negativity. I reacted with aversion to every facet of life around me. The teachers were talking too much; the cold, cloudy weather was disappointing; my fellow meditators were inconsiderately sneezing in my direction, and I already had an irritating sinus infection myself. Nothing was going right, especially me. Tired of the aversion, I decided that instead of resisting everything, I would agree to everything. I began to greet whatever arose in my awareness with a silently whispered "yes." Yes to the pain in my leg, yes to the blaming thoughts, yes to the sneezes and the irritation and the gloomy gray sky.

At first my yes was mechanical, grudging and insincere, but even so, each time I said it, I could feel something relax in me. Before long, I started to play around with it. Reflecting that I, like the Buddha, was inviting Mara to tea, I intended not only to accept what I was feeling but to actively welcome it. I began to offer the yes with a softer, more friendly tone. I even smiled from time to time—my whole drama started to seem silly. My body and mind grew steadily lighter and more open. Even the pressure in my sinuses began to ease up. The dark cloud of "no" was replaced by the expansive sky of a "yes" that had endless room for grouchiness and irritation. Critical comments continued to arise, and with yes they continued to pass. When my mind suggested that I was using a gimmick that wouldn't work for long, saying yes to the story allowed the thought to dissolve. I wasn't resisting anything or holding on to anything. Moods and sensations and thoughts moved through the friendly skies of Radical Acceptance. I felt the inner freedom that comes from agreeing unconditionally to life. I was inviting Mara to tea.

We bring alive the spirit of Radical Acceptance when, instead of resisting emotional pain, we are able to say yes to our experience. Pat Rodegast (representing the teachings of Emmanuel) writes, "So walk with your heaviness, saying yes. Yes to the sadness, yes to the whispered longing. Yes to the fear. Love means setting aside walls, fences, and unlocking doors, and saying yes . . . one can be in paradise by simply saying yes to this moment." The instant we agree to feel fear or vulnerability, greed or agitation, we are holding our life with an unconditionally friendly heart.

When I introduce the practice of yes to students, it often brings up objections or confusion. Isn't it just another shallow version of "positive thinking," a way to gloss over the reality of how hard life can be? Certainly, they object, we can't say yes to everything we experience. What if we wanted to hurt somebody? Or what if we're experiencing deep depression? Wouldn't saying yes feed those states?

Saying yes does not mean approving of angry thoughts or sinking into any of our feelings. We are not saying yes to acting on our harmful impulses. Nor are we saying yes to external circumstances that can hurt us: If someone is treating us abusively, certainly we must strongly say no and create intelligent boundaries to protect ourselves in the future. Even in that instance, however, we can still say yes to the experience of fear, anger or hurt that is arising inside us. Yes is an inner practice of acceptance in which we willingly allow our thoughts and feelings to naturally arise and pass away.

Students sometimes ask, "If we are filled with thoughts of hatred toward ourselves, won't our attempts at friendly acceptance just cover over what we really feel?" It's a good question. As we know from relating to others, we can act friendly while actually harboring tremendous judgment and distaste. The challenge at these times is, can we bring a friendly attention to just how unfriendly we feel? Can we see clearly what we are experiencing, and say yes to the huge force of no? And if we can't manage that, we can at least *intend* to be friendly.

It's also easy to mistakenly consider yes as a technique to get rid of unpleasant feelings and make us feel better. Saying yes is not a way of manipulating our experience, but rather an aid to opening to life as it is. While we might, as I experienced on retreat, say yes and feel lighter and happier, this is not necessarily what happens. If we say yes to a feeling of sadness, for instance, it might swell into full-blown grieving. Yet regardless of how our experience unfolds, by agreeing to what is here, we offer it the space to express and move through us.

I do caution my students, however, that it is not always wise to say yes to inner experience. If we have been traumatized in the past, old feelings of terror may be triggered. We might not have the balance or resiliency in a particular moment to meet our experience with unconditional friendliness, and our attempts at yes might actually end up flooding us with fear. It would be better instead to find a way to alleviate the fear, perhaps by seeking comfort with a friend, doing vigorous exercise or taking prescribed medication. For the time being, saying no to what feels like too much, and yes to what simply works to keep us balanced, is the most compassionate response we can offer ourselves.

There are many ways of sending the message of yes to our inner life. We can whisper, "It's okay" or even a welcoming "Hello"—silently or softly out loud—in response to a painful emotion. Yes might also be an image or gesture. A friend of mine mentally visualizes herself bringing her palms together and bowing to what has appeared. When she feels the grip of anxiety, anger or guilt, she imagines bowing to it with a sense of genuine respect. I sometimes lightly place my hand on my heart and send a message of acceptance and care to whatever is arising in me.

Thich Nhat Hanh calls his practice of yes "smile yoga." He suggests bringing a slight but real smile to our lips many times throughout the day, whether we are meditating or simply stopping for a red light. "A tiny bud of a smile on your lips," writes Thich Nhat Hanh, "nourishes awareness and calms you miraculously . . . your smile will bring happiness to you and to those around you." The power of a smile to open and relax us is confirmed by modern science. The muscles used to make a smile actually send a biochemical message to our nervous system that it is safe to relax the flight, fight or freeze response. A smile is the yes of unconditional friendliness that welcomes experience without fear.

When Thich Nhat Hanh visited the San Francisco Zen Center, he found the students deeply dedicated to a rigorous spiritual discipline. Toward the end of his stay, they gathered to ask for his guidance on their practice. With a little smile he offered: "You should get up a little later each morning . . . and you should smile more."

SAYING YES TO OUR LIFE

Our practice of saying yes is not limited to our immediate experience. We can say yes to the whole life we are living. Yes to our friendships, to our parenting, to our physical appearance, to our personality, to our work, to our spiritual path. However, because we are usually shooting for perfection, when we step back to take a look at "how we're doing," we often feel as if our life isn't turning out quite right. Mara appears, casting a shadow over the goodness and value of how we live.

Zen teacher Ed Brown is a brilliant cook and founder of the Greens Restaurant in San Francisco, famous for its natural foods cuisine. But during Ed's early days as a cook at the Tassajara mountain retreat center, he had a problem. No matter what recipes or variations in ingredients he tried, he couldn't get his biscuits to come out right. His unreachable standard, as he discovered, was set years earlier—growing up he had "made" and loved Pillsbury biscuits.

> Finally one day came a shifting-into-place, an awakening: not "right" compared to what? Oh, my word, I'd been trying to make canned Pillsbury biscuits! Then came an exquisite moment of actually tasting my biscuits without comparing them to some (previously hidden) standard. They were wheaty, flaky, buttery, "sunny, earthy, real" (as Rilke's sonnet proclaims). They were incomparably alive, present, vibrant—in fact much more satisfying than any memory.
>
> These occasions can be so stunning, so liberating, these moments when you realize your life is just fine as it is, thank you. Only the insidious comparison to a beautifully prepared, beautifully packaged product made it seem insufficient. Trying to produce a biscuit—a life—with no dirty bowls, no messy feelings, no depression, no anger was so frustrating.

Then savoring, actually tasting the present moment of experience—how much more complex and multifaceted. How unfathomable . . .

There is something wonderfully bold and liberating about saying yes to our entire imperfect and messy life. With even a glimmer of that possibility, joy rushes in. Yet when we've been striving to make "Pillsbury biscuits" for a lifetime, the habits of perfectionism don't easily release their grip. When mistrust and skepticism creep in, we might be tempted to back down from embracing our life unconditionally. It takes practice, learning to bounce back each time we're dragged down by what seems to be wrong. But as Ed points out, when we stop comparing ourselves to some assumed standard of perfection, the "biscuits of today," this very life we are living right now, can be tasted and explored, honored and appreciated fully. When we put down ideas of what life should be like, we are free to wholeheartedly say yes to our life as it is.

Guided Meditation: The Power of Yes

Sitting quietly, close your eyes and take a few full breaths. Bring to mind a current situation that elicits a reaction of anger, fear or grief. It may be a rift with your partner, the loss of a loved one, a power struggle with your child, a chronic illness, a hurtful behavior that you now regret. The more fully you get in touch with the charged essence of the story, the more readily you can access the feelings in your heart and throughout your body. What is it about this situation that provokes the strongest feelings? You might see a particular scene in your mind, hear words that were spoken, recognize a belief you hold about how this situation reflects on you or what it means for your future. Be especially aware of the feelings in your stomach, chest and throat.

In order to see firsthand what happens when you resist experience, begin by experimenting with saying no. As you connect with the pain you feel in the situation you have chosen, mentally direct a stream of no at the feelings. No to the unpleasantness of fear, anger, shame or grief. Let the word carry the energy of no—rejecting, pushing away what you are experiencing. As you say no, notice what this resistance feels like in your body. Do you feel tightness, pressure? What happens to the painful feelings as you say no? What happens to your heart? Imagine what your life would be like if, for the next hours, weeks and months, you continued to move through the world with the thoughts and feelings of no.

Take a few deep breaths and let go by relaxing through the body, opening your eyes or shifting your posture a bit. Now take a few moments to call to mind again the painful situation you'd previously chosen, remembering the images, words, beliefs and feelings connected with it. This time let yourself be the Buddha under the bodhi tree, the Buddha inviting Mara to tea. Direct a stream of the word yes *at your experience. Agree to the experience with yes. Let the feelings float, held in the environment of yes. Even if there are waves of no—fear or anger that arise with the painful situation or even from doing this exercise—that's okay. Let these natural reactions be received in the larger field of yes. Yes to the pain. Yes to the parts of us that want the pain to go away. Yes to whatever thoughts or feelings arise. Notice your experience as you say yes. Is there softening, opening and movement in your body? Is there more space and openness in your mind? What happens to the unpleasantness as you say yes? Does it get more intense? Does it become more diffuse? What happens to your heart as you say yes? What would your experience be in the hours, weeks and months to come, if you could bring the spirit of yes to the inevitable challenges and sorrows of life?*

Continue to sit now, releasing thoughts and resting in an alert, relaxed awareness. Let your intention be to say a gentle YES to whatever sensations, emotions, sounds or images may arise in your awareness.

Guided Meditation: Facing Difficulty and Naming What Is True

Mental noting deepens our attention so we are better able to meet painful emotions and intense sensations with a wakeful and healing presence.

Sitting comfortably, close your eyes and take a few full breaths. Is there some situation or issue in your life that you are grappling with? You might focus on an interpersonal conflict, financial pressure or stress at work. Ask yourself, "How am I feeling about this?" and bring a receptive presence to your body. Pay particular attention to your throat, chest and stomach. Is there tightness, pressure, heat? Is there a word that describes your experience—sad, restless, shaky, afraid? There is no need to strain, to run through a mental thesaurus to find the "right" word. Just notice what word arises in awareness and mentally repeat it to yourself in a soft tone. Sometimes there is no label that fits the mix of feelings that you are experiencing. In this case you might name one of the more dominant elements in the mix. The point is not to nail something down by getting it right, but to keep paying attention to the felt sense of what is real in this particular moment.

After naming your experience, gently ask yourself, while paying close attention to the sensations in your body, "Is this true? Does this word describe what I am feeling now? If not, is there another word?" Continue in this way—mentally noting your unfolding experience and checking your body to see what is most true in this moment.

You may get lost for a time in thoughts. When you realize this, gently note, "planning, obsessing, fantasizing," and return your attention to your body. Again sense and name any strong emotions or sensations that you become aware of.

Remember that labeling always remains in the background (5 percent), with the great majority of your awareness (95 percent) attending to your actual experience. When done softly and lightly, noting can create a mood that is gentle and receptive.

Guided Meditation: Embracing Life with a Smile

The compassionate Buddha is often seen in statues and pictures with a slight smile as he embraces the ten thousand joys and sorrows. When we meditate with the spirit of a smile, we awaken our natural capacity for unconditional friendliness.

Sitting comfortably, close your eyes and let the natural rhythm of the breath help you to relax. Take a few moments to let go of obvious places of tightness and tension. Now, listening to sounds and becoming aware of the space around you, allow the curved image of a smile to appear in your mind. Notice how gentleness, kindness, openness and ease arise with the idea of a smile. Sense the curved relaxed smile fill your mind and extend outward into space.

Now imagine a smile at the corner of both eyes and feel the sensations that arise there. Allow your brow to be smooth, the flesh around your eyes to be soft and relaxed. You might sense your eyes floating gently as if in a pool of warm water. Continue to soften and let go through the whole area around the eyes. Can you perceive a relaxed brightness there?

Now bring a small but real smile to your lips—the half-smile of the Buddha—and allow the feeling to relax the muscles of your face. Let the jaw be relaxed and loose, and let the tip of the tongue lightly touch the roof of the mouth. Feel now how the eyes are smiling . . . the mouth is smiling . . .

Bring the image of a smile to your throat and notice what happens. There might be a relaxing and opening. If there is tightness allow it to be held in the sense of the smile. Feel again the corners of your eyes smiling, your mouth smiling, your throat smiling.

Let the smile drift down into your chest. Imagine the shape and feeling of a smile spreading through the area of your heart. Whatever feelings might be there, allow them to float in the openness and kindness of a smile. Continuing to relax, sense the smile in your heart sending ripples of ease throughout your body—through the shoulders, along the arms and down into the torso and legs. Can you feel the openness and vibrancy of a smile at the navel, the genitals, the base of the spine?

Allow yourself to rest in the spacious and kind awareness that is engendered by a smile. When thoughts, sensations or emotions arise, can you sense how they are held with unconditional friendliness? If your mind wanders or you find yourself tightening, you can gently reestablish the smile in your mind, eyes, mouth and heart.

With practice, you will find that the smile is a simple and powerful way to reawaken the heart at any moment of the day. Rather than a full "smile-down" as described above, you can also explore simply assuming the half-smile of the Buddha whenever you remember.

FIVE

COMING HOME TO OUR BODY: THE GROUND OF RADICAL ACCEPTANCE

There is one thing that, when cultivated and regularly practiced, leads to deep spiritual intention, to peace, to mindfulness and clear comprehension, to vision and knowledge, to a happy life here and now, and to the culmination of wisdom and awakening. And what is that one thing? It is mindfulness centered on the body.

The Buddha, from the *Satipatthana Sutta*

Halfway through my son Narayan's eighth-grade year, he and I found ourselves caught in a painful and angry standoff. His grades were sliding and we struggled daily over the rules about computer play, homework, phone time, bedtime. The more I monitored, reminded and scolded, the more Narayan turned a deaf ear or became defensive and sour. When I held back and gave him some rope, he didn't hesitate to hang himself. His room was fast becoming a late-night video arcade and a permanent hangout for his friends. At least I wasn't worried about them being a bad influence—I liked them and most of them were on the honor roll. But that only deepened my frustration with Narayan.

My anger seeped into all the cracks and crevices of our daily life. If Narayan kept me waiting for a few minutes when I was retrieving him from one of his friends' houses, I would sit in the car stewing. If he forgot to feed the dog or change the cat litter, I'd pounce on him for being irresponsible. When he'd ask me to order a pizza, I'd respond vindictively, "Well, you didn't clean your room, so why should I?"

Entirely submerged in a story of right and wrong, I would barge angrily into Narayan's room every time he violated one of my rules. The demands and threats that emerged from this script only made us feel increasingly alienated from each other. Clearly my method wasn't working.

Lying awake one night, I began thinking about how fast the years were passing and how in a flash my son would be leaving home. I imagined looking back at his teen years and seeing how our misunderstandings and anger had devoured our time together. The pain of this prospect jarred me. I needed to try a different way. I regularly used the art of pausing, but I'd been so caught up in my reactions over the past few weeks that I had actually forgotten to apply it. I resolved to practice pausing before my next encounter with Narayan, hoping that would help me be more present and openhearted when we were together.

The next evening, about a half hour after the time we had agreed on for starting homework, I arrived outside his room. Through the closed door I could hear the muffled sounds of "Everquest," Narayan's favorite computer game. Anger began mounting inside me as I visualized him with his eyes glued to the glowing screen, fingers nimbly working. I realized he had been at it for hours, again disregarding our agreements. I imagined myself heaving a giant boulder into the computer screen. This had been a recurring fantasy.

Instead, I simply waited, and in that pause I began to notice the feelings and sensations in my body. The anger felt like a mounting pressure in my chest and throat. My shoulders and hands were tight, my jaw was clenched. I felt my heart pounding, felt the heat in my face. This was horribly uncomfortable—it would have been far easier to just play out my anger and barge into his room.

All our strategies of trying to control life through blaming or withdrawing are aimed at keeping us from the raw experience of just such a moment. In the pause, rather than getting lost in our reactive thoughts and actions, we become directly aware of what is happening in our body. At these times, we begin to see how interconnected our mind and body are. With anger, the body tightens, the chest fills with an explosive feeling of pressure. With fear, we might feel the grip of knots in our stomach, the constriction in our chest or throat. If shame arises, our face burns, our shoulders slump, we feel a physical impulse to shrink back, to hide. Sensations in the body are ground zero, the place where we directly experience the entire play of life.

As I stood there that night outside Narayan's door, feeling and "letting be" what was happening inside me, the sensations slowly began to shift. The pressure in my chest that wanted to explode in anger subtly gave way to a deep soreness inside, as if a fist were gripping my heart. "I'm afraid of something," I realized. Immediately the words appeared in my mind: "I'm afraid Narayan will fail in life, be unfulfilled, end up unhappy. It's all my fault that he's become so addicted to TV and videos and computers. I've let him down, not guided or inspired him to live in a healthy way."

I could sense the old familiar story of failing as a parent begin to take over. At another time I could easily have gotten lost in this trance, but I was determined to stay awake in my body. Almost before I could focus my attention on the stab of shame in my chest, another part of the story asserted itself: "I've tried to set limits, to guide him . . . and he won't listen. It's his fault I feel like this." As surges of heat and pressure rushed down my arms like waves of water, I almost stormed into Narayan's room, but I managed to turn my attention again to the tumultuous feelings in my body.

I began to sense a sinking feeling, a heavy ache pressing against my heart. As this ache grew stronger my eyes felt moist with tears. The story was no longer about what was wrong with him or with me. I was noticing what had happened between us. My aversion to his testosterone-driven attraction to violent video games and movies had created a gulf between us. As I opened to the swelling grief, I noticed the stories of blame and failure receding. In their place was a growing tenderness in my heart and mind, and an understanding that what mattered beyond all things was loving him. I didn't know what would happen when I opened the door, but I wanted to bring this awareness, this open and tender presence, into my moments with Narayan. I wanted to meet him with an accepting heart.

After knocking and hearing his mumbled "C'min," I walked slowly into his room. His attention was still fixated on the computer screen, but when he realized I was just standing there watching, he looked up with guilty eyes. "I was just getting off, Mom. What time is it anyway?" I told him, obviously noting the watch sitting on his dresser and not on his wrist. More silence. Now his look was questioning. "Are you angry? I'm sorry . . . I just lost track. But I'll get my homework done, honest. There's not much."

Pulling up a chair close to his, I sat down. "It's okay, hon, but we need to talk." What I said to him—about his study habits, about honoring our agreements—wasn't new. But *I* felt different. I was aware of my breath, of my posture, of where my hands were resting. I noticed how my face tightened when it seemed his attention was drifting. When he spoke, I listened. I heard how much he got from mastering the game he was playing. I could sympathize with his frustrations about having "lights out" when he wasn't the slightest bit tired. Inhabiting my body allowed me to be present with Narayan, and to be respectful. When I kissed the top of his head and left the room, there was a good warm feeling between us.

Bringing Radical Acceptance into our life starts at this most basic level—becoming aware of the sensations that are continually taking place in our physical being. Henry David Thoreau wrote, "Dwell as near as possible to the channel in which your life flows." By inhabiting my body with awareness, I was discovering the roots of my reactivity. I had been avoiding the unpleasant sensations that make up fear and sorrow. By opening mindfully to the play of sensations, the grip of my anger and stories naturally loosened.

This is how an embodied presence awakens us from a trance: *We free ourselves at the ground level from the reactivity that perpetuates our suffering.* When we meet arising sensations with Radical Acceptance, instead of losing ourselves in grasping and resisting, we begin the process of freeing ourselves from the stories that separate us. We taste the joy of being fully present, alive and connected with all of life. This was the Buddha's promise: Mindfulness of the body leads to happiness in this life, and the fullness of spiritual awakening.

LEARNING TO INHABIT OUR BODIES

We experience our lives through our bodies whether we are aware of it or not. Yet we are usually so mesmerized by our ideas about the world that we miss out on much of our direct sensory experience. Even when we are aware of feeling a strong breeze, the sound of rain on the roof, a fragrance in the air, we rarely remain with the experience long enough to inhabit it fully. In most moments we have an overlay of inner dialogue that comments on what is happening and plans what we might do next. We might greet a friend with a hug, but our moments of physical contact become blurred by our computations about how long to embrace or what we're going to say when we're done. We rush through the hug, not fully present.

An elderly man at one of my weekend workshops described himself as "living from the neck up." Many people are so accustomed to being out of touch with the body that they live entirely in a mental world. The fact that the body and mind are interconnected might even be hard for them to believe. In a class I led at a women's correction center, an inmate told me that she was aware of her body only when she was in pain or in a rage. Unless feelings are painfully intrusive or, as with sex, extremely pleasant or intense, physical sensations can seem elusive and be difficult to recognize. This is the basic characteristic of being in trance—we are only partially present to our experience of the moment.

Hameed Ali, author and contemporary spiritual teacher, reminds us that if we are not living with awareness of our body, we are not fully alive:

> Sincerely explore for yourself, are you here or not? Are you in your body or oblivious, or only aware of parts of it? When I say, "Are you in your body?" I mean, "Are you completely filling your body?" I want to know whether you are in your feet, or just have feet. Do you live in them, or are they just things you use when you walk? Are you in your belly, or do you just know vaguely that you have a belly? Or is it just for food?
>
> Are you really in your hands, or do you move them from a distance? Are you present in your cells, inhabiting and filling your body? If you aren't in your body, what significance is there in your experience this moment? Are you preparing, so

that you can be here in the future? Are you setting up conditions by saying to yourself, "When such and such happens I'll have time, I'll be here." If you are not here, what are you saving yourself for?

I first discovered that my body was alive with a universe of sensations during an introductory yoga class I took during my sophomore year in college. Near the end of the yoga class the teacher asked us to sit quietly with crossed legs on the floor, making sure that our hands were resting easily, comfortably on our laps or legs. She told us to take a few deep breaths, explaining that the breath offers a natural pathway out of our minds and into our bodies.

She then directed us to explore the aliveness of our body. "Let your entire awareness be in your hands," she said. "Relax and soften them, feeling your hands *from the inside.*" She guided us in slowly feeling each finger carefully from within, each palm, the tops of our hands, our wrists. I became aware first of tingling, then of pulsing areas of pressure and heat. As I relaxed into feeling the sensations in my hands, I realized that there was no distinct boundary, no sense of a defined shape to my hand. All I could perceive was a changing field of energy that felt like moving points of light in a night sky. It suddenly occurred to me that this vibrant aliveness was always going on without my conscious awareness. I had been missing out on a lot of life.

Our teacher then invited us to explore this presence and aliveness throughout our body. I noticed the knots in my shoulders, and within a few moments they relaxed simply in response to my attention. I could feel a tingling warmth spread down through my arms. As I brought awareness to the hardness and tightness in my stomach, that area also softened and loosened. I could feel energy streaming up through my chest and down through my legs. My whole body was a living, breathing field of energy. I felt a wave of gratitude—in just moments my world had become distinctly enlarged and dazzlingly alive. While I didn't know it at the time, my teacher had introduced me to meditation.

Meditation practices in all traditions typically use postures, like sitting up cross-legged as we did in the yoga class, to enable the body to be stable and still. When we are quiet, we can more readily notice our changing stream of experience: of vibration, pulsing, pressure, heat, light, tastes, images and sounds. Yet, as we quickly discover when we close our eyes to meditate, this inner world is often covered over by waves of emotions—excitement or anxiety, restlessness or anger—and an endless stream of comments and judgments, memories and stories of the future, worries and plans.

The Buddha called our persistent emotional and mental reactivity the "waterfall" because we so easily are carried away from the experience of the present moment by its compelling force. Both Buddhist and Western psychology tell us how this happens: The mind instantly and unconsciously assesses whatever we experience as pleasant, unpleasant or neutral. A titillating thought or tingling sensation—pleasant. A bad smell or sudden, loud sound—unpleasant. Noticing our breath—usually neutral. When pleasant sensations arise, our reflex is to grasp after them and try to hold on to them. We often do this through planning, and with the emotional energies of excitement and yearning. When we experience unpleasant sensations, we contract, trying to avoid them. Again the process is the same—we worry and strategize, we feel fear, irritation. Neutral is our signal to disengage and turn our attention elsewhere, which usually means to an experience that is more intense or stimulating.

All our reactions to people, to situations, to thoughts in our mind—are actually reactions to *the kind of sensations that are arising in our body.* When we become riveted on someone's ineptness and are bursting with impatience, we are reacting to our own unpleasant sensations; when we are attracted to someone and filled with longing and fantasy, we are reacting to pleasant sensations. Our entire swirl of reactive thoughts, emotions and behaviors springs from this ground of reacting to sensations. When these sensations are unrecognized, our lives are lost in the waterfall of reactivity—we disconnect from living presence, from full awareness, from our heart.

In order to awaken from this trance, the Buddha recommended "mindfulness centered on the body." In fact, he called physical sensations the first foundation of mindfulness because they are intrinsic to feelings and thoughts and are the base of the very process of consciousness. Because our pleasant or unpleasant sensations so quickly trigger a chain reaction of emotions and mental stories, a central part of our training is to recognize the arising of thoughts and return over and over to our immediate sensory experience. We might feel discomfort in our lower back and hear a worried inner voice saying, "How long will this last? How can I make it go away?" Or we might feel a pleasant tingling, a relaxed openness in our chest and eagerly wonder, "What did I do to arrive in this state . . . I hope I can do that again." We practice by seeing the stories, letting them go and dropping under them into the living sensations in our body.

We cannot cut through our chain of reactions if we are not mindful of sensations. S. N. Goenka, a contemporary teacher of vipassana meditation, warns us that if we just pay attention to passing thoughts, for instance, "deep inside, a part of the mind keeps on reacting. *Because with the thought, there's also a sensation. You must not miss this root.*"

The basic meditation instructions given by the Buddha were to be mindful of the changing stream of sensations without trying to hold on to any of them, change them or resist them. The Buddha makes clear that being mindful of sensations does not mean standing apart and observing like a distant witness. Rather we're directly experiencing what is happening in our body. Instead of seeing our hand as an external object, for instance, we carefully feel into the energy that *is* our hand in any given moment. *We train to experience the body from the inside out.*

Rather than directly experiencing sensations, we might have the notion that there is "pain in my back." Maybe we have a mental map of our body and a certain area we call back. But what is "back"? What happens when we let go of our picture and directly enter into that part of our body with awareness? In a similar way, what happens to pain when we don't label it as such?

With a mindful attention we can investigate and discover what our moment-to-moment experience of pain actually is. Perhaps we feel pressure and an ache that seems localized in a small area. As we pay deeper attention, we might notice heat or tightness. Maybe we become aware of throbbing or a sudden shooting sensation or pulling and twisting. Perhaps the sensations are no longer pinpointed in one place but begin to spread and loosen. As we continue to pay attention, we might become aware of flowing sensations arising, becoming distinctive, blending into each other, vanishing, appearing elsewhere.

Seeing this fluidity in our experience is one of the most profound and distinctive realizations that arise when we become mindful of sensations. We recognize that there is absolutely nothing solid or static about our experience. Rather, the realm of sensations is endlessly changing—sensations appear and vanish, shifting in intensity, texture, location. As we pay close attention to our physical experience, we see that it does not hold still for even a moment. At first this can be uncomfortable, even frightening.

Each time we let go of our story, we realize there is no ground to stand on, no position that orients us, no way to hide or avoid what is arising. One student at a meditation retreat told me, "When I am mindful of sensations for more than just a few seconds, I start getting anxious. I feel like I should be watching out, looking over my shoulder. It feels like there are important things that I am overlooking and ought to be thinking about." It is easy to feel that something bad will happen if we don't maintain our habitual vigilance by thinking, judging, planning. Yet this is the very habit that keeps us trapped in resisting life. Only when we realize we can't hold on to anything can we begin to relax our efforts to control our experience.

Sensations are always changing and moving. If we habitually interrupt and constrict their natural process of unfolding and transformation by resisting them or trying to hold on to them, by tightening against them in our body or telling ourselves stories, it's like damming up or diverting the course of a river. It's easy to let the river flow when sensations are pleasant. But when they're not, when we're in emotional or physical pain, we contract, pull away. Seeing this and learning how to meet pain with Radical Acceptance is one of the most challenging and liberating of practices.

REACTING TO PAIN WITH FEAR: "SOMETHING IS WRONG"

When I first got pregnant my husband and I decided we'd have a home birth, without drugs and assisted by a midwife. We considered childbirth a natural process and, since I wasn't high-risk, I wanted to be in the warmth and familiarity of my home, not a hospital. My hope was to be as wakeful and present as possible during the birth, and while I knew the pain would be intense, I trusted that my meditation and yoga practices would help me to "go with the flow."

When labor began I was rested and ready. Knowing that resisting the pain of contractions only made them worse, I relaxed with them, breathing, making sounds without inhibition, letting go as my body's intelligence took over. Like any animal, I was unthinkingly immersed, instinctively responding to the drama unfolding through me, riding the pain as a natural part of the process.

Then suddenly something shifted. When my son's head started crowning, the pain level shot up. It was no longer something I could breathe into and let surge through me. This much pain has got to mean something is going wrong, I thought. My whole body tightened, and my deep slow breaths turned into the shallow, quick breathing of panic. All my confidence was gone, all my resolve to relax into the waves of pain forgotten.

Like every aspect of our evolutionary design, the unpleasant sensations we call pain are an intelligent part of our survival equipment: Pain is our body's call to pay attention, to take care of ourselves. Dr. Jon Kabat-Zinn is known worldwide for his Stress Reduction Clinic at the University of Massachusetts, where he teaches mindfulness practices to patients suffering from chronic and acute pain. He writes:

> Symptoms of illness or distress, plus your feelings about them, can be viewed as messengers coming to tell you something important about your body or about your mind. In the old days, if a king didn't like the message he was given, he would sometimes have the messenger killed. This is tantamount to suppressing your symptoms or your feelings because they are unwanted. Killing the messenger and denying the message or raging against it are not intelligent ways of approaching healing. The one thing we don't want to do is to ig-

nore or rupture the essential connections that can complete relevant feedback loops and restore self-regulation and balance. Our real challenge when we have symptoms is to see if we can listen to their messages and really hear them and take them to heart, that is, make the connection fully.

Sometimes the messages that we receive are a call for immediate action: Burning heat—we pull our hand away from the fire. Weakness and headache—we get something to eat. Acute chest pains and shortness of breath—we call 911. At other times pain asks that we protect ourselves from further injury by resting, staying still. With childbirth, pain keeps us absolutely focused, instinctively participating in the demanding process of labor. As we are dying, like an animal that seeks solitude, pain might guide us to find an inner sanctuary of quiet and peace. If we accept pain without the confusion of fear, we can listen to its message and respond with clarity.

Yet, as I experienced in birthing, intense pain, even when it is part of a seemingly healthy process like birthing, is alarming. When I reacted with fear, I added to the unpleasant sensations the feeling and belief that something was wrong. Rather than practicing Radical Acceptance, my body and mind reacted by resisting and fighting the pain.

While fear of pain is a natural human reaction, it is particularly dominant in our culture, where we consider pain as bad or wrong. Mistrusting our bodies, we try to control them in the same way that we try to manage the natural world. We use painkillers, assuming that whatever removes pain is the right thing to do. This includes all pain—the pains of childbirth and menstruating, the common cold and disease, aging and death. In our society's cultural trance, rather than a natural phenomenon, pain is regarded as the enemy. Pain is the messenger we try to kill, not something we allow and embrace.

At that point of intensity in childbirth, I was fully at war, pitted against the pain. My midwife, used to seeing fear and resistance in response to pain, immediately assured me, "Nothing's wrong, honey . . . it's all completely natural, it's just painful." She had to say this several times before I could let it begin to sink in and, in the midst of the burning pain, the explosive pressure, the tearing and exhaustion, remember again to breathe deeply and relax. *It was just pain, not wrong,* and I could open up and accept it.

Being alive includes feeling pain, sometimes intense pain. And as we know, pain does not necessarily end in the joy of a healthy newborn. Sometimes it doesn't end at all. When it is a sign of injury, it can lead to loss in our capacity to move our body freely. It can lead to death. Given the very real relationship between pain and loss, no wonder we add on the belief that pain means "something is wrong." No wonder we respond with fear and compulsively try to manage or eliminate our pain.

But as I learned in childbirth, pain doesn't have to lead to suffering. The Buddha taught that we suffer when we cling to or resist experience, when we want life different than it is. As the saying goes: *"Pain is inevitable, but suffering is optional."* When painful sensations arise, if we meet them with clarity and presence, we can see that pain is just pain. When we are mindful of pain rather than reactive, we do not contract into the experience of a victimized, suffering self. Reacting to sensations with fear, perceiving them as "wrong," initiates the trance. As the Buddha taught, when we grasp at or resist this ground level of our experience, we set in motion a waterfall of reactivity. Fear, itself made up of unpleasant sensations, compounds the pain—now we want to get away not only from the original pain but also from the pain of fear. In fact, the fear of pain is often the most unpleasant part of a painful experience. As Jon Kabat-Zinn writes, "When you see and feel the sensations you are experiencing *as sensations,* pure and simple, you may see that these thoughts about the sensations are useless to you *at that moment* and that they can actually make things worse than they need be." When we assess physical sensations as something to be feared, pain is not just pain. It is something wrong and bad that we must get away from.

Our fear often proliferates into a web of stories. For four years I struggled with chronic illness. One of the hardest parts was how being sick became a comment on who I was and my inability to take care of myself "properly." Each time I went through a bout of fatigue or indigestion, my mind would flood with stories and interpretations: "Something's very wrong . . . maybe I'm seriously sick." I'd dwell on how I might have caused the problem. "My immune system's down. I pushed too hard and didn't get enough sleep . . . I've been drinking too much black tea, the acid must have affected my stomach." Along with a wave of tiredness or stomach cramp would arise the feeling of personal weakness, of shame. Pain was bad; it was my pain and it signaled some sort of character flaw.

When we are habitually immersed in our stories about pain, we prevent ourselves from experiencing it as the changing stream of sensations that it is. Instead, as our muscles contract around it and our stories identify it as the enemy, the pain solidifies into a self-perpetuating, immovable mass. Our resistance can actually end up creating new layers of symptoms and suffering. Perhaps the judgments and worries that tightened my muscles against the pain increased my exhaustion. When we abandon our body for our fear-driven stories about pain, we trap the pain in our body.

In moments of acute pain, our fear intensifies and the experience of "something is wrong" drives an urgent, immediate battle against pain. A friend of mine went through excruciating pain when a fragment of disc came loose and began pressing on a portion of his spinal cord: "It felt like someone had poured gasoline on my left leg and lit it." The pain was relentless and all-consuming, and he tried everything he could to escape its intensity. At one point he was taking two strong narcotics, steroids, an anti-inflammatory, and two strong sedative muscle relaxants. The drugs would knock him out for a while, but when he awoke he'd be in agony until the next dose. "Pain has a unique quality," he wrote me. "The stronger it is, the less aware you are of the rest of the world. If it is severe enough, in the end, there is only you and the pain locked in a delicate duel."

When, instead of Radical Acceptance, our initial response to physical pain is fear and resistance, the ensuing chain of reactivity can be consuming. The moment we believe something is wrong, our world shrinks and we lose ourselves in the effort to combat our pain. This same process unfolds when our pain is emotional—we resist the unpleasant sensations of loneliness, sorrow and anger. Whether physical or emotional, when we react to pain with fear, we pull away from an embodied presence and go into the suffering of trance.

When pain is traumatic, the trance can become full-blown and sustained. The victim pulls away from pain in the body with such fearful intensity that the conscious connection between body and mind is severed. This is called dissociation. All of us to some degree disconnect from our bodies, but when we live bound in fear of perceived ever-present danger, finding our way back can be a long and delicate process.

TRAUMATIC FEAR: DISSOCIATING FROM OUR BODY

As a child Rosalie had been severely abused by her father. When he was drunk he would try to reach into her underpants or climb into her bed at night and rub his body against hers until he climaxed. When she resisted him he'd hit her and threaten her with worse. If she tried to run away and hide, he would become enraged, chase after her and mercilessly beat her. On two occasions during the year before he and her mother divorced, Rosalie's father had forced her to have intercourse with him. Such severe trauma has an emotional and physical impact that can endure a lifetime. When Rosalie came to see me, she was thirty-five years old, single and mildly anorexic. She'd already been through several forms of therapy, but was still going on and off starvation diets and suffering from regular anxiety attacks. Her body was thin, rigid and tight; and she was mistrustful of everyone she knew.

Rosalie assumed that anyone who appeared to like her really just wanted to take advantage of her. She told me she thought one person she hung around with was a friend only because she didn't want to go to parties alone. Another woman, who was attractive and popular with men, must like to be around her because it "boosted her ego." While Rosalie had no trouble finding dates, intimacy never lasted for long. Not wanting to feel the humiliation of being dropped, she usually broke off the relationship at the first signs that things were going downhill. Even with people she'd known for a long time, Rosalie kept her distance. When she was going through one of her regular bouts of anxiety she'd either act as if she "had it all together" or disappear for a while.

Often the only way Rosalie could spend time with people was by getting stoned. Marijuana made everything seem okay for the time being. But, she told me, now she needed to get high every night before bed in order to sleep through the night. If she didn't smoke a joint or take sleeping pills, she'd wake up in the middle of the night in a fit of terror. The dream was always the same—she was hiding in a small dark place and someone beastly and insane was about to find her.

Neuropsychology tells us that traumatic abuse causes lasting changes by affecting our physiology, nervous system and brain chemistry. In the normal process of forming memories we evaluate each new situation in terms of a cohesive world view we have formulated. With trauma, this cognitive process is short-circuited by the surge of painful and intense stimulation. Instead of "processing the experience" by fitting it into our understanding of how the world works and thereby learning from it, we revert to a more primitive form of encoding—through physical sensations and visual images. The trauma, undigested and locked in our body, randomly breaks through into consciousness. For years after the actual danger is past, a person who has been traumatized may relive an event as if it were continually occurring in the present.

Unprocessed pain keeps our system of self-preservation on permanent alert. In addition to sudden intrusive memories, a wide range of situations, many nonthreatening, may activate the alarmingly high levels of pain and fear stored in our body. Our partner might raise her voice in irritation, and the full force of our past wounds—all the terror or rage or hurt that lives in our body—can be unleashed. Whether or not there is any present danger, we feel absolutely at risk and compelled to find a way to get away from this pain.

In order to make it through this severe pain, victims of trauma dissociate from their bodies, numbing their sensitivity to physical sensations. Some people feel "unreal," as if they have left their body and are experiencing life from a great distance. They do whatever they can to keep from feeling the raw sensations of fear and pain in their body. They might lash out in aggression or freeze in depression or confusion. They might have suicidal thoughts or drink themselves senseless. They overeat, use drugs and lose themselves in mental obsessions. Yet the pain and fear don't go away. Rather, they lurk in the background and from time to time suddenly take over.

Dissociation, while protective, creates suffering. When we leave our bodies, we leave home. By rejecting pain and pulling away from the ground of our being, we experience the dis-ease of separation—loneliness, anxiety and shame. Alice Miller tells us that there is no way to avoid what's in the body. We either pay attention to it, or we suffer the consequences:

> The truth about our childhood is stored up in our body, and although we can repress it, we can never alter it. Our intellect can be deceived, our feelings manipulated, and conceptions confused, and our body tricked with medication. But someday our body will present its bill, for it is as incorruptible as a child, who, still whole in spirit, will accept no compromises or excuses, and it will not stop tormenting us until we stop evading the truth.

When Rosalie and I started working together, it was clear that her time had come—her body was presenting its bill. During our first few sessions she poured out her life story. While she was very bright and could easily articulate her problems and their causes, it was as if she were talking about someone else's life. She let me know that when we were talking she wasn't aware of feelings in her body, yet outside of therapy she was sometimes besieged by panic or rage. At those times these feelings in her body were so intense she wanted to die.

I suggested we might work together to help her gradually feel safer in her body, and let her know that this could make a difference in a way that her previous therapies hadn't. She readily agreed, and over the next few weeks we laid the groundwork. I wanted to understand Rosalie as deeply as possible, and she needed to feel safe and comfortable with me. When she was ready, I suggested we do a guided journey, exploring parts of her inner life that might lie outside her conscious awareness.

On the day of the journey I invited Rosalie to sit comfortably and close her eyes. I guided her with the hypnotic imagery of slowly descending a long winding staircase that ended facing a closed door. I suggested that with each step she leave behind distracting thoughts and become increasingly relaxed and curious. By the time she had reached the bottom of the stairs, Rosalie's body was very still, her eyelids flickering, her face slightly flushed. She nodded when I asked if she saw a door, and I suggested that behind it she would discover something important to her healing, some gift from her unconscious mind. I reminded her that no matter what she experienced, she was safe. We were here together, and she could come back whenever she wished. Then I told her she could open the door whenever she was ready.

Rosalie stiffened. "What do you see?" I asked softly. Her voice was barely a whisper. "A little girl. She's in a closet . . . hiding."

When I asked what she was hiding from, Rosalie shook her head slightly. After a few moments I asked how old she was. "She's seven," she responded and went on quickly, "It's her dad. He's going to find her and hurt her." I reassured her that the little girl was safe right now, and suggested that by relaxing and just noticing what happened next, she would discover some way this girl might be helped. When I saw her breathing more easily, I asked what the little girl was doing now. "She's praying. She's saying it hurts too much, that she can't take it anymore."

I waited for a few moments then asked her gently, "Rosalie, what might help that little girl handle all that pain?"

She frowned. "She's all by herself . . . there's no one there." Then her words came slowly: "She needs someone to take care of her."

"Who could best do that?" I asked. Again she paused, intent and focused. Suddenly her face filled with a look of surprise and amusement: "A good fairy! I can see her there with the little girl . . . She's with her in the closet." Rosalie waited for a moment and then reported, "The fairy's surrounded by a shimmering blue light and she's waving a golden wand."

"Rosalie, does the fairy have a message for the little girl, something she wants to say?"

She nodded: "She's telling her she can do something to help. She can do something that will let her forget for a while about the horrible things going on, so she can grow up and handle it when she's stronger."

I paused for a bit and then speaking softly asked how the fairy was going to do that. Rosalie's tone was calm and deliberate: "She says she is going to touch different parts of her body with her magic wand and they will change and be able to hold all the terrible feelings for her." She paused, listening inwardly, and then continued, "The good fairy is saying that even though it's hard to be so bound up, it will be her way to survive, to be quiet and control what's happening inside her."

After a long silence, I asked Rosalie what had happened. "Well, the fairy put the little girl's rage and fear into her belly, and then she bound it up so it could stay there. And then she put a magic lock on her pelvis and vagina so her sexual feelings couldn't get her in any more trouble." Rosalie took a few shaky breaths, and I gently asked, "What else?"

Tears began rolling down her cheeks as she said, "She told her she'd have to let her rib cage tighten so she wouldn't feel the pain of her heart breaking." Rosalie was quiet and then she went on, her voice a little stronger. "She said her neck would be a fortress with very thick round walls so that she wouldn't cry out for help or scream out in anger." Rosalie fell quiet and I just sat with her in silence.

"You're doing beautifully," I told her, and then added gently, "Is there anything else the fairy wants you to know?" Rosalie nodded. "She says someday the little girl will no longer be able to hold all this in, and her body will start unwinding its secrets. She will let go of everything she has been holding for so long . . . and she will do this because *most deeply, she wants to be whole and real."* Rosalie was softly weeping, her shoulders shaking. "She just told the little girl not to worry. She would find people who cared and would hold her as she finds herself again."

Rosalie sank back in her chair, and I asked what was happening now. "The good fairy is putting her arms around the little girl and taking her to bed." After a few moments she continued, whispering, "She's telling her that when she wakes up, she will forget what happened, but she will remember when she's ready." Rosalie was quiet and when she continued her voice was tender: "The good fairy just told her, 'Until then, and for always, I love you.'"

As if she had just finished the last page of a cherished book, Rosalie reached for the shawl I leave on my couch, wrapped it around herself and lay down, curling herself into the cushions. "Is this okay?" she whispered. "I just want to rest for a few minutes." Her face looked serene, as if these were the first real moments of ease she had touched in a long, long time.

In those weeks that followed her inner journey, Rosalie slowly emerged as if from a cocoon. Even her physical movements were lighter, more fluid. I asked if she would mind if I shared her "fairy story" in one of my meditation classes. That made her happy—she gladly wished for others the new inner freedom she felt. When I told the story, a number of people cried as they realized how they too had pulled away from their bodies, how they had locked up their energy and were not fully alive. It opened up the possibility of forgiving themselves for not facing their own deep wounds, and it helped them understand that it was natural to seek relief in the face of unbearable pain.

While there are times in our life we might have had no choice but to contract away from unbearable physical or emotional pain, our healing comes from reconnecting with those places in our body where that pain is stored. For Rosalie, as for all of us, moving toward freedom requires meeting with Radical Acceptance the pain that was locked away in fear. No matter how deeply we have been wounded, when we listen to the inner voice that calls us back to our bodies, back to wholeness, we begin our journey.

HEALING OUR WOUNDS: RETURNING HOME TO OUR BODY

Rosalie's journey had given her a way to understand what had happened to her—and how she could free herself. Many of our subsequent sessions were dedicated to exploring techniques that could help her become more at home in her body.

I first introduced her to a "sweeping meditation," guiding her attention slowly up and down her body, focusing on each region—feet and legs, torso, shoulders, arms and hands, neck, head. I encouraged Rosalie to imagine breathing energy and light into the part of the body she was attending to and totally letting go and relaxing as she breathed outward. As she deepened her attention in each area, I suggested that she simply notice whatever sensations she felt there, accepting them exactly as they were.

When Rosalie told me she was having a hard time feeling sensations inside her stomach and pelvic area, I asked her what color felt healing to her. She immediately remembered the shimmering blue that had surrounded the fairy. I suggested that she imagine feeling those areas of her body bathed in that blue, letting the color wash through her with each breath. After some moments Rosalie nervously reported, "I do feel some movement, some tingling," and then, "That's enough for now." While she wasn't able to sustain her attention in that newly awakening area for very long, Rosalie was proud of her first efforts. It had taken courage to reenter the places that had felt so dangerous.

Rosalie arrived at our next session excited about a new man she had met. But by the following week excitement had turned to anxiety and her body looked rigid with fear. She *really* liked this guy and didn't want to pull away: "If I can't make peace with this fear, Tara, I won't hang in there." Rosalie knew she needed to meet her body's experience with Radical Acceptance.

I suggested she pause and, feeling into her body, sense what was most asking for her attention and acceptance. This was new for Rosalie. Up until now she had only explored a mindful presence in her body when she was relatively relaxed. That was safe, but to feel raw fear had many painful associations. Closing her eyes she became silent and still. After about a minute she put her hand on her stomach. "In here," she said. "I'm really scared . . . I feel like I could throw up." I encouraged her to let the warmth of her hand, her own gentle touch, help her bring her full awareness to the unpleasant feelings. I asked her if she could feel that area from the inside and just notice what was happening.

Rosalie took several full breaths and sank back into the couch. For the next few minutes she named what she was experiencing: the soreness and squeezing tightness in the center of her belly, the feelings of her chest rising and falling with several deep breaths, loosening and dissolving of the hard knot in her stomach, a quaking and jumpiness spreading throughout her stomach, the thought "Maybe he's the right one," stabbing fear, shaking, the image of a young child alone in the closet, the thought "I can't stand this," heat spreading up into her chest and throat, a strangling feeling in her throat, breathing in blue, opening and softening in her throat, an upwelling of sadness. When she finally looked up, her eyes were glistening: "All this is happening inside me, and I'm just holding that little girl in my arms." After a few moments she went on: "I feel like I can accept this pain, I can handle whatever I'm feeling."

In both Buddhist psychology and Western experiential therapy, this process of experiencing and accepting the changing stream of sensations is central to the alchemy of transformation. Emotions, a combination of physical sensations and the stories we tell ourselves, continue to cause suffering until we experience them where they live in our body. If we bring a steady attention to the immediate physical experience of an emotion, past sensations and stories linked to it that have been locked in our body and mind are "de-repressed." Layers of historic hurt, fear or anger may begin to play themselves out in the light of awareness. Like Rosalie, when we feel and release the past pain held in our body, we become increasingly free to meet our present feelings with a wakeful and kind heart. We discover, as Rumi writes, "The cure for the pain is in the pain."

In order to go through her pain in a way that would lead to "the cure," Rosalie needed to feel a degree of safety. A basic sense of trust had been emerging for her since her journey. Our relationship was a haven for her—she trusted that I really cared about her, and she relied on my support as she reentered her body. Her experience with the fairy had revealed her own inner wisdom, her urge to protect herself and her longing to be awake and whole. What was now giving this trust its deepest roots was actually taking the risk to open mindfully to sensations. Each time she could sense her body from the inside and accept the sensations that were arising, even the most frightening ones, she felt more confidence about her capacity to be at home there. She *could* handle whatever came up. She could find the cure through being with the pain.

Learning to bring Radical Acceptance to our physical experience is usually a gradual process. If we have a large reservoir of fear locked in our body, we begin as Rosalie did, by just "putting our toe in the river," feeling the sensations and then stepping back when necessary. While at times we may encounter no pain at all, at other times the pain may be intense. Being at home in our body does not require us to focus for sustained periods of time on overwhelming physical or emotional pain. Especially if we feel worn down, it is wise and compassionate to take breaks, to rest, to direct our attention elsewhere. If we are meditating we might direct lovingkindness to the pain or fear (see chapter 10), or rest our attention in the breath and relax our body as fully as possible. If overwhelming sensations arise during our day, we might listen to music, talk with a friend or read a novel. When we encounter an especially rough patch, we may need the support of a meditation teacher, healer or therapist to help us hold our experience with presence and care. With time, as the good fairy promised, coming home to our body can be our rite of passage. As we bring a gentle attention to the ground of sensations, we free ourselves from the reactive stories and emotions that have kept us bound in fear. By inhabiting our body with awareness, we reclaim our life and our spirit.

LETTING LIFE LIVE THROUGH US

A couple of years into my long chronic illness, I attended a six-week vipassana meditation retreat. I had been to a number of extended retreats before and loved the long days filled with silence. This retreat was during a glorious New England fall, and I was delighted to have the chance to meditate in such beauty. Given my struggles with sickness, I looked forward to this time entirely dedicated to sitting and walking meditation; I needed the inspiration I knew I would find in the talks and instructions the teachers would be giving. The retreat would be a precious opportunity to become more accepting and present with my body and mind.

The first few days went smoothly—my mind began to quiet, and I readily settled into the rhythm of the retreat. Toward the end of the week I started having stomachaches and felt so exhausted I could barely motivate myself to walk to the meditation hall. I was used to these symptoms—after much testing the medical world had labeled them with the catchall phrase of chronic fatigue and told me I had irritable bowel syndrome. At this point it was a matter of making peace with discomfort. "Okay," I figured a bit grudgingly, "I'm here to work with . . . unpleasant sensations."

For the next twenty-four hours I noted the heat and cramping in my stomach, the leaden feeling in my limbs, and tried with some success to experience them with an accepting attention. But in the days that followed, when the symptoms didn't go away, I found myself caught in the habitual stories and sinking into a funk of fear, shame and depression. "Something's wrong with me . . . with the way I'm living my life. I'll never get better." And under that, the deep fear: "I'll never be happy." The familiar trance threatened to take over, and I took that as a signal to deepen my attention.

On a clear and brisk afternoon at the beginning of the second week of retreat, I took off into the woods, and walked until I found a patch of sun. Wrapping myself in the warm blanket I had brought from my room, I sat down and propped myself against a tree. The ground, covered with leaves, offered a firm, gentle cushion. It felt good to sit here in the natural world; I felt at home in the simplicity of earth, trees, wind, sky. I was resolved to attend to my own nature—to the changing stream of sensations living through my body.

After taking some moments to release whatever obvious tension I could, I did a quick scan through my body. I noticed the aches and soreness, the sinking feeling of tiredness. In an instant I was out of my body and into my mind: "Whoa . . . I still really feel sick." Once again I watched my mind contracting with the idea that something really was wrong. Fear. It felt like thick hard braids of rope, tightening around my throat and chest. Taking a deep breath, I let go of thoughts about sickness and just felt the gripping fear. I decided that no matter what experience arose, I was going to meet it with the attitude of "this too." I was going to accept everything.

As the minutes passed, I found I was feeling sensations without wishing them away. I was simply feeling the weight pressing on my throat and chest, feeling the tight ache in my stomach. The discomfort didn't disappear, but something gradually began shifting. My mind no longer felt tight or dull but clearer, focused and absolutely open. As my attention deepened, I began to perceive the sensations throughout my body as moving energy—tingling, pulsing, vibration. Pleasant or not, it was all the same energy playing through me.

As I noticed feelings and thoughts appear and disappear, it became increasingly clear that they were just coming and going on their own. Sensations were appearing out of nowhere and vanishing back into the void. There was no sense of a self owning them. There was no "me" feeling the vibrating, the pulsing, the tingling. No "me" being oppressed by unpleasant sensations. No "me" generating thoughts or trying to meditate. Life was just happening, a magical display of appearances. As every passing experience was accepted with the openness of "this too," any sense of boundary or solidity in my body and mind dissolved. Like the weather, sensations, emotions and thoughts were just moving through the open, empty sky of awareness.

When I opened my eyes, I was stunned by the beauty of the New England fall, the trees rising tall out of the earth, yellows and reds set against a bright blue sky. The colors felt like a vibrant sensational part of the life playing through my body. The sound of the wind appeared and vanished, leaves fluttered toward the ground, a bird took flight from a nearby branch. The whole world was moving—like the life within me, nothing was fixed, solid, confined. I knew without a doubt that I was part of the world.

When I next felt a cramping in my stomach, I could recognize it as simply another part of the natural world. As I continued paying attention I could feel the arising and passing aches and pressures inside me as no different from the firmness of earth, the falling leaves. There was just pain . . . and it was the earth's pain.

When we are free of mental concepts and our senses are awake, the sounds, smells, images and vibrations we experience connect us with all life everywhere. It is not *my* pain, it is the earth's pain. It is not *my* aliveness but simply life—unfolding and intense, mysterious and beautiful. By meeting the changing dance of sensations with Radical Acceptance, we discover our intrinsic belonging to this world. We are "no thing"—not limited to any passing experience—and "everything," belonging to the whole.

In Roger Keyes's poem "Hokusai Says," the teachings of a wise Japanese artist remind us of our belonging to life, and of our capacity to open to its fullness.

Hokusai says look carefully.
He says pay attention, notice.
He says keep looking, stay curious.
He says there is no end to seeing . . .

He says everything is alive—
Shells, buildings, people fish
Mountains, trees. Wood is alive.
Water is alive.

Everything has its own life.
Everything lives inside us.
He says live with the world inside you . . .

It matters that you care.
It matters that you feel.
It matters that you notice.
It matters that life lives through you . . .

Look, feel, let life take you by the hand.
Let life live through you.

As we move from resisting our physical experience to bringing Radical Acceptance to the life living through us, we awaken from trance. We open to the fullness and mystery of our life. Each moment we wakefully "let be," we are home. As the great eighteenth-century Zen master Hakuin Zenji wrote, "This very place is the Lotus Land, this very body, the Buddha." The Lotus Land is the cherished place of awakening that is always here in the present moment. When we meet life through our bodies with Radical Acceptance, we are the Buddha—the Awakened One—beholding the changing stream of sensations, feelings and thoughts. Everything is alive, the whole world lives inside us. As we let life live through us, we experience the boundless openness of our true nature.

Guided Meditation: Developing an Embodied Presence

A mindful body scan is a valuable pathway to embodied presence.

Sitting comfortably, close your eyes and take several long, deep breaths. Then rest in the natural flow of your breath and allow your body and mind to begin to settle.

With a relaxed, open awareness, now begin a gradual and thorough scan of your entire body. Place your attention at the top of your head and without looking for anything in particular, feel the sensations there. Then letting your attention move down, feel the sensations on the back of your head, on either side of your head, through your ears. Notice the sensations through your forehead, eyes, nose, cheeks, jaw and mouth. Be as slow and thorough as you like.

As you continue the scan, be careful not to use your eyes to direct your attention. (This will only create tension.) Rather, connect directly with sensations by feeling the body from within the body. In certain parts of the body it is common to feel numbness or for there to be no noticeable sensations. Let your attention remain in those areas for a few moments in a relaxed and easeful way. You may find that as your attention deepens, when you revisit these places, you become increasingly aware of sensations.

Images or thoughts will naturally arise. Notice them passing through and gently return your attention to the sensations. Let your intention be to release all ideas and experience your physical aliveness exactly as it is.

Place your attention on the area of your neck and throat,

noticing without any judgment whatever sensations you feel. Be aware of each of your shoulders from the inside. Then let your attention move slowly down your arms, feeling the sensations and aliveness there. Bring awareness to your hands, making sure they are resting in an easy and effortless way. Feel each finger from the inside, the palms, the backs of the hands—noticing tingling, pulsing, pressure, warmth or cold. Arrive in the life of your body.

Now place your awareness on your chest, exploring the sensations in that whole area. Slowly allow your awareness to sink down into your stomach. With a soft, receptive awareness, take some moments to feel the sensations in your abdomen.

Place your attention on your upper back, feeling the sensations in the area around your shoulder blades. Moving down, be aware of the mid- and lower back, and then the entire spinal column. Continuing to let awareness sweep down the body, feel the sensations that arise through the hips, buttocks, genitals. What are the actual sensations that are arising? Move slowly down through the legs, feeling them from within. Explore the sensations in your feet and toes. At the places where your body touches the chair, cushion or floor, feel the sensations of contact, pressure and temperature.

Now open your attention to include your body in a comprehensive way. Be aware of the body as a field of changing sensations. Can you sense the subtle energy field that vitalizes and gives life to every cell, every organ in your body? Is there anything in your experience that is solid, unmoving? Is there any center or boundary to the field of sensation? Is there any solid self you can locate that possesses these sensations? What or who is aware of experience?

As you rest in awareness of your whole body, if particular sensations call your attention, bring a soft and allowing attention to them. Don't manage or manipulate your experience, don't grasp or push anything away. Simply open to the changing dance of sensations, feeling your life from the inside out. If no particular sensations call your attention, remain open to feeling energy simultaneously in all parts of the body.

If thoughts carry your attention away, gently note, "Thinking, thinking," and then reconnect with the energetic field of aliveness. Rest in this awareness of your living being, letting life live through you.

The body scan from head to feet or feet to head can be repeated over and over during a single meditation sitting. You might do a full scan, rest in attention of the whole body for a few minutes, and then scan again. You might do an initial scan slowly and then subsequent scans more quickly. You might choose to scan once, and then continue to practice by attending to predominant sensations and, whenever possible, the whole field of bodily sensations. Experiment and find out what most helps you in sustaining a relaxed and wakeful presence in your body.

In daily life, return to the experience of your body as often as possible. You can readily arrive in your body by relaxing and softening through your shoulders, hands and belly. As you move through the various circumstances of your day, notice what sensations arise in your body. What happens when you feel angry? When you are stressed and racing against time? When you feel criticized or insulted by someone? When you feel excited or happy? Pay particular attention to the difference between being inside thoughts and awakening again to the immediate experience of sensations.

Guided Meditation: Radical Acceptance of Pain

We cultivate Radical Acceptance of pain by relaxing our resistance to unpleasant sensations and meeting them with nonreactive awareness. This exercise is especially useful if you are presently distressed by physical pain.

Find a comfortable position, sitting or lying down. Take a few moments to become still, relaxing with the natural rhythm of the breath. Gently scan through your body, relaxing your brow and jaw, dropping your shoulders and softening through your hands. Try not to create any unnecessary tension in your body.

Where is the area of strong discomfort or pain that calls your attention? Bring a receptive attention directly to the unpleasant sensations in that part of your body. Notice what happens as you begin to be present with this pain. Is there an attempt, however subtle, to push the pain away? To cut it off, block it off, pull away? Is there fear? You might notice how the body and mind clench like a fist in an attempt to resist pain. Let your intention be to remain present, allowing the unpleasant sensations to be as they are.

Soften any reaction against the pain, allowing the fist of resistance to unclench and open. The more you can connect with open and spacious awareness, the more you will be able to be present with sensations and allow them to unfold naturally. Experience your awareness as the soft space that surrounds the pain and allow the unpleasant sensations to float in this awareness.

Resting in this openness, now bring a more precise attention to the changing sensations in the area of pain. What is the experience actually like? Do you feel burning, aching, twisting, throbbing, tearing, stabbing? Does the pain feel like a knot, a constricting band? Does the area feel as if it is being pressed down or crushed by a great weight? Are the unpleasant sensations diffuse or focused in their intensity? How do they change as you observe them? Investigate with a nonreactive, soft attention. Allow the sensations you may feel as a solid block of pain to unfold and move in their natural dance of change.

When resistance arises, relax again, reestablishing a sense of openness. Be aware of your entire body, including the areas that aren't painful. Let the body become like open space, with plenty of room for unpleasant sensations to arise and dissolve, fade and intensify, move and change. No holding, no tension. Inhabit the sea of awareness, and let any painful sensations float in an accepting openness.

Try not to judge yourself for reacting when pain feels like "just too much." Take care of yourself in whatever way provides ease and comfort. Over time if you practice mindful presence of pain for even a few moments at a time, equanimity will increase. You will be able to more readily let go of resistance and open to unpleasant sensations.

SIX

RADICAL ACCEPTANCE OF DESIRE: AWAKENING TO THE SOURCE OF LONGING

Men are not free when they are doing just what they like. Men are only free when they are doing what the deepest self likes. And there is getting down to the deepest self! It takes some diving.

D. H. Lawrence

From the urgent way lovers want each other to the seeker's search for truth, all moving is from the mover. Every pull draws us to the ocean.

Rumi

When I was first introduced to Buddhism in a high school world studies class, I dismissed it out of hand. It seemed irrelevant to my life—grim in its concern about attachment and, apparently, anti-pleasure. Sure, maybe we all suffer, but why dwell on it? It was the late sixties and for many of us then, hedonism was a devotional practice. We were desire junkies. Buddhism seemed to be telling me to stop seeking after romantic relationships, forgo having good times with friends, avoid the highs of marijuana and give up my adventures in nature. In my mind, freedom from desire would take the fun out of life.

Years later I would realize that the Buddha never intended to make desire itself the problem. When he said craving causes suffering, he was referring not to our natural inclination as living beings to have wants and needs, but to our habit of clinging to experience that must, by nature, pass away. On my way to understanding that, I've stumbled around, fallen down and repeatedly found myself deluded and entangled. Desire has sometimes taken me over like a tyrant; and at other times I have battled grimly, hardening myself against its strength. Eventually I would find that relating wisely to the powerful and pervasive energy of desire is a pathway into unconditional loving.

I first got a glimpse of this possibility, as may be expected, in that hotbed of desire—romantic relationship. A few years after leaving our spiritual community, my husband and I had divorced. Our marriage had been founded in a lifestyle that emphasized yogic disciplines but did not encourage much focus on personal relationships. We were good friends but not a good match as intimate partners. Not long after our divorce was final, I met a man who seemed to be exactly what I was looking for. In our few casual encounters something had clicked and I was infatuated.

In the midst of that initial rush, I left for a weeklong midwinter meditation retreat. In the six years that I had been practicing Buddhist meditation, I had attended a number of such retreats and loved the states of clarity and presence I touched there. But this time instead of settling into even a semblance of mindful presence, my immediate and compelling draw was to the pleasures of fantasy. I was in the throes of a full-blown "Vipassana Romance," as such fantasies have come to be known. In the silence and austerity of retreat, the mind can build a whole erotic world around a person we barely know. Often the object of a VR is another meditator who has attracted our attention. In the time span of a few days we can mentally live through a whole relationship—courting, marrying, having a family together. I had brought my fantasy person with me from home, and this industrial-strength Vipassana Romance withstood all my best strategies for letting go and returning to the here and now.

I tried to relax and direct my attention to the breath, to note what was happening in my body and mind. I could barely complete two cycles of mindful breathing before my mind would once again return to its favorite subject. I'd get lost in images of how we might acknowledge the huge attraction between us and head off to the Blue Ridge Mountains for a weekend together. I saw us meditating and then making passionate love. I imagined that we'd hike to the top of Old Rag Mountain, revel in the hints of early spring and in the possibility that we were, indeed, soul mates.

Then, with a stab of guilt, I'd remember where I was. Sometimes I'd look around and take in the serenity and dignity of the meditation hall. I'd remind myself of the freedom and joy of remaining present, and of the suffering that arises from living in stories and illusions. This didn't make a dent—the fantasies would take off again almost immediately. Hoping to get out of my head, I tried doing longer walking meditations on the snowy paths surrounding the retreat center. As my mind churned relentlessly onward, I felt self-indulgent and ashamed of my lack of discipline. Most of all I was frustrated because I felt I was wasting precious time. This retreat was an opportunity to deepen my spiritual practice, and there I was, caught up in wanting and off in the future.

The pain of intense wanting was more obvious on retreat, but I was all too familiar with the effect of such desire in my daily life. I knew what it was like to be at the beginning of a new relationship and pass days waiting and hoping to get a phone call. I knew what it was like to want to impress someone—a student, friend, teacher—with my intelligence or spirituality, and then leave our time together feeling embarrassed and inauthentic. I knew what it was like to keep postponing playtime with my son because I was so intent on finishing the literature review for my dissertation. How many hours of my life had I spent leaning into the future—striving to get my psychology license, longing to find the right partner, struggling to finish a book proposal? Not that I couldn't have these aspirations, but aiming my sights on the future was an uncomfortable, out-of-balance way of being. When such periods were in full swing, I was too tense to appreciate the beauty around me, too preoccupied to listen inwardly or enjoy the people I love. Now at retreat where I had every opportunity to be aware of the actual sounds, feelings and sensations arising in the present moment, my obsessive wanting self was still getting in the way.

After several days I had a pivotal interview with my teacher. When I described how I'd become so overwhelmed, she asked, "How are you relating to the presence of desire?" I was startled into understanding. For me, desire had become the enemy, and I was losing the battle. Her question pointed me back to the essence of mindfulness practice: *It doesn't matter what is happening. What matters is how we are relating to our experience.* She advised me to stop fighting my experience and instead investigate the nature of wanting mind. I could accept whatever was going on, she reminded me, but without getting lost in it.

While often uncomfortable, desire is not bad—it is natural. The pull of desire is part of our survival equipment. It keeps us eating, having sex, going to work, doing what we do to thrive. Desire also motivates us to read books, listen to talks and explore spiritual practices that help us realize and inhabit loving awareness. The same life energy that leads to suffering also provides the fuel for profound awakening. Desire becomes a problem only when it takes over our sense of who we are.

In teaching the Middle Way, the Buddha guided us to relate to desire *without getting possessed by it and without resisting it.* He was talking about every level of desire—for food and sex, for love and freedom. He was talking about all degrees of wanting, from small preferences to the most compelling cravings. We are mindful of desire when we experience it with an embodied awareness, recognizing the sensations and thoughts of wanting as arising and passing phenomena. While this is not easy, as we cultivate the clear seeing and compassion of Radical Acceptance, we discover we can open fully to this natural force and remain free in its midst.

WHAT IS DESIRE?

The Dalai Lama begins many of his talks by saying that everyone wants to be happy, nobody wants to suffer. Our desire for happiness is, most fundamentally, the desire to exist. This urge expresses itself in the way all things take form throughout the natural world. The same universal force of attraction that gathers atoms into molecules and holds solar systems spinning in galaxies also joins sperm with eggs and brings people together in communities. Buddhist monk and scholar Walpola Rahula talks about this primal desire as "a tremendous force that moves whole lives . . . that even moves the whole world. This is the greatest force, the greatest energy in the world."

As human beings our desire for happiness focuses on fulfilling our needs. According to psychologist Abraham Maslow, our needs range in a hierarchy from basic biological drives to spiritual yearnings. We need security, food and sex; emotional recognition and bonding; mental engagement and creative activity; communion and self-realization. Meeting these needs of body, mind and spirit gives us satisfaction and pleasure; denying them leaves us feeling deprived, frustrated and incomplete. We seek out experiences that enable us to survive, thrive and be fulfilled.

The catch is that no matter how gratifying any experience may be, it is bound to change. The Buddha expressed this in the first noble truth: Existence is inherently dissatisfying. When I first heard this teaching in high school in its most common translation as "life is suffering," I of course thought it meant life is nothing more than misery and anguish. But the Buddha's understanding of suffering was subtler and more profound. We are uncomfortable because everything in our life keeps changing—our inner moods, our bodies, our work, the people we love, the world we live in. We can't hold on to anything—a beautiful sunset, a sweet taste, an intimate moment with a lover, our very existence as the body/mind we call self—because all things come and go. Lacking any permanent satisfaction, we continuously need another injection of fuel, stimulation, reassurance from loved ones, medicine, exercise, and meditation. We are continually driven to become something more, to experience something else.

If our desires are simple and can be temporarily satisfied, our way of responding is straightforward. When thirsty, we drink. When tired, we sleep. When lonely, we talk to a friend. Yet, as we know, it's rarely this uncomplicated. Most of the time our wanting is not so easily satisfied. Caught in the trance of unworthiness, our desires fixate on soothing, once and for all, our anxiety about imperfection. We strive to tie up all the loose ends and to avoid making mistakes, even though we know both are impossible. We want to feel "good enough" all the time in our work, parenting, relationships, health, appearance, and life. We want others to be a certain way—always happy, healthy, loving and respectful toward us. Yet because these things don't happen, we are driven by the feeling that something is missing or wrong. Our gnawing everyday wants prevent us from relaxing and becoming aware of our deeper yearnings. We perpetually lean into the next moment, hoping it will offer the satisfaction that the present moment does not.

The Latin root of the word *desire, "desidus,"* means "away from a star." The way I like to interpret this is that stars are the energetic source of all life and an expression of pure awareness. This aliveness and wakefulness is what we long for most deeply—we long to belong to our star, to realize our own true nature. Yet because our desires habitually narrow and fixate on what by nature passes away, we feel "away from our star," away from the life, awareness and love that is the essence of who we are. Feeling apart from the source of our being, we identify ourselves with our wants and with the ways that we try to satisfy them.

THE EMERGENCE OF A WANTING SELF

One of my psychotherapy clients, Chris, grew up in a household where no one ever praised him or even said "good job." His parents didn't seem to enjoy his brightness and humor. They barely noticed his natural musical talents—he could play almost any instrument he picked up. Chris remembers a particularly painful incident that happened when he was five years old. His parents had been talking with each other for a long time in the living room. Feeling left out and hoping to get some attention, Chris pulled out his new accordion from his toy box and started to perform for them. Annoyed at this interruption, they told him to play it in his room. When he wouldn't budge, they just went off to their bedroom and shut the door. He stood in front of their closed door and played and played. They may have been trying to teach him a lesson, but he felt humiliated and abandoned. Finally he curled up on the floor and went to sleep.

By the time Chris started working with me, he had studied with several spiritual teachers, moving from one to the next, in part because, as he put it, he had "never really felt seen by any of them." In spending time with the most recent, a rabbi, Chris found himself feeling very young and insecure. He tried to curry favor by playing guitar at the temple's social gatherings, by showing off his knowledge in kabbalah classes. Whenever possible he'd strike up a conversation with the rabbi, who was perfectly friendly in response. But Chris didn't get the sense that he mattered, that the rabbi would even notice if he didn't show up.

Chris believed that if he did not stand out as a special person, he was worthless. The need to be "number one" extended to dating, friendship and work. Unless he was the center of attention, he felt he was being overlooked or rejected. Admitting this in our therapy sessions was embarrassing—he felt something was wrong with him for being so dependent on outside recognition. Chris was afraid that his neediness and insecurity would prevent him from ever finding love in his life. "It drives women away. As soon as they sense it they are turned off." It didn't seem to help that he had learned how to hold back from making overt demands or asking for reassurances. "It's my 'vibe,'" he told me. The intensity of his unfulfilled desires made him feel that he was unappealing and deserved to be rejected.

Our sense of self emerges from the ground level of all experience—our reactivity to intense pleasant or unpleasant sensations. When we want loving attention, like Chris, we are feeling certain sensations in our body—perhaps the aching of longing around the heart, as well as excitement and openness. When the answer to our need and desire is no, the physical sensations of contraction we experience are intense. We feel shame—the desire to hide—and the danger of fear. When we experience this wanting and not getting over and over, we make an enduring association: *Our wanting leads to fear and shame.* This intense cluster of reactive feelings, locked in the body, forms the energetic core of a wanting self.

We identify ourselves with these persistent feelings through the I-ing and my-ing talked about by Ajahn Buddhadasa. The tension and excitement of wanting arise, and we experience this as *my* longing for intimacy, *my* craving for touch and attention. In the same way, it's *my* fear and shame when I am rejected. We consolidate our sense of a wanting self as we tell ourselves stories about what is happening: "Something is wrong with me for wanting so much. Why don't I already have what I want? The world has it in for me, and I never get anything."

If we haven't had to deal with major threats to our physical survival, the wanting self is primarily focused on emotional survival and well-being. We all have, to some degree, experienced fear and shame when our basic needs to feel loved and understood are frustrated. If, like Chris, our needs for connection are consistently ignored or misunderstood, our wanting grows stronger, and we seek even more urgently the attention we crave. We spend our lives trying to get away from our painful feelings of fear and shame, disconnecting from and numbing our body, getting lost in self-judgment and obsessive thinking. But this only serves to increase our wanting and shame. As the cycle of reactivity repeats itself over and over, our identity as a wanting self—fundamentally deprived, isolated and unworthy—deepens.

When we can't meet our emotional needs directly, the wanting self develops strategies for satisfying them with substitutes. Like all strategies underlying the trance of unworthiness, those aimed at winning love and respect absorb and fixate our attention. We might, like Chris, be compelled to get attention by impressing others with our talent and knowledge. We might drive ourselves relentlessly to make money or have power over others. We might desperately pursue sexual conquests. Or we might feel compelled to be helpful and of service, someone needed by others. We often try to satisfy our emotional needs with the more immediate pleasures of food, alcohol and drugs. When they "work," these strategies provide immediate gratification through a temporary surge of pleasant sensations. They also numb or cover over the raw pain of shame and fear. But because they don't genuinely address our needs, our suffering continues and with it our reliance on whatever provides pleasure or relief.

Our most regularly used strategies to get what we want also become a defining part of our sense of self. The overeating, the competing, the people pleasing, feel like *me.* As we immerse ourselves in the life-consuming pursuit of substitutes, we become increasingly alienated from our authentic desires, our deepest longings for love and belonging.

LOST IN THE PURSUIT OF SUBSTITUTES

Ever since I was a teen, my drive to be productive has been a key strategy of my wanting self. When I feel insecure, producing—whether it is a finished article, a stack of paid bills or a clean kitchen—is my most readily accessible device for feeling worthwhile. This producing is not simply the natural urge to be creative and contribute to the mix of life, it is energized by fears of inadequacy and the need to prove myself. When I'm caught in the strategy, I turn to English Breakfast tea to give me the boost I think I need to remain productive throughout the day and often into the night. The price is that I become speedy, impatient and distant from those I love. I get disconnected from my body as I relentlessly urge myself onward to get yet another thing done. Feeling self-centered and bad about myself for workaholism doesn't slow me down. "Getting one more thing out of the way" seems the most reliable way to get what I want—to feel better.

At a psychotherapy conference I attended, I saw a poster that struck home. In it two homeless men are sitting on a park bench.

One is saying to the other, "I used to have a private jet, condo in Aspen and be the CEO of a Fortune 500 company . . . then I switched to decaf." It's not hard to understand why our substitutes are so attractive. Even if they don't address our deepest needs, they prop us up and for a time keep getting us the goods that give us those momentary pleasant sensations. Our efforts in pursuit of substitutes preoccupy and distract our attention enough to shield us for a time from the raw sensations of feeling unloved or unworthy. Accomplishing things *does* temporarily stave off my feelings of inadequacy. Yet underneath, my wanting self urges me on, fearful that without being productive I'll lose everything, like the executive who switched to decaf.

While having a job is usually necessary to meet our basic survival needs, where and how we work is also a key domain for substitute gratification: Work becomes an indirect means for trying to win love and respect. We might find what we do entirely meaningless, we might hate or resent our job, yet still hitch our desire for approval and connection to how well we perform. While this is true for men in particular, most of us rely on work to help us make up for fears of unworthiness. This strategy delivers the goods through money or power, through the strokes we get for our diligence and competence, through the satisfaction of "getting something done." But we can get lost in these substitutes, overlooking the fact that they will never satisfy our deepest longings.

Even when we are engaged in activities that are meaningful to us, that are creatively and spiritually gratifying, they can be "co-opted" and used to satisfy the unmet needs of the wanting self. This happens to me most often when I'm preparing talks or workshops for meditation groups or writing articles on Buddhist practice. When I remain aware that the Buddhist teachings are precious to me and I love sharing them with others, I can throw myself into what I'm doing with enormous passion. When anxiety or frustration arises,

I am able to meet it with acceptance. But sometimes that voice of insecurity and unworthiness arises, and I listen to it. Suddenly writing or preparing a presentation is linked to winning or losing love and respect and my entire experience of working shifts. The wanting self takes over. While I always intend to give a wholehearted effort, now that effort is wrapped in fear. I'm anxiously striving to be "good enough" and to reap the rewards. My love for what I do is clouded over when working becomes a strategy to prove my worth.

We are unable to give ourselves freely and joyfully to any activity if the wanting self is in charge. And yet, until we attend to the basic desires and fears that energize the wanting self, it will insinuate itself into our every activity and relationship.

D. H. Lawrence wrote: "Men are not free when they are doing just what they like. Men are only free when they are doing what the deepest self likes." When we are motivated by immediate gratification to do "just what we like," we will feel continuously driven: No amount of productivity or consuming or recognition can break through the trance of unworthiness and put us in touch with the "deepest self." As Lawrence points out, to do what the deepest self likes "takes some diving." To listen and respond to the longing of our heart requires a committed and genuine presence. The more completely we're caught in the surface world of pursuing substitutes, the harder it is to dive.

WHEN ADDICTIVE WANTING TAKES OVER OUR LIFE

As I discovered with my "Vipassana Romance," when desire gets strong, mindfulness goes out the window. Willa Cather tells us, "There is only one big thing—desire. And before it, when it is big, all is little." We can honor desire as a life force, but still see how it causes suffering when it takes over our life. Our natural hunger for food can become an ungovernable craving for food—ice cream, sweets, potato chips—comfort food or food to numb our feelings. Our longing for sex and affection can become an anguished dependency on another human being to define and please us. Our need for shelter and clothing can turn into insatiable greed, compelling us to possess three houses and closets full of unworn shoes. Our fundamental longing to belong and feel loved becomes an insistent craving for substitutes.

If we have been acutely frustrated or deprived, our fixated desire becomes desperate and unquenchable. We are possessed by craving, and our entire life is hijacked by the force of this energy. We feel like a wanting self in all situations, with all people, throughout the day. In India it is said that when a pickpocket sees a saint, he or she sees only the saint's pockets. If we are taken over by craving, no matter who or what is before us, all we can see is how it might satisfy our needs. This kind of thirst contracts our body and mind into a profound trance. We move through the world with a kind of tunnel vision that prevents us from enjoying what is in front of us. The color of the autumn leaves or a passage of poetry merely amplifies the feeling that there is a gaping hole in our life. The smile of a child only reminds us that we are painfully childless. We turn away from simple pleasures because our craving compels us to seek more intense stimulation or numbing relief.

Addictive craving is extremely difficult to endure without acting out. As Oscar Wilde put it, "I can resist anything but temptation." Temptation is an emotional promise that we will experience the pleasure we so intensely crave. Anyone who has struggled with smoking, compulsive overeating, or drug or relationship addictions knows the compelling force of these physical and mental urges. We don't want to forgo the cigarette and take a nice walk, listen to soothing music, breathe deeply. We just want what we want. While we might consciously recognize that the fix is a temporary substitute, we still feel we "have to have it."

Sarah, a meditation student who had struggled with compulsive overeating for many years, arrived at a ten-day Buddhist retreat panicked about how she would handle food. Would she get enough? Would she like what was served? Would she eat too much? She dreaded sitting at the long dining tables in silence and, without the comforting veil of conversation, eating in front of others. She feared that somehow the people around her would be able to tell by watching her that she had an eating disorder. She imagined that she would feel unbearable shame.

During the first few days of retreat, food was center stage in her awareness. When the gong sounded announcing a meal, she left the meditation hall and walked slowly toward the dining room. She told me her mindfulness was a pretense: She felt as if an irresistible magnet were pulling her. While waiting to get food in the lunch line she was squeezed by anxiety and excitement. As she ate what she had on her plate, she would plan what more she was going to get. Sarah found the food good and plentiful—so much so that she went back for seconds, sometimes thirds. Rather than sit in her original seat, she would take the additional servings to other parts of the dining hall.

At our first interview, Sarah said she felt "riddled to the core" with obsession and craving. She felt horrible shame about being such a failure, being so "unspiritual." The hardest part was that no matter how much she wanted to control her eating, no matter what her plans and intentions, she couldn't stop herself from overeating. More than anything, these futile daily attempts to control herself made her feel like a failure.

While we often don't like ourselves when caught in wanting, this dislike turns to full-blown aversion when wanting gets out of control and takes over our life. We see how we ruin our bodies and our relationships by bingeing on food or alcohol. We see how we hurt our children when we are addicted to endless achieving. We watch ourselves sabotage intimate relationships when we are driven by neediness and insecurity. As one student described it, "My wanting self is my worst enemy." When we hate ourselves for wanting, it is because the wanting self has taken over our entire life.

Desperate to get away from the pain of self-hatred, we send cruel and unforgiving messages to our wanting self. We may try to punish our wanting self by depriving ourselves of food, rest or another person's comfort. We might so badly want to destroy the part of our self that is wrecking our life that we recklessly injure our body or mind. As with Sarah, our agonizing shame of addiction takes over and prevents us from sensing "what the deepest self likes." We remain out of touch with the longing for love that drives our addiction in the first place.

REJECTING THE WANTING SELF

In the myth of Eden, God created the garden and dropped the tree of knowledge, with its delicious and dangerous fruits, right smack-dab in the middle. He then deposited some humans close by and forbade these curious, fruit-loving creatures from taking a taste. It was a setup. Eve naturally grasped at the fruit and then was shamed and punished for having done so.

We experience this situation daily inside our own psyche. We are encouraged by our culture to keep ourselves comfortable, to be right, to possess things, to be better than others, to look good, to be admired. We are also told that we should feel ashamed of our selfishness, that we are flawed for being so self-centered, sinful when we are indulgent.

Most mainstream religions—Judeo-Christian, Buddhist, Hindu, Muslim, Confucian—teach that our wanting, passion and greed cause suffering. While this certainly can be true, their blanket teachings about the dangers of desire often deepen self-hatred. We are counseled to transcend, overcome or somehow manage the hungers of our physical and emotional being. We are taught to mistrust the wildness and intensity of our natural passions, to fear being out of control. Audre Lorde tells us, "We have been raised to fear . . . our deepest cravings. And the fear of our deepest cravings keeps them suspect, keeps us docile and loyal and obedient, and leads us to settle for . . . many facets of our own oppression."

Equating spiritual purity with elimination of desire is a common misunderstanding I also see in students on the Buddhist path. This is not just a contemporary issue. The struggle to understand the relationship between awakening and desire in the context of the Buddhist teachings has gone on since the time of the Buddha himself. A classical Chinese Zen tale brings this to light. An old woman had supported a monk for twenty years, letting him live in a hut on her land. After all this time she figured the monk, now a man in the prime of life, must have attained some degree of enlightenment. So she decided to test him.

Rather than taking his daily meal to him herself, she asked a beautiful young girl to deliver it. She instructed the girl to embrace the monk warmly—and then to report back to her how he responded. When the girl returned, she said that the monk had simply stood stock-still, as if frozen. The old woman then headed for the monk's hut. What was it like, she asked him, when he felt the girl's warm body against his? With some bitterness he answered, "Like a withering tree on a rock in winter, utterly without warmth." Furious, the old woman threw him out and burned down his hut, exclaiming, "How could I have wasted all these years on such a fraud."

To some the monk's response might seem virtuous. After all, he resisted temptation, he even seemed to have pulled desire out by the roots. Still the old woman considered him a fraud. Is his way of experiencing the young girl—"like a withering tree on a rock in winter"—the point of spiritual practice? Instead of appreciating the girl's youth and loveliness, instead of noting the arising of a natural sexual response and its passing away without acting on it, the monk shut down. This is not enlightenment.

I have worked with many meditation students who have gotten the message that experiencing desire is a sign of being spiritually undeveloped. While it is true that withdrawing attention from certain impulses can diminish their strength, the continued desire for simple pleasures—delicious foods, play, entertainment or sexual gratification—need not be embarrassing evidence of being trapped in lower impulses. Those same students also assume that "spiritual people" are supposed to call on inner resources as their only refuge, and so they rarely ask for comfort or help from their friends and teachers. I've talked with some who have been practicing spiritual disciplines for years, yet have never let themselves acknowledge that they are lonely and long for intimacy.

As the monk in the Zen tale shows, if we push away desire, we disconnect from our tenderness and we harden against life. We become like a "rock in winter." When we reject desire, we reject the very source of our love and aliveness.

"IT'S NOT MY FAULT"

At our next interview, Sarah told me she had been participating in Overeaters Anonymous (OA), a twelve-step recovery program, for several years before she decided to try a vipassana retreat. She had made significant headway in OA. When she felt strong cravings she now phoned her sponsor instead of directly heading for the refrigerator. This is what I would call an "assisted pause"—together they could look at what she was feeling and explore some options on how to respond. Nevertheless, the eating binges had continued. And each time she went to an OA meeting and introduced herself as a compulsive overeater, she felt as if she were further binding her identity to being an addict. Sarah had come to the retreat hoping that meditation and prayer—the eleventh of OA's twelve steps—might help her release the grip of addiction.

Now, several days into the retreat, Sarah told me she was doubting herself even more. Without the distractions of daily life, the force of addiction and the enormity of her shame seemed more oppressive than ever. Whenever she tried to pause and pay attention to her craving for food, the agitation she felt was unbearable. Every cell in her body seemed to be reaching out to fill an impossibly big hole inside. Sarah was convinced that something was so deeply wrong with her that it could never be fixed.

I asked Sarah to close her eyes and sense into the worst part of what she was experiencing, what most wanted attention. She immediately said that, right in that moment, she wanted me to have a good impression of her. I encouraged her to bring presence to what that want was like, noticing it as a felt sense in her body. "There's a jumpiness in my chest," she reported. As we went on I suggested she remain open to any emotion, image or words that might naturally appear. When emotions surged up that felt too painful or consuming to be with, I reminded her to silently say to herself, "This too," and with a gentle attention, focus on the sensations in her body.

As we sat together, Sarah softly named the unfolding stream of what she was experiencing: "Jitteriness in my stomach. Fear: I'm not going to do this exercise right. Anger. Thinking: I'm taking too much of your time. Another thought: You must think I'm a real basket case. Soreness, squeezing around my heart. Another thought: This is what I always feel when someone pays attention or cares about me. Longing. Trembling. I want to be loved. Sadness." We sat together for about five more minutes while Sarah continued to give each wave of judgment or feeling a respectful attention. Eventually she began noticing more moments of calm. Before we ended our interview I suggested she continue to practice this way on her own. It might be hard to do when that overwhelming craving arose, I acknowledged. But even if she could manage for a few minutes to remain aware, she would be setting in motion a process that could make a profound difference. I could see a little gleam of hope in her eyes as she thanked me and left.

When she arrived at our next interview four days later, Sarah seemed calmer. Her eyes were bright. She had been meditating late one afternoon, she told me, and managed to note pretty continuously her inner stream of experience, as she had during our interview. She hadn't gotten lost very often in her usual thoughts about how bad she was for what she was feeling. She hadn't even gotten lost when her mouth watered and her stomach tightened when she smelled the cookies baking for teatime. Sarah had begun seeing how even the most acute cravings eventually subsided if she just sat still, named what was happening and, instead of wishing they'd go away, just said, "This too." "Suddenly it became clear that all my desires and thoughts and feelings are an endless, changing parade," she told me. And then, with a look of surprise she added, *"I'm not making it happen."*

For Sarah, this experience of an uncontrollable, ever-changing reality was a breakthrough that dramatically shifted how she related to herself. She *wasn't* controlling what was going on inside her, and she never had. She had not asked to be filled with craving. She couldn't stop the barrage of obsessive thoughts. She described how, during that meditation, she heard a voice whispering, "It's not my fault. It's never been my fault." It wasn't Sarah's fault that she was so filled with fear, so obsessed, so ashamed. It wasn't her fault that when her feelings got intolerable she would reach out for food. As she told me this Sarah started sobbing deeply, grieving all the moments of her life spent in blaming herself for her addiction to food, for her sneaking and pretending, for her insecurity when she was around others.

Many streams of conditioning give rise to the wanting self and the particular forms our craving takes. In Sarah's case, the genetic makeup she inherited included a predisposition to some types of addiction. She was influenced by her mother's drinking, which had bathed Sarah in alcohol even in utero. She was also affected by having a mother who was too depressed and filled with self-hatred to give her real support, and a father who was emotionally distant and critical. She was living in a culture that promised satisfaction through consuming. And most fundamental, like all living beings she was biologically primed to grasp after pleasure and avoid pain.

When I urge students to consider the chain of causes that may have led to their suffering, some take issue. Isn't that just an intellectual way to place blame on someone else and sidestep responsibility? So what if my parents neglected me. Does that give me the license to be impatient with my children, selfish with my spouse? It's certainly easy enough to say we do hurtful things to others because we were treated poorly when we were children. Yet something quite different happens when we inquire into our conditioning mindfully. I might ask a person whose parents had been neglectful to pause and honestly sense what that experience had been like. Can they feel the enormous hunger for attention that might have developed in those circumstances? How they might still need to feed themselves even when others are asking to be fed? In bringing a clear and comprehensive awareness to our situation, we begin to accept our wanting self with compassion. This frees us to move forward, to break out of old patterns.

By realizing that craving and overeating were not her fault, Sarah interrupted the painful chain of reactivity that had been driving her addiction. Merely recognizing, as she had in OA, that she was clinging to food as a substitute had not been enough to break the pattern. Forgiving and accepting the presence of the wanting self was the giant step in Sarah's transformation. Although she had to continue consciously forgiving and letting go when craving arose, when she stopped blaming herself, her ability to be present was no longer compromised by overwhelming shame.

AWAKENING FROM THE WANTING SELF

Over the remaining three days of the retreat, Sarah practiced accepting even the most excruciating wants and fears by letting herself feel them directly in her body. When she was haunted by the fear that she would never change and get better, she said, "This too," and felt the bands of tightness squeezing her chest and throat. When she doubted that anyone could ever love someone so wretched, she held the fear with "This too." When the despairing feeling that "Something is wrong with me" seemed to take over her world, she let herself feel the grief, like a swelling balloon in her heart. When craving arose, impelling her toward the relief of food, she stayed still and responded to its urgent force with "This too."

As Sarah was discovering in meditation, she could experience even the most intense craving without pushing it away or acting on it. Instead of hating her experience or losing herself in a swirl of mental activity, Sarah was saying yes to the feelings of urgency and tension and fear. Instead of trying to satisfy her craving, she was simply letting it express itself and move through her.

Sarah took a courageous step when she carried the acceptance and presence she had practiced into the arena of her greatest struggles, the dining hall. She found she was able to pay closer attention by slowing down everything she did: walking, ladling out portions of food, bringing her fork to her mouth, chewing her food. Slowing down like this was a modified way of pausing. She told me, "There were meals when one serving was enough. I could enjoy each bite because I was really there . . . being so present made me feel full."

When the impulse to stand up and get more food did arise, she would remain seated, mentally saying, "This too," feeling fully the sharp edge of tension, the squeeze of excitement, anticipation, anxiety. Sometimes the impulse would pass. Other times it didn't, and the compulsion to eat and numb her inner turmoil would keep building. If the voice of judgment arose, she would mentally whisper, "It's not my fault, it's not my fault." The reminder helped her become more gentle and open, more relaxed about the intensity of her craving. If Sarah did choose to get more food after pausing, she could accept that choice with compassion rather than condemn it or feel embarrassed, as if she had failed. By pausing and forgiving herself for the feeling of desire, Sarah had cleared the way to Radical Acceptance.

By the time the retreat ended, Sarah felt as if the grip of her addiction had begun to loosen. While the compulsions were still there, she had found a powerful and liberating way to relate to them. After hugging good-bye, she told me, "If I can remember even one time out of ten to say 'It's not my fault,' I'll be a significantly happier and freer person." She went on, "If I can just forgive myself and be present, I'll be okay."

Sarah and I spoke by phone several times in the months following that retreat. She was being considered as a candidate to head the English Department at the university where she taught, a position she had wanted for years. As the deadline for the final choice drew near, her tension mounted and so did her craving for late-night snacks. She told me that one evening after midnight, she found herself in front of the refrigerator, about to get out the milk for another bowl of cereal. But this time she remembered to pause. She took her hand off the handle and walked slowly and deliberately over to the kitchen table, pulled out a chair and mindfully sat down. She could feel the racing in her chest, but she sat very still and sent a message to herself: "Craving for food and obsessing about the job are not my fault."

As Sarah paid attention to the churning thoughts and feelings of anxiety, she realized that she not only wanted this professional success, she also deeply feared the feeling of failure that could swamp her if she wasn't selected. The tightness and pressure in her chest were so overwhelming she could barely breathe. She wanted relief; she wanted food. But as Sarah continued to pay attention to the explosive restlessness of craving, the massive pressure began to release. She felt a dissolving and opening through her chest, a growing sense of space. Filling that space was a vibrating tenderness. Sarah could now feel how deeply she longed to be accepted, valued, loved. As Sarah listened with a compassionate presence to her unfolding experience of wanting, she was freeing herself from its grip.

At the end of the month Sarah was invited to assume the position of department head. She was thrilled; this was a dream come true in her professional life. But her real triumph was a growing inner freedom. She was learning that she could accept rather than flee from or cover over her desires and cravings. She trusted that when her anxiety and judgments about her performance at work would inevitably arise, rather than reflexively turning toward food, she could offer herself a forgiving and kind presence.

Many students ask me if, after years of spiritual practice, we become free of the tug of wanting. They want to know whether we will still feel painfully attached to certain people, compulsive about working, dependent on chocolate, romance novels or the extra beer to carry us through a lonely evening. While these tendencies may persist, they often unfold to reveal complexes of wanting and shame that, in the light of mindfulness, relax their hold on us.

If we, like Sarah, have been deeply deprived emotionally, the habits of clinging or full-blown addictive behaviors will most likely be persistent and strong. Nonetheless, with time, although such wanting may continue to arise, even its most compelling and tenacious expressions need not lead to suffering. The sensations of anxiety and wanting may be unpleasant, but as we saw with pain, the suffering can be optional. We suffer when our experience of desire or craving defines and confines our experience of who we are. If we meet the sensations, emotions and thoughts of wanting with Radical Acceptance, we begin to awaken from the identity of a wanting self and to reconnect with the fullness of our being.

Whether we are on a meditation retreat or in the midst of a busy life, the practice of bringing Radical Acceptance to desire is essentially the same. We pause and relinquish our physical or mental pursuit of satisfaction long enough to recognize how our identity has contracted into the feelings and thoughts of a wanting self. In this pause we let go of blaming ourselves for the presence of wanting and kindly allow it to exist, just as it is. We invite our wanting to tea, mindfully experiencing the sensations in our body, wakefully noting the emotions and thoughts that are arising in our mind. When we are present in this way—clear, compassionate, neither grasping nor resisting—we undo the habitual patterns of reactivity that keep our body, heart and mind bound in wanting. In so doing, we enlarge our freedom to choose how we live.

WHAT WE REALLY WANT

The great Tibetan yogi Milarepa spent many years living in isolation in a mountain cave. As part of his spiritual practice, Milarepa began to see the contents of his mind as visible projections. His inner demons of lust, passion and aversion would appear before him as gorgeous seductive women and terrifying wrathful monsters. In the face of these temptations and horrors, rather than being overwhelmed, Milarepa would sing out, "It is wonderful you came today, you should come again tomorrow . . . from time to time we should converse."

Through his years of intensive training, Milarepa learns that suffering only comes from being seduced by the demons or from trying to fight them. To discover freedom in their presence, he has to experience them directly and wakefully, as they are. In one story of his feats, Milarepa's cave becomes filled with demons. Facing the most persistent, domineering demon in the crowd, Milarepa makes a brilliant move—he puts his head into the demon's mouth. In that moment of full surrender, all the demons vanish. All that remains is the brilliant light of pure awareness. As Pema Chödrön puts it: "When the resistance is gone, the demons are gone."

Without a doubt, I had been in full resistance to the desires fueling my Vipassana Romance. They were demons that, in my eyes, were consuming my spiritual life. When I finally recognized the battle I was in, the story of Milarepa came to mind. Perhaps my Vipassana Romance was not the enemy of my meditation practice after all, but a natural experience that could serve my awakening. What would it be like to greet the demon of desire, to "converse" with it as Milarepa had? I became committed to dropping my resistance so I could get to know this energy that was driving the wanting self.

Over the next few days, each time I realized I'd been lost in one of my flights of romantic illusion, I would note it as "erotic fantasy," and pay close attention to the sensations in my body and the emotions that were arising. No longer avoiding my immediate experience, I would find myself filled with waves of excitement, sexual arousal, and fear. Now, instead of resisting these feelings as demons, I just practiced accepting them and, with some curiosity, exploring them further.

The pressing ache in my chest opened into a deep grief—grief for all the lost moments of love, moments that I missed because I was too preoccupied or busy to stop and open to them. I moved back and forth between erotic passion and this profound grieving about how separate I felt from what I really longed for. When the sensations of craving or sorrow became particularly intense, I tended to become lost again, thinking about what was missing in my life, fantasizing about ways I might fulfill my longing for love. While I didn't judge the fantasies as "bad," I could see how they prevented me from being in touch with my actual experience. They kept me from tender presence—the gateway to what I most deeply longed for.

Although I became less immersed in my stories, I could see I was still holding on, trying to control the charged energies moving through me. My habitual reins—tightening my body, entertaining a running commentary on what I was doing—stopped me from letting go into the intensity and hugeness of wanting. I wasn't sure how to allow myself to love freely, without any notions or constraints. I didn't know exactly what I loved, but I knew I needed to release the resistance that was strangling my heart. Instead of focusing all that longing on a particular person, I wanted to experience the immensity of its reach.

Late one evening I sat meditating alone in my room. My attention moved deeper and deeper into longing, until I felt as if I might explode with its heartbreaking urgency. Yet at the same time I knew that was exactly what I wanted—*I wanted to die into longing, into communion, into love itself.* At that moment I could finally let my longing be all that it was. I even invited it—"Go ahead, please. Be as full as you are." I was putting my head in the mouth of the demon. I was saying yes, surrendering wakefully into the wilderness of sensations, surrendering into the very embrace I was longing for. Like a child finally held close in her mother's arms, I relaxed so fully that all boundaries of body and mind dissolved.

In an instant, I felt as if my body and mind were expanding out boundlessly in all directions—a flowing, changing stream of vibration, pulsing, tingling. Nothing separated "me" from this stream. Letting go entirely into rapture, I felt as open as the universe, wildly alive and as radiant as the sun. Nothing was solid in this dazzling celebration of life energy. I knew then that this was the fullness of loving what I love.

Kabir, the fifteenth-century Sufi poet, writes, "The universe is shot through in all parts by a single sort of love." This love is what we long for. When we bring Radical Acceptance to the enormity of desire, allowing it to be as it is, neither resisting it nor grasping after it, the light of our awareness dissolves the wanting self into its source. We find that we are naturally and entirely in love. Nothing is apart or excluded from this living awareness.

Over the next few days, each time I opened deeply to the force of longing, I was filled with a refreshed and unconditional appreciation for all of life. In the afternoons I would go outside after sitting and walk in the snowy woods. I found a sense of belonging with the great Douglas firs, with the chickadees that landed and ate seeds from my hands, with the layered sounds of the stream as it flowed around ice and rocks. Rumi writes:

A strange passion is moving in my head.
My heart has become a bird
Which searches in the sky.
Every part of me goes in different directions.
Is it really so
That the one I love is everywhere?

The "one I love" was everywhere, including within me. When we don't fixate on a single, limited object of love, we discover that the wanting self dissolves into the awareness that is love loving itself.

A few weeks after returning home from retreat, I went to a conference and ran into the man who had been the object of my passionate fantasies. We had lunch together and I could feel the distinct heat of attraction between us. But now that I was actually spending real time with him, I could also see the very glaring reasons why we weren't going to become a romantic couple. Nonetheless, when I was home alone that evening, my mind started circling once again around the possibilities of how we might get together. Because this kind of desire was now familiar, I was willing to pause. I knew that unobserved it would only fuel the wanting self. I named what was happening "Desire Story" and sat down on my meditation cushion.

Immediately thoughts about pursuing the relationship came up, and I could sense the instant contraction into an incomplete, wanting self. When I opened out of the mental movies, I could again feel the aliveness, the pulsing and vibrating, the sadness and yearning, that were right there in the moment. As at retreat, I let myself inhabit the longing. I relaxed and let it live fully through me. In the brightness of its flare, I could again sense the brightness of my own heart. It was true that I wanted to be in a romantic relationship with someone "out there." It was even more deeply true that the communion I longed for was available in that very moment. If I remained awake to this communion, desires might energize and guide my attention, but they wouldn't blind me to the fullness and beauty that are already here.

The Buddha taught that by being aware of desire, we free ourselves from identifying with it. With Radical Acceptance, we begin to shed the layers of shame and aversion we have built around our "deficient, wanting self." We see through the stories we have created—stories about a self who is a victim of desire, about a self who is fighting desire, about a self who tumbles into unhealthy desires, about a self who has to have something more, something different from what is right here, right now. Radical Acceptance dissolves the glue that binds us as a small self and frees us to live from the vibrant fullness of our being.

Longing, felt fully, carries us to belonging. The more times we traverse this path—feeling the loneliness or craving, and inhabiting its immensity—the more the longing for love becomes a gateway into love itself. Our longings don't disappear, nor does the need for others. But by opening into the well of desire—again and again—we come to trust the boundless love that is its source.

Guided Reflection: "Not Doing" When We Feel Driven by Wanting

While grasping on to what we desire is part of our conditioning, it blinds us to our deeper longings and keeps us trapped in craving. Freedom begins when we pause and pay close attention to our experience.

Reflect on an area of your life where you feel compelled by wanting mind. It might be food, cigarettes, alcohol, sex, voicing critical remarks, computer games, work or buying things. For one week let your intention be to practice pausing when you feel the urge to enact that behavior.

When you pause, become physically still and pay close attention to the nature of wanting. What does your body feel like when wanting is strong? Where do you experience the sensations of wanting most fully? Do you feel them as butterflies in the stomach? As agitation in the chest? As aching in the arms? Do you feel as if you are leaning forward, tumbling into the future? Is your mind tight and speedy? Or sluggish and dull? Notice if your experience changes during the minute or so of pausing. You might ask yourself, "What is missing right now?" and listen with your heart. If, following the pause, you move into the behavior, do so slowly and mindfully. Do you feel tension or excitement, self-judgment or fear? Notice with a clear and compassionate attention the sensations, emotions and thoughts that may arise.

While we might still pursue what we want after the pause, at least we do so aware of some of the tension and suffering that lie under our desires. Because all experience keeps changing, with time even cravings that have felt irresistible can eventually dissolve. While desire naturally arises again, the wisdom of seeing that everything passes is liberating. Observing desire without acting on it enlarges our freedom to choose how we live.

Guided Reflection: Discovering Your Deepest Longing

When we bring our myriad wants into the light of awareness, beneath them we find a deep and authentic wellspring of spiritual yearning. These core longings guide us on the path of awakening and freedom.

Sit comfortably, in a way that allows you to be present and at ease. When you feel settled, ask yourself, "What does my heart long for?" Your initial answer might be that you want to be healthy, to lose weight, to make more money, to find a partner. Ask again and listen deeply, accepting whatever spontaneously arises. Continue in this way for several minutes, asking yourself the question, pausing and paying attention in an accepting and nonreactive way. Perhaps your answer will begin to deepen and simplify. Be patient and relaxed—with time, as you listen to your heart, your deepest longing will emerge. This longing might be expressed as the longing for love, presence, peace, communion, harmony, beauty, truth or freedom.

When you recognize what you most deeply and truly long for in this moment, surrender to that longing wakefully. Say yes, allowing the energy of your deepest longing to fill your body, to suffuse your heart and awareness. What is your experience like when you fully inhabit your deepest longing? Continue to meditate, experiencing longing with an open and embodied presence.

This beautiful reflection can also be explored between two people. Sit comfortably, facing each other. Decide who will first be in the role of questioner and who will respond. After a time of becoming quiet and relaxed, one person gently asks, "What does your heart long for?" and the other responds by saying aloud what first comes to mind. Whatever the answer, the questioner simply says, "Thank you," bows or otherwise acknowledges the response, and then asks the question again. This continues for an agreed upon length of time. Before you switch roles, pause for several moments of silence so that the person who has been answering the question can inhabit his or her experience of deepest longing with a full and embodied awareness. In the same way, after the second person has had a turn responding to the question, take a few moments of silence. When the meditation is complete, you might spend a few minutes sharing your individual experience.

At any moment throughout the day, if you find yourself driven by wanting, the question, what does my heart really long for? will help you reconnect to the purity of spiritual yearning. By pausing and asking yourself at any moment, "What really matters? What do I most care about?" you awaken your naturally caring heart.

SEVEN

OPENING OUR HEART IN THE FACE OF FEAR

We have to face the pain we have been running from. In fact, we need to learn to rest in it and let its searing power transform us.

Charlotte Joko Beck

When Barbara came to me for therapy, meditation had become so unpleasant for her that she wondered if she should continue to practice. Frightening scenes from her childhood had begun to invade her morning sitting, leaving her shaken and distraught. Barbara had just returned from her first ten-day retreat, and although she had been meditating regularly for a little over a year, nothing this disturbing had happened before. Meditation had been a refuge for Barbara. She didn't want to let it go, but she just wasn't able to handle what was coming up.

She told me about one particular image that kept emerging in her meditation sittings. She and her mother had talked about the incident a number of times, and now whether the images arose from her memory or her imagination wasn't important. They were triggering unbearable fear. Barbara was an infant and her mother was bathing her in a basin on the kitchen table. She could hear the splashing of water and her mom's gentle humming. The two were engrossed in their experience, in love with each other. Suddenly her father barged in, drunk and angry, yelling at her mom: "Is that all you can ever think of . . . the baby this, the baby that . . . Did you even consider that I might come home after working hard all day and be hungry?" Shoving her mother aside, he grabbed Barbara and dunked her head underwater. She could feel the large hands pushing down on her shoulder and head, and the wild panic of drinking in water.

Barbara's mother had screamed, "No!!" and lunged for her. She wrapped Barbara in a towel and, holding her tight, said in a low voice: "Dinner will be ready in a few minutes." Her hands trembled violently as she put clothes on her daughter. Barbara lay alone in her own world—whimpering, almost unmoving. Her peaceful interlude had been shattered in an instant.

Throughout her childhood, whether her father's rage was directed at her mother or herself, Barbara would again and again feel paralyzed by the same feelings—the strangling grip of fear around her throat, the wild butterflies and sour feeling in her stomach. Even when her father wasn't home Barbara felt anxious and on edge.

Young children make sense of abusive experiences by thinking that they caused them to happen, that they were in some way to blame. Barbara grew up assuming that she brought on her father's unpredictable outbreaks. When he would suddenly start yelling at her, she would wonder, "What have I done wrong now?" Beneath that always lay the belief: "I'm bad. I'm so bad . . . that's why he hates me." Long after the waves of terror subsided, Barbara could still feel a sinking sense of shame that made her want to climb into bed and curl up under the covers. By the time she was a teen, her most persistent sense of herself was that she was a misfit—powerless, frightened and absolutely alone.

As an adult Barbara did a good job of hiding her fears from the eyes of the world. She was regarded by anyone who knew her as a highly capable, responsible person. Even her friends didn't know that she lived in constant fear that she might unknowingly offend someone, that she might make a mistake, that she might do something to invoke someone's anger. They knew only that Barbara was a wonderful listener, and they felt nourished when they were with her. Encouraged by friends to build a career on these qualities, Barbara decided to get a master's degree in education and become a high school guidance counselor. Although she felt nervous with teens, Barbara hoped she might offer them a kind of support that was missing in her own adolescence.

During her first semester at the university she met Randy, a business major. Right off, Randy adored her. She was shy and sweet, and seemed to need care. As he watched her with her nieces or with a friend having a hard time, he knew he wanted to spend his life with her. For Barbara, Randy was the perfect man. He was kind and gentle, not threatening. They moved in together while in school and married a few months after graduating.

Soon after, Barbara was hired as a guidance counselor in a small suburban high school. It didn't take long for her to notice she wasn't as witty or easygoing as the other counselors and that students rarely stopped by just to talk. When those assigned to her did come in, her fear that she might do something wrong made her stiff and distant. Meeting with parents was even worse. Her performance anxiety made everything they said sound like a comment on her own personal abilities. "I don't know what to do with her" from a parent translated in Barbara's mind into, "Why haven't you been able to guide us better?" Or, "He has terrible study habits" meant, "You could be directing him better in how he approaches his work." Her stomach would churn and the lump in her throat grow so big she could barely speak.

Barbara told me that trying to keep her fears at bay felt like locking a pack of wild dogs down in the cellar. The longer they were trapped there, the hungrier they got. Inevitably they would break down the door and invade the house. What was now happening during meditation had been going on sporadically for years. Each time the fears took over, she'd feel as if the dogs were tearing apart every room, every closet, every nook and cranny, and there was nothing she could do to stop them.

Sometimes they broke loose just before dawn. As she lay in bed, the dark shape of the picture hanging on the wall across from her would slowly come into focus. With dread, she would realize she was awake. "Oh my God . . . in a few hours I'm going to have to face another day." How could she continue pretending she knew what she was doing at work? Other people managed to handle full-time jobs, to have dinner with their in-laws or go to office parties without being flooded with apprehension. But for Barbara, everything felt like too much.

Sometimes the dogs would break through after she and Randy made love. They'd lie together and it would feel so nice to have him gently stroking her hair. Then suddenly the fear would be there—when something felt so wonderful, she was about to be blindsided. The fear would build as her mind started coming up with stories: "Maybe he'll get bored with me, tired of all my fears. Maybe he'll want to leave." Feeling frightened and alone, she'd curl up crying. Randy would wrap himself around her, trying to comfort her, not understanding what was wrong.

I regularly meet with clients and meditation students who struggle with fear. Some, like Barbara, feel overwhelmed and at times paralyzed by it. Others may not have been overtly traumatized, but as they become more aware, they realize how much fear controls their life. We all have neglected and hungry dogs in the cellar. If we make a mistake, the dogs can tear down any sense of competency we may have. If someone gets angry at us, suddenly the dogs are there, threatening to dismantle our world. If we feel rejected or betrayed, the dogs convince us that no one will ever love us.

When fear takes over in this way, we are caught in what I call the trance of fear. As we tense in anticipation of what may go wrong, our heart and mind contract. We forget that there are people who care about us, and we forget our own ability to feel spacious and openhearted. Trapped in the trance, we experience life through the filter of fear.

While all physical and emotional pain is unpleasant, the pain of fear can feel unbearable. When we are gripped by fear, nothing else exists. Our most contracted and painful sense of self is hitched to the feelings and stories of fear, to our ways of resisting fear. Yet this trance begins to lose its power over us as we meet the raw sensations of fear with Radical Acceptance. Such acceptance is profoundly freeing. As we learn to say yes to fear, we reconnect with the fullness of being—the heart and awareness that have been overshadowed by the contraction of fear.

WHAT IS FEAR?

Who doesn't know the experience of fear? Fear is waking up in the night, like Barbara, terrified that we can't go on. Fear is the jittery feeling in our stomach, the soreness and pressure around our heart, the strangling tightness in our throat. Fear is the loud pounding of our heart, the racing of our pulse. Fear constricts our breathing, making it rapid and shallow. Fear tells us we are in danger, and then urgently drives our mind to make sense of what is happening and figure out what to do. Fear takes over our mind with stories about what will go wrong. Fear tells us we will lose our body, lose our mind, lose our friends, our family, the earth itself. *Fear is the anticipation of future pain.*

The basic function of fear is to assure survival. Life-forms as primitive as the reptile experience fear. On a purely physiological level, fear is a chain of physical reactions that occur in an unvarying sequence. Western psychologists call this biological response to experience an "affect." It can unfold in an instant or endure for up to a few seconds. As the affect of fear arises, the chemistry of the body and the nervous system shifts in ways that enable several distinct responses to threatening situations. For instance, increased blood flow to the extremities of the body readies the antelope to flee. Tensing of the muscles prepares a panther to fight. Freezing and remaining motionless is the protective stance my son's gecko takes each time a human hand reaches into the aquarium. When our cats are afraid, the fur on their back bristles, making them appear larger and more dangerous in order to discourage predators. Our standard poodle crouches and appears diminutive. Similarly, a human might try to make himself smaller, protecting the places in the body that are most vulnerable—dropping the head forward, lifting the shoulders, rounding the back and contracting the chest. For each animal, as long as the danger persists, the one-pointed focus on self-preservation is maintained.

Only in mammals do cognition and memory interact with affect to create the emotion of fear. Also part of our survival equipment, the emotion of fear is shaped by the accumulated experiences of our personal history. The affect of fear that arises in response to our immediate experience combines with memories of associated past events and the affects they trigger. That's why some of us are terrified of things that hold no sense of danger for others. While the affect of fear itself lasts but a few seconds, the emotion of fear persists for as long as the affect continues to be stimulated by fearful thoughts and memories.

The emotion of fear alerts us to the possibility of negative feedback if we don't put more time into a paper for class or a report we are preparing for work. The emotion of fear lets us know that if we don't pay more attention to our marriage, we may end up divorced and alone. This more complex response to danger comes into play as we assess whether or not to seek medical attention for pain in our chest. The emotion of fear arises with any threat to our well-being, whether physical, emotional, mental or spiritual. It can guide us to respond in a healthy way or, as we each have experienced, entrap us in the trance of fear.

The real cause of our fear is not always evident. When I feel anxious, the anxiety attaches itself to whatever is going on most immediately in my life. I might be stuck in a long line at the supermarket checkout counter, afraid I'm not going to get everything else done because I'm wasting precious time. I might have the early symptoms of a flu and worry that if it gets worse I'll have to cancel clients or miss teaching my weekly meditation class. I might be helping my son with a school project due the next day and fear that if he doesn't complete the assignment in a creative or thoughtful way his grade will go down and, with it, his options in choosing a college. Regardless of the external circumstances my mind grows tight. When I pause and ask what is really bothering me, I realize that in each situation I am anticipating loss—loss of something I think is essential to my life and happiness.

The ultimate loss—the one underlying all those smaller losses I'm afraid of—is loss of life itself. The root of all our fear is our basic craving for existence and aversion to deterioration and death. We are always facing death in some form or other. I know my parents are getting older, and one day the call will come to let me know the end is near. My son, the center of my universe, will graduate from high school and leave home. People in my life are losing their memory and physical capacities. My own body is noticeably aging, getting tired, achy. Life is fragile and loss is all around. This fear of separation from the life I love—the fear of death—lies beneath all other fears.

And yet, without our fear, we would not be able to stay alive or to thrive. The problem is: The emotion of fear often works overtime. Even when there is no immediate threat, our body may remain tight and on guard, our mind narrowed to focus on what might go wrong. When this happens, fear is no longer functioning to secure our survival. We are caught in the trance of fear and our moment-to-moment experience becomes bound in reactivity. We spend our time and energy defending our life rather than living it fully.

CAUGHT IN THE TRANCE OF FEAR

We are caught in the trance of fear when the emotion of fear becomes the core of our identity and constricts our capacity to live fully. The trance of fear usually begins in childhood when we experience fear in relating to our significant others. Perhaps as an infant our crying late at night may have frustrated our exhausted mother. When we saw her frowning face and heard her shrill tone, suddenly we felt unsafe with the person we most counted on for safety. Our arms and fists tightened, our throat contracted, our heartbeat raced. This physical reaction of fear in response to disapproval may have happened repeatedly through our early years. We might have tried out something new—putting on our clothes all by ourselves and getting them backwards. We might have poured a cup of grape juice—but spilled it on the living room carpet. When we took a family trip to Grandma's, we may have wet the bed on the first night. Each time our mother's disapproving look and tone of frustration were directed at us, we felt the same chain reaction of fear in our body.

While the bodies of young children are usually relaxed and flexible, if experiences of fear are continuous over the years, chronic tightening happens. Our shoulders may become permanently knotted and raised, our head thrust forward, our back hunched, our chest sunken. Rather than a temporary reaction to danger, we develop a permanent suit of armor. We become, as Chögyam Trungpa puts it, "a bundle of tense muscles defending our existence." We often don't even recognize this armor because it feels like such a familiar part of who we are. But we can see it in others. And when we are meditating, we can feel it in ourselves—the tightness, the areas where we feel nothing.

The trance of fear not only creates habitual contraction in our body. Our mind too becomes trapped in rigid patterns. The one-pointedness that served us in responding to real threats becomes obsession. Our mind, making associations with past experiences, produces endless stories reminding us of what bad things might happen and strategizing how to avoid them. Through I-ing and my-ing, the self takes center stage in these stories: Something terrible is about to happen to me; I am powerless; I am alone; I need to do something to save myself. Our mind urgently seeks to control the situation by finding the cause of the problem. We point the finger either at others or at ourselves. As Barbara experienced, the fear of her father's rage was compounded by feeling that her own badness made him so mean to her. We might tell ourselves that inevitably we'll always ruin things for ourselves or others, or, trapped in the powerlessness of victimhood, that others will always ruin things for us. Either way, our stories tell us we are broken and need to be on guard.

Feelings and stories of unworthiness and shame are perhaps the most binding element in the trance of fear. *When we believe something is wrong with us, we are convinced we are in danger.* Our shame fuels ongoing fear, and our fear fuels more shame. The very fact that we feel fear seems to prove that we are broken or incapable. When we are trapped in trance, being fearful and bad seems to define who we are. The anxiety in our body, the stories, the ways we make excuses, withdraw or lash out—these become to us the self that is most real.

The trance of fear is sustained by our strategies to avoid feeling fear. We might learn to lie if it will shield us from someone's anger, to lash out if it gives us a temporary surge of power and safety, to try harder to be good if it will protect us from rejection. Barbara's primary strategy as an adult was to stay away from uncomfortable social situations, such as the lunchroom at work. If she was with the other teachers and counselors at a meeting, rather than participating in the casual banter, she would freeze. She was a mouse—agreeable, silent, nearly invisible—in order to stay safe.

The same was true outside of work. Randy would encourage her to join him at potlucks with friends, to go dancing or to church with him, but she usually refused. Often he stayed home with her, but occasionally when he went out on his own, fear took a different form. Something unexpected was bound to happen: Fed up with her, Randy would come home and tell her he didn't love her anymore, or he'd be killed in an accident. When Randy did come home, faithfully and on time, and try to hug her, Barbara would stiffen, an inner voice telling her, "He's just pretending to care." She couldn't let him in on how vulnerable and afraid she was—it was safer to protect herself by keeping quiet.

When we are in the trance of fear, the rest of the world fades into the background. Like the lens on a camera, our attention narrows to focus exclusively on the foreground of our fearful stories and our efforts to feel more secure. We might be having lunch with a friend or talking with a colleague at work, but their concerns and successes are outside the field of what really matters to us. Rather, we relate to them in terms of how they affect our level of fear. Is there something they have to offer—reassurance, comfort, company—that might relieve us? Do they make us feel worse about ourselves? Do they see we are afraid? Are we safe with them? We live in our own little endangered world.

Because we are responding to an accumulation of past pain, our reactions are out of proportion to what is happening in the moment. When someone criticizes us or disapproves of us, we get thrown back in time and have no access to our adult understanding. We feel as if we were a child who is powerless, alone and terrified. We lose our wallet, for instance, or are late for an appointment, and we feel as if the world is ending. Our overreaction is a further humiliation. The last thing we want is for others to know how much our life is overrun by the dogs from the cellar. If others see we are afraid, we fear we will be unappealing in their eyes—someone they pity but don't respect or want to befriend. Yet as we pretend to be okay, we sink even more deeply into feeling separate, alone and threatened.

Because the trance of fear arises from feeling cut off in relationships, we continue to feel fundamentally unsafe until we begin to experience with others some of the love and understanding we needed as children. The first step in finding a basic sense of safety is to discover our connectedness with others. As we begin to trust the reality of belonging, the stranglehold of fear loosens its grip.

THE SAFETY OF BELONGING WITH OTHERS

During one of our first sessions, Barbara told me how she used to sing when Randy was around and how much he'd loved it. In the car they often turned on a classic rock station and sang together. But something recently happened that had left her choked up around him. One morning Randy was at the breakfast table doing their taxes while Barbara was cleaning up the kitchen.

She had put on a CD and was singing along. Maybe she was a bit loud, but suddenly, over the music, she heard Randy calling out, "Barbara! Would you turn down the music so I can concentrate?" It felt like a knife had stabbed her in the chest. She flipped off the CD player and left the room. Randy followed, asking, "What did I do wrong now?" but Barbara headed into the bedroom and closed the door without answering.

After telling me this Barbara started sobbing. Randy's asking her to turn down the music shouldn't have scared her, but it did. It reminded her of something that happened in her childhood. For her twelfth birthday, her mother had signed her up for jazz dance lessons. Barbara would put music on in the living room and practice dancing for hours. On one Saturday afternoon the music suddenly stopped, and her father's belligerent voice jarred her out of her reverie. Didn't she realize she was disturbing his peace? She should either learn some consideration or get out of the house. She'd stood there, frozen, then went to her room. When this happened a second time, she quit dancing. Randy wasn't at all like her father, but she felt shut down in the same way. Maybe she'd stop singing, like she stopped dancing.

I asked Barbara if she could let herself feel in her body the fear she felt that morning with Randy. She reported that her throat felt tight and her heart was pounding loudly. "What does that fear want or need from you, Barbara?" She closed her eyes and after a moment responded, "My fear wants to know it's okay for it to be here." I asked her gently, "So . . . is it okay with you that the fear is here right now?" When she nodded, I suggested she communicate that to her fear.

Barbara was quiet for a few moments. She took a few slow, deep breaths, and I could see her shoulders relaxing with the exhales. "As soon as I sent the message saying, 'I accept you,' the fear deflated a bit . . . like a balloon." "Okay, stay with that. Could you ask the fear what it's afraid of?" Barbara paused and then responded in a flat voice: "That I don't deserve Randy. That he's too good for me." I encouraged her to note this as a thought, and remember that thoughts are not the truth.

Barbara and I were still exploring how she could best use meditation as a tool in facing her fear rather than feeling overwhelmed by it. I asked her if she would be comfortable doing some mindfulness practice together. As she noticed her experience, she could name out loud what she was aware of, and from time to time I might ask questions to guide her in deepening her attention. Barbara was enthusiastic about the idea, and over the next several weeks we interspersed our "talking" therapy with this mindfulness practice.

Supported by my presence, Barbara began witnessing the raw fear that was controlling her life. When she felt fear in her body, she noticed how her throat tightened and her voice became high and thin. She became aware of the thoughts that made nonstop predictions of what could go wrong. Barbara noticed that along with these thoughts she had a sinking feeling in her body and a mood of defeat and hopelessness. Sometimes images or thoughts would come up that were so frightening we'd stop the mindfulness practice and just talk. I noticed at these times that Barbara's gaze would fix on the floor. When I mentioned this to her, she acknowledged it was hard to look into my eyes when she was feeling so afraid.

After a month of working together in this way Barbara told me that something was changing for her: "When I'm here with you, Tara, the hungry dogs haven't gone away, but they don't seem so dangerous. I guess with someone backing me up, I feel safe enough to open the door a crack and take a look at the fear." I let her know I understood how she felt—it is easier to face the out-of-control rawness of fear when we don't feel alone. In fact, what perpetuates fear is the horrible pain of isolation. Because Barbara had another mind to help recognize the trance of fear, she could be mindful and not feel so at risk of being overpowered.

When we are feeling isolated and terrified, we can prepare the ground for practicing Radical Acceptance by first seeking out the basic safety of relationship. Barbara had wisely reached out for support when she was overwhelmed by fear. Most of us find ourselves stuck in fear from time to time, and we can greatly benefit from seeking help. In facing intense fear, *we need to be reminded that we are part of something larger than our own frightened self.* In the safe haven of belonging to others we can begin to discover the sanctuary of peace that dwells within our own being.

"TAKING REFUGE": FINDING THE INNER SOURCE OF SAFETY AND BELONGING

In our sessions together Barbara had found safety and refuge, but it was a safety that depended upon a situation external to herself. While our connectedness with others is essential on the spiritual path, genuine freedom arises as our experience of belonging finds its roots deep within us. The Buddhist practice of "taking refuge" awakens and cultivates that inner experience of safety and belonging.

In Buddhism, the three fundamental refuges are the Buddha (our awakened nature), the dharma (the path or the way) and the sangha (the community of spiritual aspirants). In these refuges we find genuine safety and peace. We discover a place to rest our human vulnerability, and a sanctuary for our awakening heart and mind. In their shelter we can face and awaken from the trance of fear.

In the formal practice of taking refuge we recite three times: "I take refuge in the Buddha, I take refuge in the dharma, I take refuge in the sangha." Even though there is a formula, this is not an empty or mechanical ritual. With each repetition we allow ourselves to open ever more deeply to the living experience behind the words. As we do so the practice leads to a profound deepening of our faith: The more fully we open to and inhabit each refuge, the more we trust our own heart and awareness. By taking refuge we learn to trust the unfolding of our lives.

Taking refuge in the Buddha may be approached on various levels, and we can choose the way most meaningful to our particular temperament. We might take refuge in the historical Buddha, the human being who attained enlightenment under the bodhi tree twenty-five hundred years ago. When the Buddha encountered Mara, he felt fear—the same painfully constricted throat, chest and belly, the same racing heart that we each experience when fear strikes our heart. By willingly meeting fear with his full attention, the Buddha discovered fearlessness—the open, clear awareness that recognizes the arising and passing of fear without contracting or identifying with it. Taking refuge in the truth of his awakening can inspire us on our own path toward fearlessness.

Those who are devotional by nature might seek safety and refuge in the living spirit of the Buddha's awakened heart and mind. Much like praying to Christ or the Divine Mother, we can take refuge in a being or presence that cares about our suffering. In taking this first refuge, I sometimes say, "I take refuge in the Beloved" and surrender into what I experience as the boundlessness of compassion. When I am feeling fear, I surrender it to the Beloved. By this, I am not trying to get rid of fear, but rather letting go into a refuge that is vast enough to hold my fear with love.

In the most fundamental way, taking refuge in the Buddha means taking refuge in our own potential for liberation. In order to embark on a spiritual path *we need faith that our own heart and mind have the potential to awaken.* The true power of Buddha's story, the power that has kept it alive for all these centuries, rests in the fact that it demonstrates what is possible for each of us. We so easily believe limiting stories about ourselves and forget that our very nature—our Buddha nature—is aware and loving. When we take refuge in the Buddha, we are taking refuge in the same capacity of awareness that awakened Siddhartha under the bodhi tree. We too can realize the blessing of freedom. We too can become fearless.

After taking refuge in the Beloved, I turn my attention inward, saying, "I take refuge in this awakening heart mind." Letting go of any notion that Buddha nature is something beyond or outside my awareness, I look toward the innate wakefulness of my being, the tender openness of my heart. Minutes earlier I might have been taking myself to be the rush of emotions and thoughts moving through my mind. But by intentionally taking refuge in awareness, that small identity dissolves, and with it, the trance of fear. By directing our attention toward our deepest nature, by honoring the essence of our being, our own Buddha nature becomes to us more of a living reality. We are taking refuge in the truth of who we are.

The second refuge, the dharma, is also richly layered in significance. A Sanskrit word, *dharma* means the truth, the way of things, the law of nature. Taking refuge in the dharma is taking refuge in the truth that everything within and around us is subject to change; the truth that if we try to hold on to or resist the stream of experience, we deepen the trance of fear. Dharma also refers to the body of teachings and practices that reveal the truth. We take refuge in the "skillful means" that awaken us to our Buddha nature and to our natural wisdom and compassion.

For Barbara finding the dharma was, at first, like finding a life raft in a stormy sea. Resting in mindfulness of the breath and noting her experience offered a reliable way to steady herself and touch a little peace. But when the practice seemed to be leading to torment, not peace, Barbara didn't know what to do. As our practice deepens, inevitably layers of buried fear are uncovered. When this happens it is important to find a refuge that can provide safety and balance. Sometimes the wise course is to seek help, as Barbara did. Sometimes it is best to set aside the practice of vipassana and instead cultivate lovingkindness for ourselves and others (see chapter 10). As Barbara came to understand, the dharma is not a rigid set of rules or practices: When we take refuge in the dharma, we take refuge in whatever ways of paying attention help us awaken from the trance of fear and realize our true nature.

Because dharma is the law of nature, communing with the natural world is also a way of taking refuge in the dharma. When I sit by the Potomac River and watch the swirling currents, when I lean against a great sycamore tree and sense how its life will continue beyond my own, I intuitively grasp how my existence is vivid, changing, empty of any solid self. As we feel our belonging to the natural rhythms of life, the illusion of being separate and threatened begins to dissolve.

The third refuge is sangha. During the Buddha's lifetime he taught that the sangha—the community of monks and nuns—was an essential support on the path of spiritual awakening. Traditionally, sangha has meant all those walking the path of dharma, the path of spiritual freedom. They too woke up in the middle of the night feeling frightened and alone. They too felt the quaking fear of loss and the terrifying certainty of death. When we know that others before us have broken the painful patterns of fear, our faith that we too can awaken deepens. When we attend a meditation retreat, our fellow practitioners and teachers are the sangha that offers safety and support as we face our fear.

As Buddhism has been integrated into the West, the meaning of sangha has come to include all our contemporaries who in various ways are consciously pursuing a path of awakening. We are held by sangha when we work individually with a therapist or healer, or when a close friend lets us be vulnerable and real. Taking refuge in the sangha reminds us that we are in good company: We belong with all those who long to awaken, with all those who seek the teachings and practices that lead to genuine peace.

A minister I know who lives in Washington, D.C., told me that ever since the terrorist attacks of September 11, she has been fearful of leaving behind her six-year-old daughter when she travels. She fears that while they are apart one of them might be killed. Distraught before leaving for a weeklong meditation retreat, she found refuge in a sangha big enough to hold her fears: "When I imagine all the other mothers around the world who cherish their children and right now are fearing for their lives, my heart feels different," she wrote to me. "The fear is still there, but even more profound is a feeling of shared grief . . . and compassion. We are facing together the possibility of immeasurable loss." While her own fear had isolated her and made her feel vulnerable, when it became *our* fear she no longer felt alone. The compassion that arose in her heart was far greater than her fear. By taking refuge in the sangha of mothers who so love their children, she awakened what the Taoists call "the invincible shield of caring," the safety of abiding in the heart.

I like to take refuge in the sangha by remembering the people I love, allowing feelings of warmth and tenderness to fill my body, heart and mind. These visceral feelings of togetherness infuse my further reflections, as I bring to mind those I'm not so personally close to, and then all living beings everywhere. When I'm feeling anxious, isolated or hard-hearted, taking refuge in the sangha in this way softens the edges and diminishes the power of the trance. At times, I might even think of my dog, and as my heart feels comforted by our bond, open gradually to feel belonging with others.

Because we are all so different in the ways our fears and needs take shape, one of the three refuges might be more accessible and nourishing than another. We can begin with whichever one we most easily sense a natural affinity for. As feelings of safety and connection arise, we can then more easily open to the others. The Buddha, the dharma and the sangha are interconnected—they are mutually supportive and each naturally involves and unfolds into the others.

As with any spiritual practice, developing a genuine sense of refuge can take time. Over the years, taking refuge nourishes a profound and liberating faith in our belonging. The Buddha taught that *our fear is great, but greater still is the truth of our connectedness.* Taking refuge transforms our relationship with fear. When we feel the safety of belonging, we can begin to meet fear with Radical Acceptance.

MEDITATION AND MEDICATION

I was confident that Barbara, desperate as she was, would in time release the painful grip of fear through her work in psychotherapy and meditation. But for some people, no matter how hard they try, something else is needed to engender safety and bring fear to a manageable level. Whether the cause is life trauma or genetic predisposition, the brain chemistry and nervous system of some people lead to intolerably high levels of fear. For them prescribed medication for depression and anxiety may provide additional, and possibly critical, aid in finding the safety that enables them to trust others and to pursue spiritual practices.

The use of antidepressants by those involved in meditation practice is a hot topic. Students have asked me, "If I take Prozac, isn't that as good as giving up? Aren't I admitting that meditation doesn't work?" Those who have been advised by a doctor to consider medication come to me distraught, afraid of becoming dependent on it, afraid they'll never function again without it. Some wonder if taking medication doesn't directly undercut the process of spiritual awakening: "Don't medications numb the very experiences we are trying to unconditionally accept?" One student even asked me, "Wouldn't liberation be impossible if we were on medication? It's hard to imagine the Buddha reaching for Prozac while under the bodhi tree."

It is true that some of the most widely used antidepressants can create a sense of distance from acute fear, a degree of emotional numbing. It is also possible to become at least psychologically dependent on any substance that provides relief. But when fear is too overwhelming, medical intervention, at least for a period of time, may be the most compassionate response. Like insulin for a diabetic, medications shift an imbalanced chemistry toward normalcy. For some this can be a critical and wise step on the spiritual path. I've seen students who were utterly incapacitated by fear finally able to face it with mindfulness and lovingkindness once they started on medications. As a psychiatrist friend says, medications make it possible for some people to "stop anxiously doing, and just sit there."

Medication and meditation can work together. As medications shift the biological experience of fear, mindfulness practice can help undo the complex of reactive thoughts and feelings that sustain the trance of fear. One of my meditation students, Seth, a composer and pianist, took antidepressants after struggling unsuccessfully for years with debilitating anxiety, shame and depression. Seth dreaded performances and the expectation of perfection that surrounded them. He told me, "Knowing how to write and play music is my life. When I feel like I am blowing it, I lose it completely. I feel totally worthless." When Seth began taking antidepressants his fear level dropped significantly. The familiar stories and self-judgments would still arise, but because the fear was less intense, he was able to see that his thoughts were just thoughts, not the truth about how things were. Gradually, as Seth deepened his meditation practice, he became familiar with a new and different sense of himself. Rather than rejecting himself as sick and broken, he began wanting to care for and comfort himself.

After two years, Seth decided to stop taking antidepressants. While his fear had decreased, he had also lost a certain degree of his natural sensitivity and empathy, and his libido was diminished. Within a few months of discontinuing the medication, Seth began to experience once again waves of acute fear and, at times, oppressive depression. But now when the old stories made their appearance, he could note them mindfully rather than getting lost in them. Taking medication had driven a wedge into the trance of fear, and it no longer was so engulfing. While his emotions were still intense, his fear wasn't fueled by overwhelming self-judgment and shame. He no longer identified himself as a broken person. Perhaps from time to time he might seek relief again from medications, but Seth now had a strength to his spiritual practice and a faith in himself that gave him a genuine sense of inner freedom.

There are no absolute recipes for the process of waking up from the trance of fear. In making choices on our path, it is important to ask ourselves whether or not they will serve awakening and freedom. Our best answers are found by honestly looking into our intentions. What is our intention in doing therapy, in taking medication or doing a particular style of meditation? Are we using meditation as a way of escaping from painful relationships or unwanted responsibilities? Do we truly intend to face and accept fear? Are our choices helping us relax and become more kind? As we seek pathways to safety, we ask these questions and then experiment to see what works.

WIDENING THE LENS OF ATTENTION: MAKING ROOM FOR FEAR

With the help of our sessions, Barbara was able to meditate alone at home again. She had learned that when strong fear came up, she could take refuge or practice lovingkindness. Gradually, as her sense of safety deepened, Barbara would begin to open more directly to the arising of fear. In the meantime, we continued to face her fear together in our sessions.

Barbara had arrived in my office one day, looking pale and tired. She'd been having a hard time sleeping, she told me. One of the students she worked with, Marty, had gotten involved with drugs and was on the verge of being kicked out of school. Barbara had begun to dread their twice-a-week meetings. Marty was sullen and hard to reach, and Barbara didn't know how to help her climb out of her hole. Each meeting was making Barbara feel more and more inadequate.

Barbara's voice was strained, her hands clenched. Anxiety had so narrowed her focus that she didn't have access to the natural intuition and warmth that would enable her to be present and open with Marty. I knew if Barbara could widen the lens of her attention, her enlarged perspective would make all the difference. She'd be able to hold both her anxiety *and* Marty's suffering with compassion.

I asked Barbara to close her eyes and imagine her next meeting with Marty. Immediately she tightened. "Try visualizing yourself sitting on a park bench," I suggested softly. "Simply name whatever experience arises, say a friendly hello and invite it to sit beside you." Barbara nodded her agreement: "There's a squeezing pressure in my chest. My stomach feels tied up in knots . . . Okay, they're sitting next to me." After a pause she added, "A voice is telling me, 'You'll blow it . . . you're hopeless.'" I reminded her, "Just say hello to that too, and invite it to sit down."

After an extended silence I asked Barbara what was happening. With a little laugh she answered, "The fear's lined up next to me on the bench, but at least it's not on top of me. I have room to breathe!" I encouraged her to go ahead and breathe more fully, to relax her hands and release whatever other tension she felt. "Now, sitting there on the park bench, can you open your attention to include the sounds around you? Notice the vastness of the sky extending out in all directions and continue listening to sounds as they arise and disappear in that openness. With the fear still right there next to you, can your mind become one with this great space of sky?"

Barbara's face softened, and she took a deep breath. Nodding slowly she told me, "The fear is still here, but now it seems so much smaller." I encouraged Barbara to let go into that soft, wakeful space surrounding and holding her fear. *"Just allow the fear to float in awareness."* By the end of our session, Barbara was able to imagine having a conversation with Marty, feel the anxiety well up in her chest and just let it untangle and begin to dissolve in awareness.

Being mindful of fear requires being both open and awake. As Barbara experienced, *opening her mind* allowed her to be present without constriction. *Being awake* enabled her to recognize and fully experience whatever was arising. Both of these aspects of mindfulness are essential in widening the lens. If we don't remain awake, spaciousness can become spacing out. We can seek openness as a way of avoiding fear rather than meeting it with mindfulness.

When we relate *to* fear rather than *from* fear, our sense of who we are begins to shift. Instead of being a tense and embattled self, we reconnect with our naturally spacious awareness. Instead of being trapped in and defined by our experiences, we recognize them as a changing stream of thoughts and feelings. Because our mind is so habitually contracted, widening the lens requires regular practice. While we cultivate this wakeful openness through mindfulness meditation, we can also use the tool of widening the lens, as Barbara would discover, right in the midst of challenging circumstances.

Marty showed up late for her next counseling session, sat down across from Barbara and said, "This is a waste of time. No one cares about me anyway, here or anywhere." Wildly searching for something "right" to say, Barbara just looked at Marty, aware of the rising tide of panic in her own body. Suddenly she noticed that in her mind she had noted "panic," said hello to it and placed it on a park bench next to her. Then, spontaneously, she imagined Marty on the park bench, too. Taking a full breath she glanced out the window behind Marty, and in seeing the sky remembered that vast space of awareness. It was holding her fear, the sounds of the ticking clock and the swirling colors of the van Gogh poster on her office wall. It could hold Marty too. In those few short moments Barbara's mind had been released from her gripping fear of failing. When she turned her attention back to Marty, she saw a confused and hurting person sitting across from her. Barbara's heart filled with tenderness. With an openness that surprised both of them, she asked, "Marty, please tell me, what's happening?"

Marty began crying, her words coming out between sobs, "I'm sorry. I'm so sorry. I'm just ruining everything . . . for everyone." Barbara moved closer and even though she felt a bit awkward, she placed her hand gently on the girl's shoulder. "It's okay, hon," she murmured in a comforting tone. "*You're* okay. Things will work out." By opening the lens of awareness wide enough to relate to her own fear, Barbara had made room for Marty's as well. In cultivating Radical Acceptance of fear, we see again and again how the wings of mindfulness and compassion are interrelated. For Barbara, widening the lens and establishing a mindful presence gave rise to her natural caring.

Widening the lens makes a full and accepting presence possible. Imagine the difference between a herd of wild stallions enclosed in a small corral and those same horses galloping through wide-open plains. This is the difference between seeing life with a narrow focus and widening the lens to a more spacious view. When our field of awareness is open and vast, there is plenty of room for the stallions of fear to kick up dust as they stampede through.

When I am meditating and become aware of a strong clutch of fear, I often take a few minutes to widen the lens. But after I've created a little physical and mental room, the only way to deepen a wholehearted presence is to directly feel the fear. Otherwise the comfort of feeling spacious might tempt me to avoid feeling the unpleasantness of my immediate experience. *Being genuinely awake in the midst of fear requires the willingness to actively contact the sensations of fear.* This intentional way of engaging with fear I call "leaning into fear."

LEANING INTO FEAR

In a popular teaching story, a man being chased by a tiger leaps off a cliff in his attempt to get away. Fortunately, a tree growing on the side of the cliff breaks his fall. Dangling from it by one arm—tiger pacing above, jutting rocks hundreds of feet below—he yells out in desperation, "Help! Somebody help me!!" A voice responds, "Yes?" The man screams, "God, God, is that you?" Again, "Yes." Terrified, the man says, "God, I'll do anything, just please, please, help me." God responds, "Okay then, just let go." The man pauses for a moment, then calls out, "Is anyone else there?"

In the face of fear, letting go of what seems to be our lifeline is the last thing we want to do. We try to avoid the tiger's mouth and the jutting rocks by accumulating possessions, by getting lost in our mental stories, by drinking three glasses of wine each evening. But to free ourselves from the trance of fear we must let go of the tree limb and fall into the fear, opening to the sensations and the wild play of feelings in our body. We must agree to feel what our mind tells us is "too much." We must agree to the pain of dying, to the inevitable loss of all that we hold dear.

Letting go into fear, accepting it, may seem counterintuitive. Yet because fear is an intrinsic part of being alive, resisting it means resisting life. The habit of avoidance seeps into every aspect of our life: It prevents us from loving well, from cherishing beauty within and around us, from being present to the moment. This is why Radical Acceptance of fear is right at the center of our spiritual awakening.

About midway into a ten-day retreat I was leading, one of the students, Eric, met a fear he couldn't avoid. He told me that during a meditation the day before he'd had a life-changing experience. It started with a lot of agitation and anxiety he was feeling about his mother and his wife, Julie. His mother recently had a stroke and might never again be able to walk or talk. Julie was struggling with chronic depression. Eric felt powerless to help—and powerless before the rising tide of anxiety that threatened to overtake him.

Remembering the teaching I had given the night before about relating to fear, Eric decided to inquire into what he was feeling. Remaining aware of the sensations of anxiety in his body, he asked himself, "What is really asking for attention?" Suddenly, a traumatic scene from his childhood arose in his mind. Eric was about six years old, and he and his baby brother were playing on a dock at the lake by their summer house. His brother went too near the edge and fell off into the water. Eric screamed for help, not knowing what to do. But help came too late. All his life Eric had always believed that his brother drowned because he hadn't been able to save him. Now, in meditation, all those feelings were rising to the surface, and Eric felt as if he would explode. His mind was racing a million miles an hour: He thought about his guilt. His fears about his wife. How things could get worse. He urgently wanted to do something but didn't know what. Suddenly Eric's body went numb.

The numbness was familiar. Eric frequently found himself feeling distant and detached when Julie would tell him how she had nothing to look forward to, nothing to give her any hope. He cared but, as he put it, "I wasn't able to be in the trenches with her. I couldn't really relate." At those times, when his body felt lifeless and his heart hard, his mind would struggle to come up with how to make things better. Now during the sitting Eric knew that beneath this numbness was a huge well of pain. If he went near it, he feared he would drown. But Eric had asked what wanted attention, and this was his answer. He was ready to meet the fear he had been pushing away for so long.

Leaning into fear does not mean losing our balance and getting lost in fear. Because our usual stance in relating to fear is leaning away from it, to turn and face fear directly serves as a correction. As we lean in, we are inviting, moving toward what we habitually resist. Leaning in allows us to touch directly the quivering, the shakiness, the gripping tightness that is fear.

Whether it is a familiar but vague feeling of anxiety or a strong surge of fear, leaning in can help us become aware and free in the midst of our experience. We might wake up after a disturbing dream, we might have just gotten a call from our doctor's office about a suspicious mammogram, we might hear a rumor of our company downsizing, we might have read a new warning about a potential terrorist attack. In any of these circumstances, a good way to begin the process is to pause and ask ourselves, "What is happening right now?" Like Eric, we can ask, "What is asking for attention?" or, "What is asking for acceptance?" It is especially important to address this inquiry to the sensations we feel in our throat, heart and stomach. These are the areas in our body where fear expresses itself most distinctly.

When we begin to face fear by focusing on sensations, what often happens is our mind immediately produces a story. We might get lost in our plans on how to respond to a frightening situation. Or we might fixate on fearful beliefs and assumptions: "I'm afraid I am a failure," "I'm afraid I'll never find love and intimacy," or "I'm afraid so-and-so will see how stupid and uninteresting I am and push me away." We might remember a recent conversation where our insecurity seemed obvious and embarrassing. Or we might, as Eric experienced, plunge into a past memory in which we came face-to-face with a feeling of powerlessness.

The key to awakening from the bonds of fear is to move from our mental stories into immediate contact with the sensations of fear—the squeezing, pressing, burning, trembling, quaking, jittering life in our body. In fact, the story—as long as we remain awake and don't get stuck in it—can become a useful gateway to the raw fear itself. While the mind will continue to generate stories about what we fear, we can recognize the thoughts for what they are and drop under them again and again to connect with the feelings in our body.

The stories that fed Eric's anxiety and powerlessness had led him to the deeper level of fear he had been trying to numb out all these years. Now he opened to the fear and asked, "How big are you?" Instantly his feelings of apprehension intensified, and the swelling pressure of fear exploded through his chest. His terror felt as if it could fill the entire meditation hall. Rather than pulling back, Eric silently said yes. His heart was pounding loudly, and in his stomach he felt cramping and a strong feeling of nausea. An excruciating tension was building in his chest, as if a wall of muscle were trying to push the fear back, trying to surround and contain it. He again asked the question, "How big are you?" As if released by his question, the feeling of terror broke all bounds; it could fill the universe. Like the utter horror that seizes us if our child runs out into a busy street, the urgency of fear strangling Eric felt as if it would never subside, never be released. "If I open to this," Eric thought, "I'll be annihilated. This fear will kill me."

Eric was saying yes and yet fighting at the same time, and the battle itself was compounding the intensity. Fear was ripping through his heart. In an instant he realized the fear would kill him if he didn't allow it to exist in its fullness. Something deep inside him knew he had to let go. As Eric put it, "I finally just wanted to surrender into something bigger than fear. I wanted to give up trying to control what was going on in me." That basic longing finally won out, and Eric let go into the fear. "It felt like my body and mind were breaking apart, that I was lost in a storm of burning winds, and my ashes were being dispersed in all directions."

Leaning into fear can be as terrifying as Eric found it to be. Even when the process is not so intense, it's never comfortable. In fact, letting go into fear may feel, as Charlotte Joko Beck puts it, like "lying down on an icy couch." It can be extraordinarily difficult to let ourselves relax in that situation. We want to hold back because it feels as if we might die of the pain. Nevertheless, if we can let the hard edges of fear press into us, the sharpness stab us, the violence pull us apart, something amazing happens. Eric told me, "When the chaos subsided, my mind was absolutely still. It was as if a screaming, thundering cacophony of sound had suddenly stopped, and I was resting in deep silence. It was vast and completely empty . . . yet it felt indescribably tender."

As Eric experienced, when we are no longer trying to control fear and cling to life, our armor drops away and we experience a deep and pure freedom. The other side of resisting fear *is* freedom. *When we stop tensing against life, we open to an awareness that is immeasurably large and suffused with love.*

A few weeks later Eric came to my weekly meditation group. He looked different—I noticed his shoulders weren't slumped, he was standing straight, and his chest seemed more open. He told me that he'd returned from the retreat to find his wife sunk into a bout of depression and hopelessness. He could feel the anxiety rising and automatically tensed. But rather than armoring against the fear and shutting down, Eric felt his heart open. "I was struck by how sad it makes me to see Julie miserable," he told me, "and how much she matters to me. So I just let her know that and held her . . . for a while." With a slightly embarrassed smile, he added, "You know, Tara, it's taken me a long time to realize that I can just hold her without trying to fix her." Rather than pulling away, Eric had discovered his capacity to remain accepting and kind in the face of anxiety.

When the trance of fear arises, instead of getting caught up in worrying or looking for something to eat, instead of getting busy and trying to fix things, we can choose to lean in. Naturally there are times when fear is too strong and we don't feel safe enough to engage with it. If we are feeling contracted and small, we may first need to widen the lens of awareness before bringing our full attention to fear. But in those moments when we can courageously lie down on the icy couch of fear and allow ourselves to experience its sharp edges, we are carried into the love and awareness that are beyond the reach of fear.

THE GIFT OF FEAR

Barbara arrived at one of our final sessions smiling brightly and eager to tell me something that had just happened. That morning she had been meditating at home and that terrifying memory had surfaced of being shoved under water by her drunk father. As the fear began to swell, she remembered to pause and breathe deeply. She'd faced her fears many times over the past months, both in therapy and in meditation. She could handle this one now. As her throat tightened, she called on the fearless heart of the Buddha and imagined his compassionate presence holding the fear. When the childhood images threatened to carry her away, she came fully into the present and, listening to the sounds of the crickets and birds outside her window, felt as if the natural world was helping to hold the fear as well. When her mind felt spacious enough, she let herself lean into the sharp, clutching pain in her chest. By the end of the sitting, she actually felt the "calm after a storm." She could still see the images, but they didn't seem to trigger the feelings in her body. "The memory might come back, but somehow I don't think the pain of it is going to take me over again—ever."

Just as I was about to celebrate her breakthrough, Barbara went on. "As I was driving over here, I passed by the church in my neighborhood. There's always a message up on the announcement board. Today it read: *What happens underwater? The Holy Spirit enters.*" We both sat quietly for a few moments, fully letting in the power of that message. Then Barbara continued: "You know, I can see now that my father was the first to baptize me. Strange as it seems, he was the one who set in motion my whole spiritual unfolding." I told her it didn't seem strange at all: "The pain of that experience—and all the times he hurt you—*have* been baptisms. They awoke in you a deep yearning for peace, for love . . . a yearning that's guided you powerfully on the spiritual path." She nodded slowly, her eyes soft and moist. "It's true. Maybe this longing is the voice of the Holy Spirit . . . and I'm finally learning to listen more carefully."

Before Barbara left I let her know how much I honored her devotion to spiritual practice. "It takes courage to listen deeply . . .

and that's what you've done. Instead of giving up on meditation—or on life—you were willing to keep paying attention." As we sat quietly for a few moments I realized what made me most happy for Barbara. "By facing fear," I told her, "you've opened to a love great enough to hold the fearful one inside you."

When we come face-to-face with the fear and pain in our psyche, we stand at the gateway to tremendous renewal and freedom. Our deepest nature is awareness, and when we fully inhabit that, we love freely and are whole. This is the power of Radical Acceptance: When we stop fighting the energy that has been bound in fear, it naturally releases into the boundless sea of awareness. The more we awaken from the grip of fear, the more radiant and free becomes our heart.

Several months after we ended therapy I saw Barbara at a daylong meditation workshop I was teaching. During our lunch break, she came to show me something. It was a brochure from The Dance Place. Barbara had registered for a ten-week jazz series, and she and Randy had already started taking swing-dancing classes together. The weekend before, she told me, they'd had a "great time" when they visited her parents. I knew Barbara had gotten closer to her father since he'd joined AA, and her mother "was like a new person." Besides, Randy's presence there always made her feel safe. But this time a "real breakthrough" had occurred. After the four finished dinner, Barbara went into the living room and put on a tape of music from their dance class. Accompanied by a loud and cheerful band, she and Randy gave a lively demonstration of the steps they had just been taught. Her parents clapped and then insisted on trying the moves themselves! At one point her father had turned to her and said, "Barb, you used to dance when you were little. You were good. Why did you stop?" She smiled without answering. Inside she felt a pang of sadness, the hurt of not having been known. But her old fears were no longer stopping her from dancing, and that filled her with the light of hope. "It's not only dancing, Tara," Barbara said, "it's everything. I feel like my life is in front of me, and I'm free to live it."

OUR ULTIMATE REFUGE

As long as we are alive, we feel fear. It is an intrinsic part of our makeup, as natural as a bitter cold winter day or the winds that rip branches off trees. If we resist it or push it aside, we miss a powerful opportunity for awakening. Rilke writes:

> *You nights of anguish. Why didn't I kneel more deeply to accept you,*
> *Inconsolable sisters, and, surrendering, lose myself*
> *in your loosened hair. How we squander our hours of pain.*
> *How we gaze beyond them into the bitter duration*
> *To see if they have an end. Though they are really*
> *Seasons of us, our winter . . .*

If we are waiting only for our fear to end, we will not discover the pure and loving presence that unfolds as we surrender into the darkest of nights. Only by letting go into the stream of life and loss and death do we come into this freedom.

Facing fear is a lifelong training in letting go of all we cling to—it is a training in how to die. We practice as we face our many daily fears—anxiety about performing well, insecurity around certain people, worries about our children, about our finances, about letting down people we love. Our capacity to meet the ongoing losses in life with Radical Acceptance grows with practice. In time we find that we can indeed handle fear, including that deepest fear of losing life itself.

Our willingness to face our fear frees us from trance and bestows on us the blessings of awareness. We let go of deeper and subtler layers of resistance until there is nothing left to resist at all, there is only awake and open awareness. This is the refuge that has room for both living and dying. In this radiant and changeless awareness we can, as Rilke puts it, "contain death, the whole of death . . . can hold it in one's heart gentle, and not . . . refuse to go on living." Radical Acceptance of fear carries us to this source of all freedom, to the ultimate refuge that is our true home.

Guided Meditation: Meeting Fear with an Open and Engaged Presence

You will benefit from cultivating an open and engaged presence as described in this exercise during those times when you are not experiencing feelings and sensations linked to trauma. If your fear is related to trauma or feels overwhelming, the practice of being with fear may lead to emotional flooding and be inappropriate. In these cases, rather than facing fear on your own, it is important that you seek support from trusted friends, guidance from a meditation teacher or skillful help from a therapist.

Find a comfortable place to sit where the view is not distracting or confined. You might look out a window or at a blank wall or an uncluttered space in your house. With your eyes open, rest your gaze on a point slightly above your line of sight. Soften your eyes so that they are unfocused and you are also receiving the images on the periphery of your vision. Relax the flesh around your eyes, letting your eyeballs float gently in their sockets. Take a few moments to do a quick scan through your body, releasing any tension, especially in the shoulders, hands and belly.

Now with a receptive awareness, begin noticing the arising and disappearing of sounds in the space around you. Spend a minute or two simply listening. Be aware of nearby sounds, noticing their beginnings and endings. Notice the spaces between sounds. Become aware of more far-off sounds, then open to the most distant sounds you can detect. Relax and open into the awareness that includes even the most distant sounds you detect. Sense how everything you perceive—sights, sounds, tastes, sensa-

tions, moods—arises and passes away within boundless awareness.

Continue with your eyes open, downcast or, if you prefer, closed. Let your attention rest softly on the out-breath, letting go into space with each exhale. Follow each breath as it dissolves outward into open space. Feel that your entire body and mind could follow the out-breath and dissolve into space. Sense that your awareness is mingling with endless space, absolutely open, boundless.

As the breath comes in, simply rest in openness, listening and awake, doing nothing. Then again let go outward with the exhale. Inhaling, rest in receptive, spacious awareness. Exhaling, relax into openness. You can meditate with the breath in this way for as long as you like.

Now resting in this natural openness, bring to mind a situation that evokes fear. Ask yourself: "What is the worst part of this situation? What am I really afraid of?" While your inquiry may arouse a story, if you stay alert to the sensations that arise in your body, the story becomes a gateway to accessing your feelings more fully.

Paying particular attention to your throat, chest and stomach area, discover how fear expresses itself in you. You might kindly invite the fear: "Be as much as you really are." Now, as you breathe in, let the breath directly touch the place of most pain and vulnerability. Bring your full attention to the sensations of fear. As you breathe out, sense the openness of space that holds your experience. Feel the fear as if floating and untwisting itself in this openness.

What does the fear actually feel like? Where in your body do you feel it most strongly? Do the sensations change or move to different parts of your body? What is their shape? What color, if any? How do you experience fear in your mind? Does it feel contracted? Is your mind racing or confused?

With each in-breath, feel your willingness to gently connect with the waves of life that are unpleasant and disturbing. Breathing out, let go and feel how the waves of fear belong to a larger world, an ocean of openness. You can surrender your fear into this vast and tender space of healing. Breathing in, you contact the immediate sensations with a kind and clear attention. Breathing out, you realize your belonging to the boundless awareness that has room for all of life's fears.

If you feel defended or numb, focus on your physical sensations and contact them fully with the in-breath. If you feel as if the fear is "too much," emphasize breathing out—letting go into openness and safety. It can help to begin again by listening to sounds or opening your eyes. You might remember the spaciousness of the world or reflect with compassion on all those who at this moment are also feeling fear. You might bring to mind a person or spiritual figure or place in nature that conveys a sense of safety. Once you feel that you belong to a larger world, again attend to the way that fear expresses through your body and mind. With time, you will discover an artful balancing of touching fear and remembering openness.

You can practice being with fear as it arises anytime during the day. Using your breath, allow yourself to touch the sensations of fear, and exhaling, let go into openness. This way, the energy does not get buried and begin to fester. Instead of reinforcing a fearful self who is running from life, you become increasingly confident and feel more fully alive.

EIGHT

AWAKENING COMPASSION FOR OURSELVES: BECOMING THE HOLDER AND THE HELD

All you need is already within you, only you must approach yourself with reverence and love. Self-condemnation and self-distrust are grievous errors . . . all I plead with you is this: make love of your self perfect.

Sri Nisargadatta

God created the child, that is, your wanting,
So that it might cry out, so that milk might come.

Cry out! Don't be stolid and silent
With your pain. Lament! And let the milk
Of loving flow into you.

Rumi

We were three days into a weeklong meditation retreat when Daniel came in to see me for his first interview. He plopped down in the chair across from me, and immediately pronounced himself the most judgmental person in the world. "When I meditate, whatever I'm thinking or feeling . . . I end up finding something wrong with it. During walking practice or eating, I start thinking I should be doing it better, more mindfully. When I'm doing the lovingkindness meditation, my heart feels like a cold stone." When Daniel's back hurt while he was sitting, or when his attention wandered and he got lost in thought, he would rail at himself for being a hopeless meditator. Daniel confessed that he even felt awkward coming in for an interview, afraid that he would be wasting my time. While others were not exempt from his barrage of hostility, most of it was directed at himself. "I know that Buddhist teachings are based on being compassionate," he said bitterly, "but it's hard to imagine they'll ever rub off on me."

Being hard on ourselves like Daniel is familiar to many of us. We often distance ourselves from emotional pain—our vulnerability, anger, jealousy, fear—by covering it over with self-judgment. When we push away parts of ourselves, we only dig ourselves deeper into the trance of unworthiness. We might clearly perceive the faults and shortcomings of ourselves and others, we might recognize we are judging, we might acknowledge that we are stuck in anger or craving or fear. We might even say we accept what we see, but Radical Acceptance has two wings—compassion as well as mindfulness. We cannot be accepting of our experience if our heart has hardened in fear and blame.

In the previous two chapters we've seen how a degree of compassion has helped people use the tools of mindfulness skillfully in facing desire or fear. When Sarah, who struggled with a food addiction, remembered, "It's not my fault" and forgave herself, her heart opened and softened in a way that made mindful presence possible. Barbara could not face her fear until she had taken refuge in our therapy relationship, and learned to find a container of safety and refuge on her own. While thus far the emphasis has been on using the wing of mindfulness to free ourselves from suffering, in this and the next two chapters we're going to focus on ways to directly awaken the wing of compassion.

If we are trapped in self-judgment like Daniel, our first and wisest step toward the freedom of Radical Acceptance is to develop compassion for ourselves. If we've injured someone and are embroiled in guilt and self-recrimination, compassion for ourselves allows us to find a wise and healing way to make amends. If we are drowning in grief or sorrow, arousing compassion helps us remember the love and connection in our life. Rather than pushing them away, we free ourselves by holding our hurting places with the unconditional tenderness of compassion.

Compassion means to be with, feel with, suffer with. Classical Buddhist texts describe compassion as the quivering of the heart, a visceral tenderness in the face of suffering. In the Buddhist tradition, one who has realized the fullness of compassion and lives from compassion is called a *bodhisattva.* The bodhisattva's path and teaching is that when we allow our hearts to be touched by suffering—our own or another's—our natural compassion flowers. The bodhisattva's aspiration is simple and powerful: "May all circumstances serve to awaken compassion." When we are going through a divorce, afraid for our child, facing disease, facing death—whatever is happening can be a gateway to the clear and limitless compassion, which is the essence of Radical Acceptance.

My understanding of the bodhisattva path is that we are all awakening beings, each of us learning to face suffering, each of us discovering the compassion that expresses our deepest nature. As we come to trust in suffering as a gateway to compassion, we undo our deepest conditioning to run away from pain. Rather than struggling against life, we are able to embrace our experience, and all beings, with a full and tender presence.

To cultivate the tenderness of compassion, we not only stop running from suffering, we deliberately bring our attention to it. Buddhist compassion practices usually begin with being aware of our own pain because once our hearts are tender and open to our own suffering, we can more easily extend compassion to others. Sometimes we most easily connect with tenderness by first focusing our attention on the suffering of others and then bringing attention to our experience. Either way, as we feel suffering and relate to it with care rather than resistance, we awaken the heart of compassion. As we practice responding to our suffering with the kindness of compassion, our hearts can become, as Buddhist teacher Sharon Salzberg says, as wide as the world.

HOLDING OURSELVES WITH COMPASSION

When I asked Daniel how long he had been turning so harshly on himself, he paused for several moments. He said it had been for as long as he could remember. He had joined his mother in relentlessly badgering himself from an early age, ignoring the hurt in his heart. As an adult he treated his heart and body with impatience and irritation. Even in the face of a tormenting divorce and a long bout of chronic back pain, Daniel hadn't been able to acknowledge how real and intense his suffering was. Instead, he criticized himself for having screwed up the marriage and for not having the sense to take proper care of himself.

I asked Daniel if he could tell me what happened in his body when he was judging himself. He pointed to his chest and said his heart felt bound by tight metal cords. I asked if he could feel that right in this moment. To his surprise, Daniel heard himself saying, "You know, this really hurts." I gently asked him how he felt about the pain in his heart. "Sad," he responded softly, his eyes welling up with tears. "It's hard to believe I've been carrying this much pain for so long."

I suggested he put his hand on his heart, on the place where he most felt the pain. I asked if he might send a message to the pain:

"How would it feel for you to say, 'I care about this suffering'?" Daniel glanced at me and then looked down again: "Strange, I think." I encouraged him to try, to just whisper the words softly. As he did so, and then repeated the phrase slowly two more times, Daniel's shoulders began to shake with quiet sobbing.

We've all felt the power of someone's care to melt our armor. When we feel upset, often not until someone cares enough to listen or give us a hug are we able to melt down and cry. When someone says to us, as Thich Nhat Hanh suggests, "Darling, I care about your suffering," a deep healing begins.

We might quite readily offer such care to others, but we can learn to offer this same kind of gentle attention to ourselves. With the tenderness we might bring to stroking the cheek of a sleeping child, we can softly place a hand on our own cheek or heart. We can comfort ourselves with words of kindness and understanding.

Offering ourselves such care might feel strange and unfamiliar at first, as it did for Daniel. Sometimes extending compassion to ourselves in this way feels downright embarrassing. It can trigger a sense of shame about being needy and undeserving, shame about being self-indulgent. But this revolutionary act of treating ourselves tenderly can begin to undo the aversive messages of a lifetime.

Over the next few days, whenever Daniel became aware of judging himself or others, he would check into his body to see where he was feeling pain. Usually he would find his throat, heart and stomach tightened in fear, and his chest heavy and sore. With a very gentle touch, Daniel would place his hand on his heart and say, "I care about this suffering." Because he was sitting in the front of the meditation hall, I noticed that his hand was almost permanently resting on his heart.

One afternoon Daniel came to tell me about something that had happened earlier that day in meditation. A scene had arisen in his mind of being at his mother's house engaged in an angry exchange with her. As he tried to explain why it wasn't irresponsible for him to take a week off to meditate, he could hear her disdainful reply: "You lazy bum, why don't you do something worthwhile with yourself?" This was the same kind of demeaning message that, in his youth, had made him want to shrivel up and disappear. He felt his chest fill with the heat and pressure of rage. In his mind he heard himself shouting, "You fucking bitch, you don't understand! You've never understood. Can't you shut up for just a minute and see who I am!!"

Daniel could feel the pain of anger and frustration like a knife stabbing at his heart. He was just about to launch into a diatribe at himself for being such a wimp for not standing up to her, and for being a meditator filled with such hatred. Instead he placed both hands on his heart and whispered over and over, "I care about this suffering. May I be free from suffering." After a few minutes the stabbing anger had subsided, and in its place he could feel warmth spreading through his chest, and a softening and opening around his heart. Feeling as if the vulnerable part of him was listening and taking comfort, Daniel said, "I'm not leaving you. I'm here and I care." Throughout the rest of the retreat, Daniel practiced like this, and some of the painful knots, the wounds of his young, anguished self slowly began to release.

When he came in for his final interview, Daniel's whole countenance was transformed. His edges had softened, his body was relaxed, his eyes bright. In contrast to his former awkwardness and hesitancy with me, Daniel seemed glad to be there. He said that the judgments and self-blame had continued but not with such unrelenting cruelty. No longer imprisoned by constantly feeling something was wrong with him, he was beginning to notice the world in new ways—other students seemed more friendly; the acres of forest were an inviting, magical sanctuary; the dharma talks stirred up a childlike fascination and wonder about "how it all is." He felt energized and somewhat bewildered by the fresh sense of possibility in his life. By holding himself with a compassionate presence, Daniel was becoming free to participate more fully in his world.

Because, like Daniel, we become so addicted to judging and mistrusting ourselves, any sincere gesture of care to the wounded places brings about radical transformation. Our suffering becomes a gateway to the compassion that frees our heart. When we become the holder of our own sorrows, our old roles as judge, adversary or victim are no longer being fueled. In their place we find not a new role, but a courageous openness and a capacity for genuine tenderness, not only for ourselves but for others as well.

REACHING OUT FOR COMPASSION

At a weekend workshop I led on Radical Acceptance, one of the participants, Marian, shared her story about the shame and guilt that had tortured her. Marian's daughter Christy, in recovery for alcoholism, had asked her mother to join her in therapy. As their sessions unfolded, Christy revealed that she had been sexually abused throughout her teen years by her stepfather, Marian's second husband. When Marian was asleep or not at home, he'd enter Christy's bedroom and lock the door so that her younger sister wouldn't surprise them. Almost every week he would arrive drunk, demand that she give him oral sex and then swear her to silence. He told her that if word ever got out, he'd beat her so badly that she'd wish she'd never been born. He also threatened to start doing the same thing with Christy's little sister. Sometimes he cried, saying that if Christy's mother ever found out, it would destroy her. She'd probably kill herself.

With each new revelation from her daughter, Marian felt her soul plunging deeper into a bottomless pit. Her days became a living nightmare. She would relentlessly rerun the mental movie of her husband sneaking into Christy's room and forcing the girl sexually. Rage would overcome her and she would plot violent acts of vengeance against this man who had harmed her daughter. Only slowly did it dawn on her how much she herself was to blame.

Imagining herself clueless, asleep downstairs after perhaps too much wine, Marian felt wracked by self-hatred. Her mind fueled her misery with its endless assaults of "If only I had known" and "How could I be so blind." Compassion for herself was not only impossible, Marian was convinced it would have been wrong. She was the mother, she told herself. What had happened to Christy was her fault. She deserved to suffer.

Then at one session what Marian had feared all along happened. Christy verbally attacked her. "You just slept through my whole adolescence," she shouted. "I was being violated and had nowhere to turn. No one was there to take care of me." Christy's face was red and her hands clenched into tight fists. "There, I've done it. I've told you the truth and *now you'll disappear again.* I was afraid to tell you then, and now I know why. You can't handle the truth. You can't handle me. You never could. I hate you," screamed Christy. "I hate you. I hate you."

Marian felt the words pierce her heart. As she watched Christy dissolve into great heaving sobs, Marian knew what she'd heard was true. She had indeed hidden away from Christy's pain by sleeping. She hadn't been able to handle her daughter's involvement with drugs, her clashes with teachers, her truancy and suspensions from school, because she couldn't handle anything about her own life. Much like her first marriage, her relationship with her second husband had quickly disintegrated after he had an affair. Her way of managing depression was through drinking with her friends and oversleeping. By the time she entered therapy and finally divorced, both her girls had left home. Now she knew how tragically she had failed Christy and her sister, how she had failed in everything that was important. There was no reason to go on living.

We have all harmed others and felt as if we were bad because of our actions. For Marian the unavoidable truth was that she had played a direct role in Christy's suffering. When we, like Marian, face the truth that we have hurt others, sometimes severely, the feelings of guilt can tear us apart. Even when the damage is not so great, some of us still feel undeserving of compassion or redemption. At times like these, the only way to find compassion for ourselves is by reaching out to something larger than the self that feels so small and miserable. We might take refuge by calling on the Beloved, on Buddha or the Divine Mother, God or Jesus, the Great Spirit, Shiva or Allah. We reach toward the loving awareness that is great enough to offer comfort and safety to our broken being.

As a Catholic, Marian had found through prayer moments of deep peace and communion with a loving God. But in her despair, she now felt alone in the universe. Sure God existed, but she felt too sinful and wretched to reach out to him. Thomas Merton writes, "True love and prayer are learned in the hour where prayer has become impossible and the heart has turned to stone." Marian's hour had come

Fearing she might harm herself, Marian sought counsel from an elderly Jesuit priest who had been one of her teachers in college. Crying, she collapsed in the overstuffed chair he offered. "Please, please help me," she pleaded. He listened to her story and sat quietly with her as she wept. When she calmed down, he gently took one of her hands and began drawing a circle in the center of her palm. "This," he said, "is where you are living. It is painful—a place of kicking and screaming and deep, deep hurt. This place cannot be avoided, let it be."

Then he covered her whole hand with his. "But if you can," he went on, "try also to remember this. There is a greatness, a wholeness that is the kingdom of God, and in *this* merciful space, your immediate life can unfold. This pain," and he again touched the center of her palm, "is held always in God's love. As you know both the pain and the love, your wounds will heal."

Marian felt as if a great wave of compassion was pouring through the hands of the priest and gently bathing her, inviting her to surrender into its caring embrace. As she gave her desperation to it, she knew she was giving herself to the mercy of God. The more she let go, the more she felt held. Yes, she had been blind, and ignorant, she had caused irreparable damage, but she wasn't worthless, she wasn't evil. Being held in the infinite compassion of God, she could find her way to her own heart.

Feeling compassion for ourselves in no way releases us from responsibility for our actions. Rather, it releases us from the self-hatred that prevents us from responding to our life with clarity and balance. The priest was not advising Marian to ignore the pain or to deny that she had failed her daughter, but to open her heart to the love that could begin the healing.

Now, rather than being locked inside her tormenting thoughts, Marian could remember the possibility of compassion. When remorse or self-hatred would arise, she would mentally say, "Please hold this pain." When she felt her anguish as being held by God, she could face it without being ripped apart or wanting to destroy herself. As her mind began to settle and clear, Marian was able to reflect on what she could do, how she could help Christy.

Two weeks later when they met again in a therapy session,

Christy was guarded and cold. Silently, Marian took a seat next to her on the couch. When Christy didn't withdraw, Marian moved a little closer. She told her she knew that she had failed her terribly. "I should have been there to protect and comfort you . . . and instead I let you down. I was so wrapped up in my own pain that I couldn't see yours." She paused, looking earnestly into her daughter's eyes. "I can't tell you how sorry I am. I know I can't make your pain go away, Christy, but I want to be with you as you find yourself. I'm *not* going to disappear again."

Gently taking Christy's hand, Marian told her the story of what had happened with the priest. Drawing a soft circle in the center of her palm, she whispered his words, "This place cannot be avoided. Let it be." Then covering Christy's hand with her own, she went on, "But in this merciful space that is the kingdom of God, your life can unfold." By the time they embraced, both were in tears. Holding her sobbing child, Marian felt filled with a tender compassion—for both of them. Christy let herself be held, surrendering into the unexpected strength and sureness of her mother's love. There was no way either of them could bypass the raw pain of yet-unhealed wounds, but now they could heal together. By reaching out and feeling held in God's mercy, Marian had discovered the compassion that could hold them both.

Marian's story stirred up deep feelings in those participating in the workshop on Radical Acceptance. Many told of their "hour where prayer has become impossible," times when they felt too worthless to be loved. As a group we explored some ways we might reach out at these times to a source of compassion, and through it learn to hold ourselves. We explored how the wise compassion at the heart of Radical Acceptance begins with regarding our own being with unconditional care.

When we feel separate and alone, we long to be held like a child in the compassionate heart of an all-loving mother, a merciful and accepting father. At these times we can reach out and offer our brokenness to this healing embrace. As Rilke puts it:

> *I yearn to be held*
> *In the great hands of your heart—*
> *Oh let them take me now.*
> *Into them I place these fragments, my life . . .*

When we feel held by a caring presence, by something larger than our small frightened self, we begin to find room in our own heart for the fragments of our life, and for the lives of others. The suffering that might have seemed "too much" can awaken us to the sweetness of compassion.

MINDFUL PRAYER: "MAY THIS SUFFERING AWAKEN COMPASSION"

We might think of Marian's devotional style of praying as peculiar to Christianity and other God-centered religions, yet no matter what we believe, as human beings we all tend to reach out to something in moments of desperation. We might call out for relief from a migraine, beg to be selected for a job, pray for the wisdom to guide our child through a difficult time. Maybe we whisper, "Oh please, oh please," and feel that we are asking "the universe" for help. When we feel disconnected and afraid, we long for the comfort and peace that come from belonging to something larger and more powerful.

Students of Buddhist practice often wonder if this kind of prayer reinforces the notion of a separate and wanting self. We do seem to be beseeching someone or something greater than our small and frightened self. And who exactly are we praying to? I grew up Unitarian, and I remember how we used to joke about addressing our prayers "To Whom It May Concern." Following the path of the Buddha, we might have the same question. While prayer does suggest a dualism of self and other, it can be a direct path to the nondual experience of fully belonging.

Although not always highlighted in the West, prayer and devotion are a living stream in Buddhism. The earnest wishes expressed in the practices of lovingkindness and compassion—may I be happy, may I be free from pain and suffering—are forms of prayer. Our prayers of aspiration and our longing for relief from suffering may not necessarily be directed to anyone or anything. But we might also address them to the Buddha or one of the other great teachers or bodhisattvas we regard as embodiments of the awakened heart and mind. When done with mindfulness and sincerity, this kind of devotional prayer becomes a way to awaken our own heart and mind.

When we are suffering and turn to prayer, no matter what the apparent reasons for our pain, the basic cause is always the same: We feel separate and alone. We reach out to be relieved of this pain of isolation. Celtic poet and scholar John O'Donohue, in his book *Eternal Echoes,* writes: "Prayer is the voice of longing; it reaches outwards and inwards to unearth our ancient belonging." This is a beautiful description of what I call mindful prayer. We reach not just outward to know our belonging, but *with mindful prayer we also turn inward and listen deeply to the suffering that is giving rise to our prayer.* When we are willing to touch the pain of separation, our longing carries us to the tender and compassionate presence that is our awakened nature.

I experienced the transforming power of mindful prayer some years ago when I was suffering from a broken heart. I had fallen in love with a man who lived two thousand miles away, on the other side of the country. Because we had very different desires about having a family and about where to live, we couldn't weave our lives together and the relationship ended. The loss was crushing—for many weeks I was swamped in obsessing about him, sobbing, overwhelmed with grief. I stopped listening to the radio because classic rock songs often left me weeping. I avoided romantic movies. I barely talked with friends about him because even saying his name out loud would freshly reopen the wound.

I accepted my grieving process for the first month or so, but as it went on and on, I started feeling ashamed of how big and dominating my sense of desolation was. On top of that, I felt that something must be wrong with me for being such an emotional wreck. The man was moving on, dating other people. Why couldn't I do the same? I tried to wake up out of the stories, I tried mindfully letting the pain pass through, but I remained possessed by feelings of longing and loss. I felt more excruciatingly lonely than I had ever felt in my life.

In the room where I meditate, I have a Tibetan scroll painting (called a *thanka*) of the bodhisattva of compassion. Known as Tara in Tibet and Kwan Yin in China, she is an embodiment of healing and compassion. It is said that Kwan Yin hears the cries of this suffering world and responds with the quivering of her heart. One morning, about a month into my meltdown, as I sat crying in front of the thanka, I found myself praying to Kwan Yin. Like Marian, I didn't feel any compassion for myself. I felt crushed and worthless. I wanted to be held in Kwan Yin's compassionate embrace.

Off and on over my years of Buddhist practice, I had prayed to Kwan Yin, primarily relating to her as a symbol of compassion that could help me awaken my own heart. But I hadn't really prayed to her in the way Marian had prayed, reaching out to her as a spiritual presence, as a being larger than my small self. Now, in my desperation, it was different. Kwan Yin was no longer just a symbol of inspiration, she was the Beloved—a boundless and loving presence who, I hoped, could help relieve my suffering.

For a few days I did find some comfort by reaching out in this way. But one morning I hit a wall. What was I doing? My ongoing ritual of aching and praying and crying and hating my suffering was not really moving me toward healing. Kwan Yin suddenly seemed like an idea I had conjured up to soothe myself. Yet without having her as a refuge, I now had absolutely nowhere to turn, nothing to hold on to, no way out of the empty hole of pain. What felt most excruciating was that the suffering seemed endless and utterly worthless.

Even though it seemed like just another concept, I remembered that, for the aspiring bodhisattva, suffering is the trusted gateway to awakening the heart. I remembered that when I had remained present with pain in the past, something had indeed changed. Suddenly I realized that maybe this situation was about *really* trusting suffering as the gateway. Maybe that was the whole point—I needed to stop fighting my grief and loneliness, no matter how horrible I was feeling or for how long it continued.

I recalled the bodhisattva's aspiration: "May this suffering serve to awaken compassion," and began quietly whispering it inside. As I repeated the prayer over and over, I could feel my inner voice grow less desperate, more sincere.

I knew it was true—I could awaken to the love I yearned for by directly touching the fullness of this suffering. The moment I let go into that truth, the change began.

The fourteenth-century Persian poet Hafiz wrote:

Don't surrender your loneliness
So quickly.
Let it cut more deep.

Let it ferment and season you
As few human
Or even divine ingredients can.

Something missing in my heart tonight
Has made my eyes so soft,
My voice
So tender,

My need of God
Absolutely
Clear.

That day in my meditation room, as I let the loneliness cut more deep, I could scarcely bear the searing pain of separation. I was longing, not for a particular person but for love itself. I was longing to belong to something larger than my lonely self. The "something missing in my heart" felt like an aching, gaping hole. The more fully I reached inward to that gnawing emptiness instead of resisting or fighting it, the more deeply I opened to my yearning for the Beloved. Like Hafiz's need for God, my yearning for communion felt absolutely clear.

As I let go into the yearning, the sweet presence of compassion arose. I distinctly sensed Kwan Yin as a radiant field of compassion surrounding me, cherishing my hurting, vulnerable being. As I surrendered into her presence, my body began to fill with light. I was vibrating with a love that embraced the whole of this living world—it embraced my moving breath, the singing of birds, the wetness of tears and the endless sky. Dissolving into that warm and shining immensity, I no longer felt any distinction between my heart and the heart of Kwan Yin. All that was left was an enormous tenderness tinged with sadness. The compassionate Beloved I had been reaching for "out there" was my own awakened being.

We might begin our prayer by reaching out, and in that way remember the warmth and safety of connectedness. Yet we ground our prayer by reaching inward to the raw feelings of loneliness and fear. Like a great tree, mindful prayer sinks its roots into the dark depths in order to reach up fully to the light. When the pain is deep, the more fully we touch it, the more fully we release ourselves into boundless, compassionate presence.

Many of my therapy clients and students have discovered that mindful prayer dramatically alters the landscape of their daily life. Sometimes many times a day, in the face of discontent and suffering, they pause to listen inwardly, to touch the pain and to reach out toward love and compassion. Although this may seem most natural for people with devotional temperaments, I've found that people who have considered themselves "not the praying type" are often surprised by how mindful prayer transfigures their life. Rather than being caught in the suffering of judgment and fear, they find their true home in the tenderness of their hearts.

We can also turn to mindful prayer at those times when we get caught in our smaller anxieties about daily life. Perhaps we're told our flight has been canceled due to mechanical difficulties, or we feel hurt because we were not invited to a social gathering, or we find we are in a jam because the baby-sitter just called in sick. If we can remember at these moments the aspiration that these circumstances might awaken compassion, our experience shifts. By mindfully feeling our discomfort and calling on compassion, our heart naturally becomes more spacious and relaxed. Our suffering, rather than being worthless or an obstacle, becomes the path to inner freedom.

Like any form of meditation, mindful prayer becomes more vibrant and powerful with practice. When we remember over and over how much we long to be tender and kind, and let ourselves fully inhabit that longing, compassion naturally awakens. As Hafiz wrote:

> *Ask the Friend for love.*
> *Ask Him again.*
>
> *For I have learned that every heart will get*
> *What it prays for*
> *Most.*

Whenever we feel closed down, hurt or unforgiving, by simply breathing in and gently touching the rawness of our pain, we can begin to transform our suffering into compassion. Keeping our gaze on the bandaged place, as Rumi says, allows the light to enter. As we breathe out, we can feel our longing to connect and let go into the immensity of the light. We can surrender into the radiant love we yearn for. Breathing in and breathing out, we hold our pain and let our pain be held in a boundless heart of compassion.

WE ARE THE HOLDER AND THE HELD

As our heart transforms suffering into compassion, we experience being both the holder of our sorrows and the vulnerable one who is being held. Daniel found he could hold his wounds in his own healing awareness. As Marian released her desperation into the boundless mercy of God, she found the compassion that could hold not only her own but also her daughter's suffering. Through mindful prayer I found how holding and being held unfold into a compassion that transcends all sense of separation. Both the holder and the held dissolve into loving awareness.

When we understand our pain as an intrinsic gateway to compassion, we begin to awaken from the imprisoning story of a suffering self. In the moments when we tenderly hold our anger, for instance, we cut through our identity as an angry self. The anger no longer feels like a personal flaw or an oppressive burden. We begin to see its universal nature—it's not *our* anger, it is not *our* pain. Everyone lives with anger, with fear, with grief.

A beautiful Sufi teaching shows us how our pain is not personal, it is an intrinsic part of being alive:

Overcome any bitterness that may have come
because you were not up to the magnitude of the pain
that was entrusted to you.
Like the Mother of the World,
Who carries the pain of the world in her heart,
Each one of us is part of her heart,
And therefore endowed
With a certain measure of cosmic pain.

Understanding that the pain in our life is an expression of universal suffering opens us to the fullness of Radical Acceptance. Rather than being a problem, our depression, fear and anger are "entrusted to us," and can be dedicated to our awakening. When we carry our pain with the kindness of acceptance instead of the bitterness of resistance, our hearts become an edgeless sea of compassion. We, like the Mother of the World, become the compassionate presence that can hold, with tenderness, the rising and passing waves of suffering.

Guided Meditation: Becoming the Holder of Suffering

Compassion begins with the capacity to hold your own life with a loving heart. Whenever you're aware that you are suffering, if you offer yourself care—through attention, words and touch—compassion will naturally awaken. This meditation is especially useful when you are feeling emotional pain. Even if you do not immediately feel compassion for yourself, your willingness alone can reconnect you to your loving heart. Because compassion is intrinsic to your nature, it inevitably flowers.

Find a comfortable position and take a few moments to breathe naturally and relax. Turn your attention to the hurt or grief, shame or fear you may be feeling. You might use your breath to deepen your attention to this suffering—breathing in and directly touching the feelings of vulnerability; breathing out and sensing the space of awareness that holds your experience. Invite the painful feelings to express their fullness, allowing them to swell and intensify through your body and mind.

Begin offering words of care to the place within you that feels most vulnerable. You might silently say, "May I be free from suffering," or as Thich Nhat Hanh suggests, say to yourself, "Darling, I care about this suffering." Your prayer might be more specific: "May I be free from fear," or, "May I feel safe and at peace." As you continue to offer your caring prayers you might also place your hand on your cheek or your heart, letting the tenderness of your touch express compassion.

Be aware of how your heart feels as you offer care to your suf-

fering. Do you feel sincere, open or tender? Or do you feel mechanical, blocked or numb? If you feel distant and disconnected, without any judgment simply affirm your intention to be present and kind and continue offering these gestures of care. If your intention to be compassionate is genuine, with time your heart will naturally soften and open.

As you extend care to yourself, notice how the sensations and feelings of emotional pain change. Do they become more intense? Do they begin to subside? Does the emotion you first felt transform into a different one? You may find that embracing yourself with kindness brings up a deep sadness. Whatever you are feeling, hold your pain with the same presence and tenderness you would offer to a beloved and frightened child.

Feel free to experiment with whatever communicates genuine care to your inner life. You might softly whisper aloud the words of care. You might physically hug yourself, or imagine holding yourself as a child. Take the time to listen inwardly and sense what particular weave of words or gestures feels most healing. It may be as simple as acknowledging with tender care that you are hurting. With practice you will begin to find that when fear or hurt arises, you respond with a spontaneous and gentle compassion.

Guided Meditation: Invoking the Presence of the Beloved

There are times we feel alone and afraid and wish we could curl up in the lap of the Buddha or some other manifestation of love and wisdom. When you long to be held in this way, allow yourself to reconnect with your own awakened heart by first reaching out to whatever you experience as the Beloved, the embodiment of compassion.

Sitting comfortably and quietly, take a few full breaths. With a gentle and open attention, notice the fear or vulnerability you are feeling in your body and mind. Connect with your longing to be held in unconditional love.

Bring to mind the image or sense of a person, a spiritual figure or a deity you associate with compassion. You may see the face of your grandmother or your dearest friend. You may see an image of the Buddha, Kwan Yin or Christ, or you may call to mind an all-merciful God. With a silent prayer, ask this being to be present with you. You may experience the being gazing at you with unconditional love. Look into the eyes that regard you with understanding and complete acceptance. Placing your attention on your heart and aware of your longing, experience this compassionate being as absolutely present and available, as wanting to be here with you.

Now imagine this being's presence as a radiant and boundless field of light. Visualize and feel that you are surrounded by this warm luminosity, held in this being's loving embrace. See how fully you can surrender, letting your hurt and fear, pain and sorrow dissolve into this merciful presence. Allow your entire body, heart and mind to release into and merge with this loving awareness. If you contract again in doubt or fear, gently feel your suffering and reach out once more toward this compassionate presence.

As you practice invoking an embodiment of compassion, you discover that it is the pathway home to your awakened heart. Each time you dissolve into oneness with the Beloved, trust in your true nature deepens. You become the compassionate presence that holds all suffering with tenderness.

NINE

WIDENING THE CIRCLES OF COMPASSION: THE BODHISATTVA'S PATH

I live my life in widening circles
That reach out across the world.
I may not ever complete the last one,
But I give myself to it.
Ranier Maria Rilke

On Narayan's sixth birthday I gave him an ant farm. My son spent hours watching with fascination as the little creatures magically created their network of tunnels. He named several and followed their struggles and progress closely. After a few weeks he pointed out the ants' graveyard and watched with wonder as several of them dragged the bodies of their dead comrades and deposited them there. The following day when I picked Narayan up after school he was visibly distressed. He told me that on the playground the kids had made a game out of stepping on ants. He was horrified that they were hurting these friends he so admired.

I tried to comfort him by explaining that when we really spend time with any living beings—as he had with the ants—we find out that they are real. They are changing, animated, hungry, social. Like us, their life is fragile and they want to stay alive. His playmates hadn't had the chance to get to know ants in the way he did, I told him. If they had, they wouldn't want to injure them either.

Whenever we wholeheartedly attend to the person we're with, to the tree in our front yard or to a squirrel perched on a branch, this living energy becomes an intimate part of who we are. Spiritual teacher J. Krishnamurti wrote that "to pay attention means we care, which means we really love." Attention *is* the most basic form of love. By paying attention we let ourselves be touched by life, and our hearts naturally become more open and engaged.

The Dalai Lama once remarked, "I don't know why people like me so much. It must be because I value *bodhichitta* [the awakened heart/mind]. I can't claim to practice [it], but I value it." We care about the awakened heart because, like a flower in full bloom, it is the full realization of our nature. Feeling loved and loving matters to us beyond all else. We feel most "who we are" when we feel connected to each other and the world around us, when our hearts are open, generous and filled with love. Even when our hearts feel tight or numb, we still care about caring.

In describing his own spiritual unfolding, Mahatma Gandhi said, "I hold myself to be incapable of hating any being on earth. By a long course of prayerful discipline, I have ceased for over forty years to hate anybody. I know this is a big claim. Nevertheless, I make it in all humility." When we look at our own lives and at the history of humanity, we realize that hatred, anger and all forms of dislike are a pervasive and natural part of being alive. Aversion arises because we are so deeply conditioned to feel separate and different from others. As Gandhi found, only by dedicating ourselves to some form of intentional training can we dissolve this tendency and embrace all beings with Radical Acceptance.

Serving the poor and dying of Calcutta was to Mother Teresa a practice of viewing each person as "Christ in his distressing disguise." By doing so she was able to see beyond the differences that might have hardened her heart and to serve with unconditional compassion each person she touched. As we train ourselves to see past surface appearances, we recognize how we are all the same. For Mother Teresa this meant that each person carries a spark of divinity. According to the Buddha's teachings, our true nature is timeless, radiant awareness. To accept ourselves and others with unconditional compassion means recognizing both the pure awareness that is our essence *and* our natural human vulnerability.

Up until this point in the book, we have been exploring how to bring the mindfulness and compassion of Radical Acceptance to our inner life. Just as we awaken compassion for ourselves by touching our own fear, anger and grief, when we bring clear attention to the vulnerability of others, our hearts become open and tender. Compassion for ourselves naturally leads to compassion for others. While love describes our basic feeling of relatedness, compassion for others is the flavor of love that arises when we see this truth of our shared suffering.

Living our lives with a wise and compassionate heart is the essence of the bodhisattva's path. As we saw in the last chapter, the bodhisattva's aspiration, "May all circumstances serve to awaken compassion," can guide us in holding whatever arises in our life with acceptance and care. As we transform suffering into compassion, we realize our interconnectedness with all of life. This profound realization gives rise to a second and key aspect of the bodhisattva's aspiration: "May my life be of benefit to all beings."

In traditional texts this aspiration is expressed as the bodhisattva's vow to refrain from entering nirvana—ultimate freedom—until all other living beings are also free. While the language of this vow may be interpreted in different ways, its intent is clear: Out of compassion, the bodhisattva dedicates his or her life and practice to relieving suffering. The selfless spirit of this vow invites us to remember our belonging and deepen our capacity for limitless compassion. Like the bodhisattva of compassion, we can aspire to become spacious and tender enough to hold the suffering of all beings with care. In this chapter we will look at how, by paying attention to the suffering of others, our compassion grows in ever-widening circles. As Gandhi discovered, we can train ourselves to include everyone in our heart.

WE ARE IN THIS TOGETHER

Kim arrived at a New Year's retreat on "Awakening the Heart of Compassion" feeling utterly humiliated from a mishap at work. After printing out five thousand brochures for her company, she found that she had missed several very obvious typos. In a nasty exchange with a coworker, Kim had defensively tried to deflect some of the blame, suggesting that if he had covered the phones instead of staying so long at the holiday luncheon, maybe she wouldn't have been so distracted. She punctuated her remarks by angrily sweeping a neatly piled stack of brochures off her desk. Now, alone with her own mind, Kim found herself rerunning this scene, squirming with shame as she recalled the tone of her voice and how she had just stood and watched as her coworker stooped to collect the brochures.

In our first interview, I encouraged her to let go of the story and just drop down into the feelings of fear and shame as they arose in her body and mind. She told me she felt a deep ache in her chest and a vise around her throat. Using as a base the traditional compassion meditation we had introduced at the retreat, I guided Kim to begin with awakening compassion for herself. "Holding those painful areas with care, you might repeat the phrases you learned: 'I care about this suffering. May I be free of suffering.' "

When I could see that Kim had relaxed, I asked if she could think of any family members or friends who'd also felt embarrassed by mistakes and emotional reactivity. Kim brought to mind her mother and her brother. As she remembered times when they'd felt ashamed and humiliated, Kim felt a welling up of tenderness for them. Thinking of her mother and brother, Kim silently whispered to them: "I care about your suffering; may you be free from suffering."

Continuing with the compassion practice, Kim expanded the circle of her caring by bringing to mind people she was familiar with but didn't know well—others at the retreat, people she saw working out at the gym, parents of her children's friends. Still feeling the rawness of her own self-doubt, Kim could imagine how some version of that same fear she was feeling might live behind the aloofness or arrogance, busyness or defensiveness she noticed in some of them. As she let in a sense of each person's vulnerability and offered her prayer of care, Kim felt an intimate bond arising.

With her heart feeling more open, Kim brought to mind the coworker with whom she'd felt so irritated. She remembered the hurt look in his eyes when she lashed out. She recalled his habitual look of worry, his physical tightness and self-deprecating remarks and recognized that he too feared being unworthy and incompetent. Kim felt a surge of remorse and then sadness as she realized she had probably struck him in a very vulnerable spot. With a full and focused attention she continued for the next few moments offering him her care, praying that he might be free of fear.

I guided Kim to the last step in the compassion practice—opening her heart and attention boundlessly, extending care to all beings who suffer, to all who feel insecure and alienated. When Kim finished the meditation and opened her eyes, her face had softened and her body had relaxed. Sitting back in her chair now, she rested her hands openly and easily in her lap. She gave me a smile that was both sad and sweet and said, "When I remember that other people feel the same kind of insecurity that I do, then it's not like I'm bad—I'm just human." She paused and then added, "I can feel how we're all in it together."

This practice of intentionally reflecting on suffering—our own and that of others—is the basic form of Buddhist compassion meditations. We include the suffering of those we cherish, those we barely know, those we find difficult and those we have never met, out to the widest circle. While we might not formally reflect on those in each domain during every meditation, the practice deepens our capacity for compassion. As Kim found, when we reflect on the suffering of others, we realize we are not alone in our pain. We are connected through our vulnerability.

Without a genuine willingness to let in the suffering of others, our spiritual practice remains empty. Father Theophane, a Christian mystic, writes about an incident that happened when he took some time off from his regular parish duties for spiritual renewal at a remote monastery. Having heard of a monk there who was widely respected for his wisdom, he sought him out. Theophane had been forewarned that this wise man gave advice only in the form of questions. Eager to receive his own special contemplation, Theophane approached the monk: "I am a parish priest and am here on retreat. Could you give me a question to meditate on?"

"Ah, yes," the wise man answered. "My question for you is: What do they need?" A little disappointed, Theophane thanked him and went away. After a few hours of meditating on the question and feeling as if he were getting nowhere, he decided to go back to the teacher. "Excuse me," he began, "perhaps I didn't make myself clear. Your question has been helpful, but I wasn't so much interested in thinking about my apostolate during this retreat. Rather

I wanted to think seriously about my own spiritual life. Could you give me a question for my own spiritual life?" "Ah, I see," answered the wise man. "Then my question is, What do they *really* need?"

Like so many of us, Father Theophane had assumed that true spiritual reflection focuses on our solitary self. But as the wise man reminded him, spiritual awakening is inextricably involved with others. As Theophane focused on the needs of those he had been given to serve, he would recognize their vulnerability and longing for love—and realize that their needs were no different from his own. The question the wise man suggested was wonderfully crafted for awakening in Theophane the true spiritual depth that comes from paying close attention to other human beings.

THE TRANCE OF THE UNREAL "OTHER"

When we are caught in our own self-centered drama, everyone else becomes "other" to us, different and unreal. The world becomes a backdrop to our own special experience and everyone in it serves as supporting cast, some as adversaries, some as allies, most as simply irrelevant. Because involvement with our personal desires and concerns prevents us from paying close attention to anyone else, those around us—even family and friends—can become unreal, two-dimensional cardboard figures, not humans with wants and fears and throbbing hearts.

The more different someone seems from us, the more unreal they may feel to us. We can too easily ignore or dismiss people when they are of a different race or religion, when they come from a different socioeconomic "class." Assessing them as either superior or inferior, better or worse, important or unimportant, we distance ourselves. Fixating on appearances—their looks, behavior, ways of speaking—we peg them as certain types. They are HIV positive or an alcoholic, a leftist or fundamentalist, a criminal or power monger, a feminist or do-gooder. Sometimes our typecasting has more to do with temperament—the person is boring or narcissistic, needy or pushy, anxious or depressed. Whether extreme or subtle, typing others makes the real human invisible to our eyes and closes our heart.

We each have our own complex and largely unconscious system of classifying others. When I read the newspaper or watch the news, I regularly run into my own anger and dislike toward public figures who are rich, Caucasian, usually male, powerful and conservative. As I hold tightly to my views of right and wrong, I type these senators, corporate executives and editors-in-chief as the "bad guys," as part of the problem. They become characters in an upsetting movie, not living, breathing humans.

In her novel *Stones from the River,* set in Nazi Germany, Ursula Hegi reveals the suffering of the "other" in a startling way. The story is told through the eyes of a courageous woman, Trudy, who risks her life to hide the Jews living in her small town. Trudy is an insightful and appealing character. She is also a dwarf. As the story unfolds we begin to see, through Trudy's eyes, the pain of being the "other." She longs for her neighbors and townspeople to know her, to see past her small awkward body and broad outsized face. Trudy can well identify with those she gives refuge to because she too suffers the nonverbal and spoken slights that let her know she doesn't belong.

Reading this story was a jarring awakening for me. I wondered how many people each day I am unable to see and respond to because I unknowingly classify them as "other." I could easily have lived in Trudy's village and turned my head away in embarrassment, not wanting to look too closely at this human "oddity" when she and I passed each other on the street. Our capacity to look away from the realness and the suffering of others has horrendous consequences. For years, much of the world turned away from the plight of the Jews in Nazi Germany. Today we might not recognize the realness of the massive number of people dying of AIDS, the horror of living in the Middle East, in Afghanistan, in the many war-torn and devastatingly poor places on this globe.

In the summer of 1991, I was flying across the country, talking with the woman sitting next to me. She told me her son was in the air force and had safely returned from Desert Storm, the war with Iraq. Then she leaned toward me with a smile and spoke softly: "You know, it went really well. Only a few of our boys died." My heart sank. Only a few of our boys. What about all the Iraqi boys and women and children? What about the millions who were yet to die from radioactive contaminants, or from starvation and disease during the economic embargo that followed the war? *Our boys.*

Once someone is an unreal other, we lose sight of how they hurt. Because we don't experience them as feeling beings, we not only ignore them, we can inflict pain on them without compunction. Not seeing that others are real leads to a father disowning his son for being gay, divorced parents using their children as weapons. All the enormous suffering of violence and war comes from our basic failure to see that others are real.

Our immediate response of attraction or aversion, of interest or inattention, is part of our biological programming for survival. How a person looks, the way they smell and speak, alerts us to whether or not they are from the same tribe. When we are trapped in this biological trance, we can only read behaviors and opinions as signs of friend or foe. While this evolutionary conditioning to perceive difference is powerful, we also have the capacity to relax our armor. We can enlarge our sense of tribe. This is an experience of Radical Acceptance that is at the center of the bodhisattva's path. We can learn to see our shared vulnerability and realize our belonging with all beings.

ENLARGING OUR TRIBE: SEEING BEHIND APPEARANCES

In the mid-1970s I worked as a tenants' rights activist with poor families in Worcester, Massachusetts. Through organizing tenants' unions we would try to pressure landlords into assuring fair rents and decent living conditions. One of these unions was comprised of families renting from one of the most notoriously callous slumlords in the city. The union's leader, Denise, was a forceful and articulate woman who worked hard to galvanize the group into action to fight a steep rent increase that no one could afford.

Over the many months it took to build the union, I had become friends with Denise and her family. I joined them for dinner, played with the children and was privy to their struggles. Their apartment had been vandalized several times, and there was no way to keep out the rats and cockroaches. Denise's oldest son was in jail, another was a drug addict. Her current husband was unemployed and they were in debt. Feeding and clothing her young children and keeping the heat on were challenges she faced regularly. I admired her willingness to put such a dedicated effort into her role as union leader when she had so much to handle at home.

Two days before we were about to begin a rent strike that Denise was coordinating, I found a note from her under my door. It said she was leaving the union. I was surprised and disappointed, but I had an idea of what had happened. Landlords frequently co-opted tenant leaders as a way of crippling the unions. As it turned out, Denise had been bought off with the offer of a new double lock, a rent break and a part-time job for her son.

The other tenants felt betrayed and demoralized. Denise was "two-faced" and "spineless," they said. Whenever they saw her on the sidewalk, they would cross over to the other side of the street.

They didn't let their children play with her children. She was an outsider, one of "them." In the past, when union leaders had been bought out, I'd felt the same. They were obstructing our progress.

With Denise it was different. I understood how desperately she was trying to help her family. I had seen how, like me, she felt anxiety about her life, how she too wanted love. The poet Longfellow writes, "If we could read the secret history of our enemies, we should find in each man's life sorrow and suffering enough to disarm all hostility." I had read enough of Denise's secret history for her to be real to me; I cared about her.

On the other hand, while it was possible for me to feel openhearted toward Denise despite her actions, I certainly didn't feel the same toward the landlords. They were in my "bad guy" category. A number of years later I had the perfect opportunity to face someone in this category and look more deeply. A friend of mine knew a CEO from a very large corporation who wanted to set up a mindfulness program for his company's employees. My friend wanted me to discuss the program with this man over lunch. The CEO fit exactly my rich white man stereotype. He had been the focus of a well-publicized class action suit for systematically denying women the same opportunities for upward mobility as men. The discrimination was particularly egregious toward African American women. I agreed to talk with him but felt uncomfortable about the meeting, expecting that we'd be coming from very different and unfriendly planets.

Close up, he turned out to be quite human and real. He bragged a bit and was obviously eager to be liked. His mother had had triple bypass surgery several weeks earlier. His oldest son had juvenile diabetes. On the weekends his wife complained that he didn't play enough with the children. He did want to, he was crazy about them, but invariably urgent calls on his cell phone would pull him away from the games of Ping-Pong, the barbecues or the videos they were watching together. He wondered, "Can mindfulness help me to relax when everywhere I turn is another demand?" It didn't matter that we probably disagreed on most political and social issues. I liked him and I wanted him to be happy.

Even if we don't like someone, seeing their vulnerability allows us to open our heart to them. We might vote against them in an election, we might never invite them to our home, we might even feel they should be imprisoned to protect others. Still, our habitual feelings of attraction and aversion do not have to overrule our basic capacity to see that, like us, they suffer and long to be happy. When we see who is really in front of us, we don't want them to suffer. Our circle of compassion naturally widens to include them.

LIVING IN A WORLD WHERE EVERYONE IS REAL

One of the most remarkable things I've noticed about the Dalai Lama is how he treats everyone equally. While one newspaper photo shows him lovingly embracing Jesse Helms, another shows him with his arms around a poor Tibetan refugee. When the Dalai Lama says, "My religion is kindness," he is expressing his commitment to live with the unconditionally open and loving heart of compassion. Kindness is a facet of the jewel of compassion. It is the desire to help that arises when we remember that we are connected with every living being we meet. Each person is precious, each person is fragile, each person matters.

At the funeral of a beloved rabbi, a younger man who had only recently begun his studies with the rabbi turned to one of those who had been a disciple for decades. "What most mattered to our master?" he asked. The disciple smiled as he answered, "Whomever he was with at that moment." Like the Dalai Lama, this rabbi did not reserve his time and energy for just those with money and power, for just his family or closest disciples. He brought his wholehearted attention to each person he was with and offered the gift of a fully compassionate and wakeful heart.

Even if we don't push others away with anger or hatred, we can easily overlook people and unknowingly withhold our kindness. This can be most striking in relation to those whom Buddhist compassion practices describe as "neutral" people—those who evoke neither a negative nor positive response. They might be the postman, children in the carpool, the spouse of a friend, a distant relative. In teaching compassion practices I sometimes ask students to choose someone they see regularly but are not personally involved with. When they have brought this person to mind, I invite them to consider, "What does he or she need?" "What does this person fear?" "What is life like for this person?"

Vicki came up to me after one of these meditations to report that a wonderful thing had happened since she'd begun doing this practice. When seeing colleagues at work, neighbors walking their dogs, clerks at stores, she had been saying in her mind, "You are real. You are real." Rather than being backdrops for her life, she was finding them come alive to her. She'd notice a gleam of curiosity in the eyes, a generous smile, an anxious grinding of teeth, a disappointed and resigned slope to the shoulders, the sorrow in a downcast look. If she stayed a moment longer, she could also feel their shyness, their awkwardness, or their fear. Vicki told me, "The more real they are to me, the more real and warm and alive I feel. I feel a closeness in just being humans together. It doesn't matter who they are . . . I feel like I can accept them as part of my world."

When we stop to attend and see others as real, we uncover the hidden bond that exists between all beings. In her poem "Kindness," Naomi Shihab Nye writes:

Before you learn the tender gravity of kindness
you must travel where the Indian in a white poncho
lies dead by the side of the road.
You must see how this could be you,
how he too was someone
who journeyed through the night with plans
and the simple breath that kept him alive.

We are all journeying through the night with plans, breathing in and out this mysterious life. The "tender gravity of kindness" naturally awakens as we pay attention to others.

WHAT DO WE DO WHEN OUR HEART SHUTS DOWN?

Some years ago I found myself feeling irritated with and imposed upon by a client in a psychotherapy group I was leading. Tom would stay after each meeting, asking me questions that seemed unnecessary or commenting at length on that evening's session. During the group sessions it was clear that he was also provoking resentment from others. One night, when a young man revealed that his wife's nonstop judging was making him feel tense and self-conscious when they were together, Tom told him with an air of authority that he should pretend to be confident because otherwise his wife would never respect him. The young man's face flushed and he said nothing for the remainder of the evening. During several other sessions I had to interrupt Tom's long stories about how he had faced and solved problems similar to those brought up by others. He clearly wanted to feel important and be a center of attention, and no matter what I tried, he continued to grab the limelight.

When, at the end of our fifth session, I saw Tom once again waiting for everyone else to leave, my heart sank. I felt myself angrily wishing him away. Breathing deeply, I walked over and took a seat beside him. He told me that he needed to talk about the problems he was having fitting in with this group. While this was a reasonable request, I felt hard and tight. I knew he wanted my interest and attention, but I didn't want to give it. As Tom began telling me what was wrong with the particular combination of people—overly sensitive women; passive, emotionally repressed men—my irritation spiked. I felt intolerant, impatient and filled with disdain. I thought to myself, "Fine then. Why don't you just leave? That will solve everybody's problem."

As I was finding, it is not always easy to feel compassionate in response to another's needs. Rather, we might feel resentful, imposed upon, disgusted, powerless, guilty, afraid. When our hearts harden in defense, it does not mean we are failing as bodhisattvas. It just lets us know that we need to befriend what is happening inside us before compassion for others can naturally arise.

As Tom and I continued talking, part of my attention went inward. I could see that behind my intolerance was a feeling of being violated. He was taking my time, preventing others from feeling safe in the group and speaking disparagingly about group members. As I felt the heat and swelling pressure of anger in my chest, I started turning on myself. "I'm supposed to be helping him, not reacting to him . . . he's the one who's really suffering." But as I noticed how agitated I was feeling, I realized I was suffering too. Gently I told myself, "It's okay, it's okay." Simply acknowledging this pain helped me to relax and remember to send a message to my own heart: "I care about this suffering."

Relating kindly to my anger enabled me to open and pay attention to what Tom was feeling. Now as I beheld this person before me, I mentally asked, "What do you really need?" It was as if I could hear his heart speaking. I sensed that he desperately wanted me to keep him company, to see him and care about him. He was afraid I would misunderstand him and not value him as a helpful person with a lot to offer.

My feelings of irritation and superiority began to soften. I had been using the roles of "client" and "therapist" to distance from Tom, and now we were here together, both of us vulnerable and suffering human beings. The more I saw Tom as a real, hurting, sensitive person, the more tender I could feel toward him and the pain he was living with.

I reached out and touched Tom's arm. We both talked—and listened. We ended up laughing together when he joked that our session was interfering with his weekly viewing of *Frasier* and in close competition for his loyalty. I no longer had one foot out the door—I was engaged and caring. When I did give Tom some feedback about his role in the group, he listened without becoming defensive. I shared with him how much I loved Father Theophane's question, "What do they really need?" and he was eager to let this guide him. When we wound up the conversation, he was no longer hanging on, trying to prove himself or get something more from me. He left the room with a light step, as if he felt nourished. I too felt a sense of lightness. I had stepped out of my angry superiority and returned home to feeling connected and tender.

As it turned out, Tom took to heart the practice of asking, "What do they really need?" In one group session, he even told the young man he had offended how sorry he was. "You remind me in some ways of my son. I wanted you to look at me as a knowing father, but I did the same thing wrong with you that I did raising my son. I forgot to find out what you really needed." Tom swallowed, hard. "I just wanted to help and didn't know how." The young man was visibly touched. After some moments he responded, his words slow but sure. "What I have been really needing, from my wife and everyone, is to feel like I matter. You just made me feel that way."

It turned out that the person I had tagged as "most unwanted other" ended up playing a key role in opening up everyone in the group. While Tom's initial insensitivity had made him the lightning rod for blame, once he opened up, others could acknowledge that the hurt, fear or anger they'd expressed had little or nothing to do with Tom. The deep intimacy that subsequently flowered in our group was based on the willingness of each participant to be present with his or her own pain and, because of that, open to the pain of others. Softening our hearts together opened up our circle of compassion—we were real and mattered to each other.

SEEING THROUGH EACH OTHER'S EYES

Sometimes the very people we are closest to become unreal to us. We might easily assume we know what life is like for them and forget that, like us, they are always changing, their experience is always new. We lose sight of how fully they too are living with hurts and fears, how hard life can be on the inside.

Jeff and Margo came to therapy because their marriage was sliding downhill. Jeff had been a vigorous person until eight years ago when he contracted Lyme disease on one of their camping trips. Month by month the aches and fatigue were increasing. His fingers had swollen and stiffened, so he could no longer do his job as a fine carpenter. Although he tried to remain hopeful, his depression was deepening. Margo did what she could—working overtime, making meals, cleaning the house—but she felt as if Jeff didn't really appreciate her efforts. "I'm never enough," she said.

The way Jeff saw it was that Margo begrudged the whole situation. He could tell by the grim set of her jaw and her terse words. And she made him feel guilty, as if it were his fault that he was sick and couldn't do his part.

In our sessions we did a simple psychodrama process known as "role reversal." First, as Margo listened carefully, Jeff described how much shame and frustration he felt about being sick. He felt impotent, as if he were a wimp who couldn't be counted on for anything. He talked about how scared he was about his future, and also how lonely he felt because Margo didn't seem to register the enormity of what had happened to him. He had lost his health, his life as he had known it.

When he was done, they switched chairs. Assuming his posture, and, as well as she could, even his facial expressions and tone of voice, Margo became Jeff. Speaking from his world, she talked about how it was to live with Lyme disease. When they returned to their original places, Jeff let her know that hearing her relate his experience so clearly helped him feel more understood by her.

When it was Margo's turn to describe her experience, she began by talking about feeling unappreciated. But then, after a few moments of silence, she blurted out, "I've just felt so helpless. You've been plagued by sickness. You, the person I love. And I can't make you feel better. And I don't know where it's going to end up." Margo was angry at life, not at Jeff. And under the anger, she felt deep grief about how hard their life had become. When they switched places, Jeff spoke as Margo, describing what it was like to feel powerless, to feel their life was being ruined and there was nothing she could do about it.

When the process was complete, Margo and Jeff held each other, both in tears. He hadn't realized that she was suffering with such feelings of frustration and grief. And she had no idea how lonely he felt without her understanding. Their mutual accusations of "You make me feel . . ." had turned into "What can I do to help?"

Thoreau writes, "Is there a greater miracle than to see through another's eyes, even for an instant?" As Margo and Jeff were finding, seeing through another's eyes is at the very heart of compassion. We don't have to do the formal process of role reversal in order to understand how life is for our spouse or child, sister or friend. We can imagine how it would feel to be in this person's body and mind, living in his or her circumstances. As we allow ourselves to fully open to their conscious and vulnerable being, we feel naturally close and tender. Hafiz writes,

It happens all the time in heaven,
And some day
It will begin to happen
Again on earth—

That men and women . . .
Who give each other
Light,
Often will get down on their knees

And . . . With tears in their eyes,
Will sincerely speak, saying,

"My dear,
How can I be more loving to you;
How can I be more
Kind?"

If we ask ourselves when meeting anyone—friend or stranger—"How can I be more kind?" inevitably we will recognize that every being needs to be listened to, loved and understood. While we might become aware of this first with those in our immediate circle, it is possible to pay attention and care for all living beings. *The more fully we offer our attention, the more deeply we realize that what matters most in life is being kind.* As we open to the vulnerability of others, the veil of separation falls away, and our natural response is to reach out a helping hand.

THE CIRCLE OF ALL BEINGS

In a touching Sikh story, an aged spiritual master calls his two most devoted disciples to the garden in front of his hut. Gravely, he gives each one a chicken and instructs them, "Go to where no one can see, and kill the chicken." One of the men immediately goes behind his shed, picks up an ax and chops off his chicken's head. The other wanders around for hours, and finally returns to his master, the chicken still alive and in hand. "Well, what happened?" the teacher asks. The disciple responds, "I can't find a place to kill the chicken where no one can see me. Everywhere I go, the chicken sees."

To this man, the chicken was real. It was conscious and felt pain. As we bring a kind attention to our own conscious and vulnerable being, we become more alert to how all beings are sentient, how they hurt and want to stay alive. While we may not be inclined to think we have much in common with a chicken, when we deepen our attention—much as my son had done with the ants—we tap into the fundamental vibrancy and fragility that marks all living beings. Poet Gary Lawless writes:

When the animals come to us,
Asking for our help,
Will we know what they are saying?
When the plants speak to us
In their delicate, beautiful language,

Will we be able to answer them?
When the planet herself
Sings to us in our dreams,
Will we be able to wake ourselves, and act?

When we know that the animals and plants are part of who we are, we can listen and respond. Ignoring the trees is like ignoring our lungs when they are congested and we can't breathe. Extinction of the songbirds means the end of our living music. When the planet herself calls to us in our dreams, if we are in touch with the truth of our mutual belonging, our hearts naturally stir with care. We remember that the web of life is our home.

The bodhisattva's aspiration, "May my life be of benefit to all beings," is a powerful tool for remembering our belonging and widening the circles of our compassion. In resolving to help all suffering beings, the bodhisattva is not assuming a grandiose role or holding to some unreachable ideal. If we see ourselves as small and separate individuals trying to take on the world as our responsibility, we set ourselves up for delusion and failure. Rather, our aspiration to be of benefit arises from the radical realization that we all belong to the web of life, and that everything that happens within it affects everything else. Every thought we have, every action we take has an impact for good or for ill. An aboriginal woman from Australia speaks from this sense of relatedness in a powerful way: "If you have come to help me, then you are wasting your time. But if you have come because your destiny is bound up with mine, then let us work together."

When we feel our togetherness, there are countless ways to express our care. Some people focus their lives on creating a loving home for their families; others on changing laws that will help poor children get better nutrition and education. Some people pray for hours in solitude and others are always on the phone. While it is easy to get caught up in believing we should be doing something more or different, what really matters is that we care. As Mother Teresa teaches, "We can do no great things—only small things with great love."

Just as a bright sun causes ice cubes to melt, in the moments when we feel connected and kind, we create a warm environment that encourages others around us to relax and open up. Each time we widen the circle of caring—with a smile, a hug, a listening presence, a prayer—the ripples flow out endlessly. When we offer comfort to the person sitting by our side, our kindness spreads through the world. Whether offered inwardly or to others, the bodhisattva's compassion is a gentle rain that touches, without bias, all of life.

Guided Meditation: Tonglen—Awakening the Heart of Compassion

The Tibetan practice of tonglen cultivates the all-embracing heart of compassion. *Tonglen* means "taking in and sending out." Linked to the flow of the breath, this practice trains you to open directly to suffering—your own and that of all beings—and offer relief and care. The following meditation is a version of tonglen that can help you awaken compassion in the face of suffering.

There are times when tonglen may be inappropriate. If you are struggling with the terror of having been abused, with unrelenting depression or severe emotional imbalance, tonglen may cause emotional flooding, or a deepened feeling of being stuck. In these situations, rather than practicing tonglen, seek guidance from a therapist, a teacher familiar with this practice, or a trusted spiritual guide.

Sit in a way that allows you to be relaxed and alert. Feeling the natural rhythm of your breath, let your body and mind settle.

The traditional practice of tonglen begins with a flash of remembrance, recognizing the awakened heart and mind. With your eyes open, take a brief moment to sense the immensity of space and the natural openness and emptiness of awareness.

Now bring to mind an experience of suffering. It might be your own pain or the suffering of someone close to you—a friend or family member, a pet or other living being. Let yourself feel this suffering in an immediate, vivid, close-in way. Let it be real to you—the loss, hurt or fear. As you breathe in, allow this pain to come fully into your body and heart. If it is another being's pain, feel it as if it is your own. Open to the intensity of sensations, whatever they are.

Now as you breathe out, let the pain you are experiencing be released. Let go into the openness of awareness, letting the pain be ventilated in the freshness of open space. With the exhale, offer whatever prayer or expression of care comes naturally for you. For instance, "May you be free of suffering; I care about your suffering; I wish you could be happy and peaceful."

You might find that at first you don't actually feel connected to the suffering of hurt, fear or grief. If this is the case, for a few minutes you might let your primary focus be with the in-breath and the "taking in" of pain. Pay special attention to the sensations that arise in your body. Then, as you begin to experience the suffering more fully, resume a balanced practice of taking in suffering and sending out relief.

Without any judgment, be aware of how you are relating to suffering. At times you may feel a courageous willingness to open to the intensity and rawness of pain. At other times you may feel fearful and your heart may be defended or numb. If you feel resistance, you can do tonglen with the sensations of resistance. (You can do tonglen with whatever experience arises.) Breathe in the feelings of fear or numbness, touching them fully. Breathe out forgiveness, offering the resistance into the spaciousness of awareness. Whether you are feeling willing or resistant, continue practicing with the breath, taking in the raw sensations of suffering and sending out relief, letting go into openness.

Now bring to mind all the other beings in the world who experience the same kind of suffering that you have been reflecting on. Sense how, while stories may differ, our actual experience of physical pain and emotional distress is the same. If you are meditating on the pain of feeling inadequate and rejected, in this moment millions of other people are feeling the same pain. Sensing the realness of this suffering, begin to breathe in on behalf of all those who suffer in this way. Breathe in the insecurity, grief or hurt that all these beings are feeling, and experience the intensity and fullness of their pain in your heart. As you breathe out, release this enormity of suffering into boundless space. Let it be held in boundless awareness. As before, with the out-breath offer whatever prayer might alleviate the suffering.

Continue breathing in and out, opening to the universal experience of this suffering and letting go into spaciousness with prayer. As your heart opens to the enormity of suffering, you become that openness. By offering your tenderness, your awareness becomes suffused with compassion. Continuing to breathe in suffering and breathe out care, sense your heart as a transformer of sorrows.

Whenever you become aware of suffering, you can practice tonglen. You might see on the TV news a family who has just lost their home in a flood or fire. You might be traveling on the freeway and see a car accident. You might be at an AA meeting, listening as someone describes his or her struggle with alcoholism. Right on the spot you can breathe in, letting yourself feel the immediacy and sharpness of that hurt and fear. Exhaling, release the pain into the openness of awareness, with a prayer for relief. After spending some minutes in this way, enlarge the field of compassion, breathing for all beings who are suffering from loss or trauma or addiction.

TEN

RECOGNIZING OUR BASIC GOODNESS: THE GATEWAY TO A FORGIVING AND LOVING HEART

Like a caring mother
Holding and guarding the life
Of her only child,
So with a boundless heart
Hold yourself and all beings.
Buddha

I am larger and better than I thought.
I did not think I held so much goodness.
Walt Whitman

Amy arrived at her therapy session flushed and agitated. During the two months I'd been seeing her, she had been quiet, almost repressed. The main issue we'd worked on together was lack of self-worth. In this session, Amy launched into telling me how she discovered that her husband had been having an affair. Over the past half year he'd been spending an increasing number of weekends away on "work-related projects." Suspicious, Amy had decided one day the previous week to look through the e-mail he received on his company account. Numerous messages from one woman, a colleague at work, had a tone of intimacy that left her shaking with rage. When Amy confronted Don that evening, he went pale and then, looking defeated and sad, nodded and said, "You're right. It's true." He wanted to keep talking, to explain, but she couldn't listen. She told him it was all over and that she'd never be able to forgive him.

After admitting his infidelity that first evening, Don had ended the affair. He pleaded with Amy to forgive him, to give their marriage a chance. Too angry to give him any assurances, Amy at first maintained a stony silence. Later she told him that if it weren't for their daughter, Celia, she would already have ended the marriage.

Ever since that night, she said, her mind had been flooded with thoughts about how he had misled her, telling her he needed to attend a conference, or stay late at work, or go to a team planning meeting. Her anger at being betrayed burned in her chest like an immense red fire. He was a sleazy liar. A heartless fiend. Everything he said was part of a web of deception. The whole marriage was a sham.

When we have been betrayed, one of our first reactions is to lash out in blame. We create a story of good and bad and aim our anger at the one who has caused us pain. With deep resentment, we build a case against them, often with enough evidence to prove we should eliminate them from our life altogether. The word *resentment* means "to feel again." Each time we repeat to ourselves a story of how we've been wronged, we feel again in our body and mind the anger at being violated. But often enough our resentment of others reflects our resentment of ourselves. When someone rejects us, he or she might be reinforcing a view we already hold—that we're not good enough, not kind enough, not lovable enough.

While at first Amy focused her resentment and anger on Don, she soon turned them against herself. Don's affair had confirmed her worst fear: She deserved to be thrown aside. Every way in which she felt inadequate was reinforced by his rejection. She might appear warm and caring to the world but inside she felt fake, wooden, grotesque. Don was the one who knew her best and he had rejected her. Now, lost in the trance of unworthiness, Amy was convinced she was unlovable.

Especially when things seem to be falling apart—we lose a job, suffer a serious injury, become estranged from a loved one—our lives can become painfully bound by the experience that something is wrong with us. We buy into the belief that we are fundamentally flawed, bad and undeserving of love. Like Amy, we forget our goodness and feel cut off from our heart. The Buddha taught, however, that no matter how lost in delusion we might be, our essence, our Buddha nature, is pure and undefiled. Tibetan meditation master Chögyam Trungpa writes, ". . . every human being has a basic nature of goodness." Basic goodness is the radiance of our Buddha nature—it is our intrinsic wakefulness and love.

This doesn't mean we can do no wrong. But in sharp contrast to our cultural conditioning as heirs of Adam and Eve, the Buddhist perspective holds that there is no such thing as a sinful or evil person. When we harm ourselves or others, it is not because we are *bad* but because we are *ignorant.* To be ignorant is to ignore the truth that we are connected to all of life, and that grasping and hatred create more separation and suffering. To be ignorant is to ignore the purity of awareness and capacity for love that expresses our basic goodness.

To recognize this basic goodness in everyone takes courage. Trungpa calls this the task of the spiritual warrior, and says that the essence of human bravery is "refusing to give up on anyone or anything." This can be especially hard when we're trying to see the goodness in a murderer, the CEO of a corporation that pollutes the planet, a child molester. Basic goodness can be buried under an ugly tangle of fear, greed and hostility, and seeing it doesn't mean overlooking harmful behavior in ourselves or others. To radically accept life depends upon clearly seeing the full truth of it. Novelist and mystic Romaine Rolland says, "There is only one heroism in the world: to see the world as it is, and to love it." Seeing the world as it is means seeing not only the vulnerability and suffering of each person, but also the basic goodness of each person. When we embrace ourselves and others with Radical Acceptance, we are seeing past the roles, stories and behaviors that obscure our true nature.

Seeing the goodness in others begins with seeing the goodness in ourselves. Even when we feel ashamed or depressed, resentful or insecure, we don't give up on ourselves. In traditional Buddhist teachings there are formal meditations designed to free us from trance and reconnect us with the goodness and loving awareness that is our true nature. These often begin with forgiveness, for it releases the armor of resentment and blame that surrounds our heart and prevents us from feeling the goodness in ourselves and others. The practices of lovingkindness awaken the love that is the flower of our goodness.

The Radical Acceptance at the center of these practices depends upon a leap of faith. Our trance thoughts may tell us that something is wrong, but we dare to let go of them and trust in the possibility of goodness. Our body may be filled with painful emotions, but instead of running away, we entrust ourselves to the healing power of compassionate presence. We may have protected ourselves by closing our heart, but instead, for the sake of love, we refuse to push anyone, including ourselves, out of our heart. When we are willing to leap, our faith is not disappointed, for when we peel off the layers of delusion, we find the goodness and love that are always there.

FORGIVING OURSELVES: RELEASING THE BLAME THAT BINDS OUR HEART

At our next session, Amy poured out a litany of her personal failings. She was an inadequate mother. She was a bad wife. Everywhere—at home, at work—she was a fumbling, failing person. She was acutely aware of how distant she and her fourteen-year-old daughter, Celia, had become from each other. They seldom really talked, and Amy knew little about what Celia thought or felt. It shouldn't have been such a surprise that Don would turn to another woman. Who would want to be faithful to someone as bitchy and selfish as she was? She was always criticizing how messy he was, the way he planned their vacations, the way he drove the car. A particular episode stood out in her mind. One night during the past year they had been lying in bed together, and Don had started telling her about an argument he had with his boss. Amy had interrupted angrily: "Okay, just say it. Did you go and ruin your chances for a promotion? Did you screw up?" Don got out of bed and stood for a moment in the dark. "No, Amy," he said simply and left the room. He didn't come back to bed that night or the next. After telling me this, Amy sat back and looked down at the floor. In a weary voice she said, "I don't know who I am more mad at . . . Don or myself."

Whether our anger and resentment is directed at another or at ourselves, the result is the same—it removes us from the deeper pain of our hurt and shame. As long as we avoid these feelings, we remain trapped in our armor, locked away from love for ourselves and others.

As we have seen over and over, the way out begins with Radical Acceptance of our pain. When we release our stories of blame and let ourselves directly experience the feelings of shame and fear in our body, we begin regarding ourselves with compassion. Rather than living in reaction to past events, rather than identifying ourselves as an angry person, a betrayed person, a bad person, we free ourselves to meet the present moment with wisdom and kindness. This is the essence of forgiveness. Whether we are angry with ourselves or others, *we forgive by letting go of blame and opening to the pain we have tried to push away.*

But when we have deeply turned against ourselves, forgiveness can seem impossible. Like Marian in her guilt over Christy's sexual abuse, when we feel we've caused great suffering, we can't imagine feeling compassion for ourselves. I asked Amy, "Do you think you could forgive yourself for being that critical person, for making those mistakes?" She responded without hesitation, "No! Forgiving myself would just let me off the hook . . . how would that make me a better mother or a better wife?" I gently continued, "Is there anything else that stops you from forgiving yourself, Amy?"

With some bitterness she replied, "Why should I forgive myself? It wouldn't help those I've already hurt. I've already ruined my family. It's too late." But I knew that a part of Amy desperately wanted to remove the noose of self-hatred around her neck. I asked, "What would happen if, just for a short time, you put aside your story of being a bad person?" She said she didn't know, but she was willing to try it.

As I guided her to placing her attention on the feelings in her body, Amy said she felt as if she were dropping into a deep hole of shame, a swamp of badness. Within moments, a memory from years ago sprang into her mind. Amy saw herself in her office at home, irritated by Celia's persistent whining. She literally dragged her daughter by one arm into their den and, turning on the TV, forbade her to leave the room. She left her locked in for two hours, ignoring her periodic cries to be let out. After telling me this she asked, "Tara, how am I supposed to forgive myself for treating my child like that? I feel so ashamed of myself."

I suggested to Amy that, instead of trying to forgive *herself,* she might just send a message of forgiveness to the shame. "Can you forgive the shame for existing?" I asked. Amy nodded, then whispered, "I forgive this shame . . . I forgive this shame." She was silent for what seemed a long time, so I asked what was happening. "Well," she began slowly, "it doesn't feel like shame anymore. Now it's more like fear." I let her know that she could be with the fear in the same way, letting it be there, feeling it, offering it forgiveness. After a few minutes Amy said, "I know what I'm afraid of—that I'll never be close to anyone. I push everyone away. I don't want anyone to see what I'm really like." Crying, Amy covered her face. I gently reminded her to forgive this too, the fear and now this grief. If she wanted, I told her, she could simply say, "Forgiven, forgiven." Hugging her knees into her chest and rocking back and forth, Amy forgave and opened to the grief that had lain buried under her resentments. "There were so many times when I could have been loving but wasn't . . . with Celia, with Don, with my friends."

No matter what appears—burning rage, gnawing anxiety, cruel thoughts or utter despondency—by offering forgiveness directly to each, we give permission to our inner life to be as it is. Rather than forgiving a "self," we forgive the experiences we are identified with. While resistance keeps us stuck by hardening our heart and contracting our body and mind, saying, "I forgive this," or, "forgiven," creates a warmth and softness that allow emotions to unfold and change.

When her grief finally subsided, Amy's body became very still, her face relaxed. She let her head rest against the back of the chair, and her breathing grew long and slow. When she looked at me, her eyes were red and swollen, yet peaceful. Still curled up in her chair, Amy told me about coming home from second grade and finding a stray dog sniffing around their garbage. It was "love at first sight," she said, and when it seemed her parents were going to take the dog to a shelter, Amy cried and cried. As it turned out, the family adopted Rudy, and he became the first of a string of stray creatures—including several more dogs, kittens and an injured bird—that Amy took into her care. Amy's face softened as she said, "Everyone used to say I was so kind to animals . . . I just loved them. They were my friends." She joked about how Don's mild but real allergies were the only line of defense against her now creating a full-blown menagerie.

Then in a quieter voice she said, "You know, I do care about people . . . about animals . . . I've always been like that." As she spoke these words I could tell that she was beginning to open the door to her own healing: "Amy, you *are* a good person. I hope you can let yourself trust this." I asked her if she had any photographs of herself with her pets. If so, she might spend some time with them. She might also take a look at some of her baby pictures, just to see what she noticed.

As we ended the session I reminded Amy that forgiving ourselves and learning to trust our goodness can take a long time. I told her that some days I need to forgive myself over and over—twenty times, thirty times. I usually don't use a formal meditation to do so; I simply recognize that I'm judging or disliking myself and bring compassion to the pain I'm feeling. I consciously hold the intention to let go of blame and try to be more kind to myself.

Each night before going to sleep, I suggested, she might do a "forgiveness scan," scanning to see if she was holding anything against herself from the day. She might have made a mistake at work or said something condescending to her husband. If she realized that she was down on herself, she could feel the pain of her self-blame, the fear or anger or shame, and send the message "forgiven, forgiven." She might also gently remind herself that she was doing the best she could.

Forgiving ourselves is a process that continues through our whole life. We are so used to replaying the story of what is wrong with ourselves and others that living with a resentful, tight heart can become our most familiar way of being. Thousands of times we might find ourselves caught in stories of what we are doing wrong. Thousands of times we might drop under our blame to where the deeper pain lives. With each round of freeing ourselves through forgiveness, we strengthen our recognition of our basic goodness. As Amy found, we begin to trust again that we care about life.

With time, forgiving ourselves utterly transfigures our life. We all know stories of prisoners on death row who, through honestly facing the suffering they caused, were able to forgive themselves. By opening to the enormity of pain, their hearts became tender and awake. Other inmates, guards, prison chaplains and relatives could recognize the glow of their inner freedom. These prisoners were not letting themselves off the hook. While taking full responsibility for their actions, they were also able to recognize the truth of their basic goodness.

We might worry, as Amy did, that forgiving ourselves is in some way condoning harmful behavior, or giving ourselves permission to continue in hurtful ways. When we forgive ourselves, we are not saying, "I couldn't help doing what I did . . . so I might as well forget about it." Nor are we pushing away responsibility when we release our blaming thoughts. Feeling guilty and bad about ourselves for something we've done might temporarily restrain us from doing harm, but ultimately blaming and hating ourselves only leads to further harmful actions. We can't punish ourselves into being a good person. Only by holding ourselves with the compassion of forgiveness do we experience our goodness and respond to our circumstances with wisdom and care.

LEARNING TO SEE OUR OWN GOODNESS

Amy barely spoke to Don for the next few weeks. He was sleeping on the living room couch, and she wasn't really sure what to do next. She told me she didn't want to end the marriage, but she just couldn't pretend everything was normal and let him get away with what he'd done. Despite Amy's pain and uncertainty, I could see in our sessions that something was shifting and opening inside her.

Amy came to our next session with a small packet of photos. She laid them out on the coffee table, and we sat side by side on the couch to look at them. One was of Amy as an infant cradled to her mother's breast, and we both smiled at the sweet, wide-eyed little person in the picture. In another she was about two, sitting on her father's shoulders, hugging his head and laughing. Amy grinned. "You know, it makes me happy to see her happy!" In the others, taken when she was eight or nine, Amy was with her adopted friends—cuddling Rudy, lying in bed with their kitten Sam sleeping on her chest, carefully holding a small bird in her hands. As we looked at her with her animals, Amy told me she could remember how it felt to be a good person. "When you told me that last week, Tara, it was hard to take it in. But looking at these, I think I can feel it right now. That goodness and innocence—they're still inside me."

To even consider remembering her goodness depended on Amy's letting go of her belief that she was bad and unlovable. In our previous session she had started the process of forgiveness, opening to her pain and holding it with compassion. She said the forgiveness scan had also helped. One night as she remembered how distracted and inefficient she'd been with her real estate clients she simply let herself feel the anxiety and shame in her body and forgave it for being there. Amy smiled and said, "I realized I could be uptight and still be a good person."

As Amy began collecting her photos, I got up and took a book off my office shelf and turned to one of my favorite poems. I read aloud to Amy a few lines written by the poet Kabir:

We sense that there is some sort of spirit that loves
birds and animals and the ants—
perhaps the same one who gave a radiance to you in
your mother's womb . . .

"This makes me think of you, of *your* loving spirit, Amy . . . I think those animals you cared for helped you remember who you were." Smiling in agreement, she patted the stack of photos. "These belong on my altar. If there was ever a time I needed regular reminding, this is it."

Reflecting on our own goodness is considered a skillful means in Buddhist practice, because it opens our hearts and invigorates our faith in our spiritual unfolding. If we're caught up in considering ourselves bad, we contract and hide. In contrast, if we trust our goodness, we open up to others, we feel inspired to help others, we move forward on our spiritual path with dedication and joy.

There are several practices that are traditionally offered as ways to remember our goodness. We might begin by simply reflecting on certain qualities or behaviors that we appreciate in ourselves. For instance, when I recall instances of being kind to someone, I can taste the sweetness of being caring and generous. I might remember a time when I put aside my own agenda to stop and listen deeply to someone, or spontaneously gave a friend a book she might like.

When I feel moved by the music of Mozart or awed by a starry night sky, I feel part of the goodness and beauty of life. When life strikes me as funny, I feel real and human and basically good.

Sometimes though, the idea of appreciating myself can feel awkward or self-serving. When this is the case, it feels more honest to acknowledge my basic desire to be happy, to recognize that I, like all human beings, long to be loved, yearn to feel my goodness. When I pay attention to the depth of these longings, I reconnect to a genuine feeling of warmth toward myself.

Sometimes the easiest way to appreciate ourselves is by looking through the eyes of someone who loves us. A friend told me that when he sees himself through the eyes of his spiritual teacher, he remembers how deeply devoted he is to seeking the truth. One of my clients realizes he is lovable when he remembers how his grandfather used to delight in his boyish curiosity and inventiveness. Sometimes seeing ourselves through the eyes of a close friend can help us to remember our good qualities. Our friend might love our humor and warmth, our passion about saving the environment, our honest willingness to say what's really going on in our lives. We don't have to limit our appreciators to the human world. I once saw a bumper sticker that said: "Lord, help me to see myself the way my dog sees me." We might ask ourselves what makes our dog happy to see us. Even if the answer is that he just wants to get fed or walked, our animal's appreciation of our constancy reflects an aspect of us that is worthy. The practice of looking through the eyes of one who loves us can be a powerful and surprisingly direct way to remember our beauty and goodness.

Through the simple practice of seeing our own goodness, we undo the deeply rooted habits of blame and self-hate that keep us feeling isolated and unworthy. The contemporary Indian master Bapuji lovingly reminds us to cherish our goodness:

My beloved child,
Break your heart no longer.
Each time you judge yourself you break your own heart.
You stop feeding on the love which is the wellspring of your vitality.
The time has come, your time

To live, to celebrate and to see the goodness that you are . . .

Let no one, no thing, no idea or ideal obstruct you
If one comes, even in the name of "Truth," forgive it for its unknowing
Do not fight.
Let go.
And breathe—into the goodness that you are.

Every time we betray ourselves by not seeing our goodness, we break our heart. When we judge ourselves for falling short, we break our heart. Although Amy had been breaking her heart for years, she was now beginning to see her goodness and move toward healing. Because how we see ourselves is so deeply influenced by our relationships, for Amy this trust in her goodness would be deepened when she felt forgiven by another.

THE BLESSING OF FEELING FORGIVEN

Driving home one late afternoon from the office, Amy found herself stuck in rush-hour traffic. She arrived home with little time to prepare dinner. Don was out of town, and her new boss and her husband were coming over for the evening. When she walked into the kitchen, she discovered the countertops stacked with dishes covered in tomato sauce, and several half-drunk cans of soda sitting around. Amy exploded. She stormed into Celia's room, turned off the blaring music and sent her daughter's friends home.

When the door shut behind them, she lit into Celia. "How could you be so thoughtless! You knew we were having company." Celia started to say, "All you had to do was ask me," but Amy interrupted her, yelling that she shouldn't have to go around pleading for help. "Your friends and your music are all that matter . . . You don't give a damn about anything else." Amy slammed Celia's door as she left the room.

In the silence that followed, Amy could hear the echo of her voice screaming. Her heart was pounding, and her breath was fast and shallow. Suddenly an image of her daughter as a toddler came into her mind, and she remembered how Celia used to pick bouquets of dandelions for her. Another image immediately arose of her and Celia weaving spring flowers into each other's hair, turning themselves into May queens. Amy turned and knocked softly on the door. Celia opened it and stood waiting. "I can't believe it, Celia. I can't believe I'm doing this to you." Amy sat down on the bed, and it all came pouring out. She was sorry for making their lives so miserable, sorry for what was happening between her and Celia's dad, sorry for the kind of mother she was, sorry for not being there enough for Celia, sorry, sorry, sorry.

Celia was silent for a while, then she said, "Mom, no one's perfect, but I've always known you loved me. Isn't that what counts?" Amy looked into her daughter's clear blue eyes and knew she was speaking the truth. Celia had never doubted that her mother cared about her. Even when Amy was anxious and frazzled and critical, Celia had felt her love and known it was unshakable. Certainly she'd felt angry at her mother and sometimes didn't want to be around her, but she knew Amy was there if she needed her. Amy felt a great wave of relief. Instead of feeling guilty and despicable, she felt forgiven.

In the following days, when Amy noticed herself being bitchy and critical, when she remembered Celia's sweet blue eyes, the painful grip of self-blame began to relax. Even though the habit of judging herself continued, the feelings of badness didn't build up until they took over. Because Celia had forgiven her, Amy was gentler and kinder toward herself.

To know we are forgiven can be deeply liberating, especially when the acceptance embraces our failings with compassion. I heard a moving story about a woman in the hospital dying of AIDS. She had lived the last decade of her life addicted to heroin, not caring where she got her next fix, just so long as she got it. The only person she had ever loved was her daughter, and yet even this love had not stopped her from destroying her own life.

One day a young Catholic priest was making his rounds at a community hospital and he came upon this woman, emaciated and with the yellow tinge of an afflicted liver. He sat down next to her bed and asked how she was doing. "I'm lost," she replied. "I've ruined my life and every life around me. There is no hope for me. I'm going to hell."

The priest sat in silence a few moments. Then he noticed a framed picture of a pretty girl on the dresser. "Who is that?" he asked. The woman brightened a little. "She's my daughter, the one beautiful thing in my life."

"And would you help her if she was in trouble or made a mistake? Would you forgive her? Would you still love her?"

"Of course I would!" cried the woman. "I would do anything for her! She will always be precious and beautiful to me. Why do you ask such a question?"

"Because I want you to know," said the priest, "that God has a picture of you on his dresser."

In his message of unconditional forgiveness and love, the priest was giving back to this woman her goodness and innocence. From a

Buddhist perspective, when we can regard our mistakes and transgressions with the eyes of compassion, we release the ignorance that keeps us bound in hating and blaming ourselves. We see that our imperfections don't taint our basic goodness. This is what it means to feel forgiven. Aware of our true nature, we know nothing is wrong.

Feeling forgiven is a sure way to open the heart. This power is recognized in traditional Buddhist practices. Before beginning the meditation practice of sending lovingkindness to all beings, we first silently ask forgiveness of anyone we may have harmed, intentionally or unintentionally. Even this basic gesture of asking forgiveness softens our heart. We can open further to the possibility of being forgiven by reflecting on specific people we may have harmed and silently asking their forgiveness.

As Amy found, feeling forgiven by others can allow us to more deeply forgive ourselves. Another step in the traditional forgiveness practice is offering forgiveness to ourselves. When we have released the painful armor of self-blame by feeling forgiven by ourselves and others, we can then in our meditation sincerely offer forgiveness to others.

FORGIVING OTHERS: NOT PUSHING ANYONE OUT OF OUR HEART

Like every part of living, forgiving has its own natural process of unfolding. Often we are not ready to forgive ourselves, not able to forgive someone who has injured us. We can't will ourselves to forgive—forgiving is a product not of effort but of openness. This is why the intention to forgive is such a key element in the process. To be willing but not quite ready to forgive holds the door open a crack.

Having the courage not to push anyone out of our heart is difficult enough when we've been harmed by someone we know. But as spiritual warriors our intention not to give up on anyone may be most severely tested when we are deeply violated by someone with whom we have no loving ties. How do we forgive a stranger who rapes our daughter, a political terrorist who kills our friend with a bomb?

A student at one of my meditation retreats told me of her struggle to forgive the man who left her son unable to walk for life. One evening she had picked up Brian from a bar mitzvah class, and on the way home a drunk driver crossed over the median and struck their car. She suffered minor injuries, but Brian was pinned to the ground when their car turned over, his legs crushed. Forgiveness was a long and painful process. Thousands of times she felt the burn of anger and the anguish of loss storm through her. She also felt the hardening of her heart when hatred wanted to take over. Knowing that the only way to find her way back to love and freedom would be through forgiveness, she took on the intention to forgive the man. Gradually over the years, as she allowed the feelings to course through her, forgiving them as they arose, her heart widened to include him. Without knowing any particulars, she knew he too suffered. She knew he had not intended to cause them pain. Eventually, by remembering the goodness of all beings, she opened to hold him with a forgiving heart.

We maintain the intention to forgive because we understand that not forgiving hardens and imprisons our heart. If we feel hatred toward anyone, we remain chained to the sufferings of the past and cannot find genuine peace. We forgive for the freedom of our own heart.

For the first six months after discovering Don's affair, Amy's hurt and rage had been so intense she couldn't imagine ever forgiving him. But as her heart opened in forgiving herself, it began to dawn on her that in time she might feel different about Don. She told me one day that she actually intended to forgive him—when she was ready.

It happened almost imperceptibly. Amy would notice how kind he was to Celia, how carefully he listened to her, and her heart would soften a little. When a friend of theirs got sick, she saw how helpful Don was, driving him to the doctor's office, getting take-out food for him each evening. And he certainly was trying hard enough to be nice to her, clearly making efforts to compliment her when she got dressed for work, making sure he told her exactly where he was going and how she could reach him when he was out of town. At dinner one night, she found herself laughing at a story Don was telling about the performance of his company's amateur volleyball team. As he went on, she remembered how much she appreciated the way he could put a comic spin on just about anything. There were still many moments when the full feeling of betrayal would sweep through her, but something was changing.

Amy wasn't sure just when it happened, but she told me that one day she found herself looking at the photographs of their wedding hanging on the hallway wall, and she realized Don wasn't really a bad person. He had made a big mistake, and maybe it had brought home something really painful to her about herself. But he wasn't evil or malicious. "There never was a moment in time when I thought, 'Okay, I forgive him,'" she told me. "Just somewhere along the line, I no longer needed to push him away so hard."

It may not have been entirely clear to Amy, but I could see that over the course of our work together, the better she felt about herself, the more open she felt toward Don. Seeing her own goodness opened her up to seeing his. As sometimes happens when one partner in a couple has an affair, over time Amy and Don did find their way back to each other, and to a deeper and more honest relationship. Both had changed, but I attributed their success in large part to Amy's willingness to accept and forgive the feelings hidden beneath her sense of unworthiness.

Our intention and willingness to forgive, to let go of resentment and blame, does not mean that we excuse harmful behaviors or allow further injury. For Amy, forgiving didn't mean she approved of Don's way of expressing dissatisfaction with the marriage, or in any way condoned his deceit. She insisted that they do couple's counseling, and she continued in therapy herself. Forgiving didn't mean she became a doormat or denied feeling angry at times. Nor did it mean she would sit back if her husband ever again betrayed their marriage. She could see Don's goodness and still set boundaries.

When we forgive, we stop rigidly identifying others by their undesirable behavior. Without denying anything, we open our heart and mind wide enough to see the deeper truth of who they are. We see their goodness. When we do, our hearts naturally open in love.

SEEING THE GOODNESS IN OTHERS

When Narayan was younger, I used to sit by his bed while he was sleeping and reflect on who he was. While I watched his sweet face and gently breathing form, I'd do a practice of intentionally trying to see past his physical appearance to who he really was. Whatever thoughts or images came to mind, I'd notice and put aside. My heart would warm to remember how he asked questions, or played with our dog, or said, "Love you, Mama." But I'd ask again, "Who are you, really?" The question guided me beyond all my ideas of him, and revealed his nature to me as awareness, as aliveness loving life. I'd also direct the question "Who am I?" to myself, and look behind the idea of being the mother, behind my identification with a physical body, behind any thoughts of what I was doing there, sitting by the side of his bed. Again, what was revealed was pure awareness and love. We were the same. There was no separation between us, no difference in who we both really are.

Like myself, most parents have watched their sleeping children and felt a pure and uncomplicated upwelling of tenderness. When they are sleeping, we don't have to say no to the tenth cookie, hurry them up for the carpool or fend them off when we are trying to get through a phone call. When they are sleeping, we can deepen our attention and see through to the sweetness and innocence of their soul. In our attempts to give up on no one, a useful practice can be to imagine others as infants or children. Another method that can lead us to the precious being outside personality and roles is to imagine that we are seeing someone for the last time, or even that they have already passed away. By letting go of our habitual ways of defining others, we can see the radiant awareness, the goodness of their true nature.

Most of us, however, fall into the habit of pinning a narrow and static identity on those around us. All too often this is based on behaviors we find unpleasant or annoying. We might fixate on how stubborn or rude our child is, or how a colleague brags about his accomplishments. If someone has offended us, we feel wary and guarded each time we see them. If our partner makes a cutting remark to us before leaving for work in the morning, we are ready for more of the same in the evening. We forget that every person, including ourselves, is new every moment.

In his play *The Cocktail Party,* T. S. Eliot writes:

> *What we know of other people*
> *Is only our memory of the moments*
> *During which we knew them. And they have*
> *Changed since then . . .*
>
> *We must*
> *Also remember*
> *That at every meeting we are meeting a*
> *Stranger.*

While we can of course recognize patterns of behavior in ourselves and others, our collection of assumptions doesn't define a person. When we stop and ask, "Who are you really?" we are led to a deeper understanding. As I found with Narayan, we see inherent goodness, we see Buddha nature, and invariably we respond with love.

AWAKENING THE HEART OF LOVINGKINDNESS

The quality of tenderness and love and goodwill that naturally awakens in us in response to seeing goodness is known in Buddhism as *metta,* or lovingkindness. While lovingkindness is intrinsic to who we are, it can also be cultivated through a refined set of practices that have been passed down in an unbroken line of teachings over the past twenty-five hundred years.

When we feel love for someone, we spontaneously wish for their happiness and well-being. This response has been formalized in what is known as the practice of lovingkindness. Traditionally, we begin this meditation by reflecting on the goodness in ourselves and offering simple phrases of care: "May I be happy. May I be peaceful. May I be filled with lovingkindness." These are the standard phrases used, but any prayer for well-being that resonates with our heart is an expression of lovingkindness. Like the widening circles of compassion, lovingkindness begins with ourselves and then opens out to include others: those we love, those we consider "neutral," those we may have a hard time feeling goodwill toward, and ultimately all beings everywhere.

When we send lovingkindness to those we love, we begin with someone in whom we most easily perceive goodness. If our heart becomes most tender when we reflect on our child or on our grandmother, then we begin with them. We might remember what makes that person so dear to us and offer them the phrases of care. As we say, "May you be happy" and feel into the meaning of that prayer, we can imagine them brightening and glowing with happiness. As we do so, our feelings of warmth grow even stronger and we more deeply appreciate who they are.

Widening our circle to include in lovingkindness those we experience as challenging requires the courage of the spiritual warrior. Even with those who bring up feelings of anger or dislike in us, we seek to find some small quality we can appreciate. When I'm feeling dislike for someone, I find it helpful to imagine that person being warmed and comforted in the embrace of someone who loves them. Or I might think of them as sincerely praying, or being filled with wonder as they walk through newly fallen snow. When we imagine someone in these ways, the idea is not to invent something or deny our perceptions or feelings. Rather, we are looking beyond our habitual judgments in order to see the beauty that is truly there. The Dalai Lama says, "Everyone wants to be happy. Nobody wants to suffer." Even if there is little that seems good about those we feel distant from, we can still remember that, like us, they want to be happy and free from suffering. While it can be very hard to send wishes of lovingkindness to those we have difficulty with, by doing so we enlarge the capacity of our hearts to love unconditionally.

Matt loved his mother dearly, but her insecurity and neediness sometimes "gave him the willies," as he put it. She had relied on him throughout his adult life to reassure her that she was doing okay, that she was making good decisions, that she was all right. Matt moved to the other side of the country, partly to get away from her. He'd visit her regularly and always showed up when needed, but he often found himself pushing her away when they were together, pulling out of an overwarm embrace, keeping his personal life to himself. At times just thinking about something she said or did made him feel cynical and resentful. His tendency to mistrust others and withhold his affection was most full-blown with his mother. I'd known Matt for years, and many times he talked about how guilty he felt about his reaction, but he just didn't know how to get in touch with his feelings of love.

One day Matt called me, and I could immediately tell something was wrong. Angry and frustrated, he told me he had just returned from yet another trip across the country to see his mother, who was supposedly dying. This was the sixth time in three years that he had disrupted his life to fly to her deathbed, and each time she had, against all odds, recovered. She would beg him to stay, telling him how afraid she was to die, afraid she wouldn't go to heaven. He'd do what he could to comfort her, but as he told me, "Honestly, Tara, I feel like she's pulling me into a black hole. Sometimes I wish she'd just die already."

Matt had been meditating for a couple of years, and while we never discussed his practice I knew he'd be open to a suggestion: "Matt, probably the best thing you can do is practice lovingkindness—for your mother *and* yourself." He had tried doing that some months earlier, he told me, but the effort had been sporadic, half-hearted. "It's going to be hard," he said, "but I'll try again. It doesn't feel good to be closed down to someone I love."

Even when it's hard to appreciate goodness in someone, we can send lovingkindness anyway. At first we might feel fake or irritated; our good wishes may feel hollow or flat. But if we can regard those feelings with kindness and continue the practice, a surprising thing happens. *By simply offering care, our care begins to wake up.*

Each morning after meditating, Matt would sit for a few minutes to practice lovingkindness. Remembering good things about himself did begin to ease his heart a bit. Sending wishes for happiness to his friends and neutral people was easy and felt good. When he got to his mother, at first the practice felt rote, but he said the phrases anyway: "Mother, may you be happy. May you feel peaceful. May you feel filled with lovingkindness." Some days he'd just repeat over and over, "May you accept yourself just as you are."

Day by day, Matt found he was spontaneously remembering a little of what he appreciated about his mother. He remembered how she was the one in their neighborhood who brought food and cheerful company to those who were ill or in need. He remembered her bright smile of happiness for him when he got accepted at his favorite college, her joyful tears as he walked down the aisle with the woman he loved. Over the weeks, his wishes for her happiness grew sincere. He wanted her to be peaceful and to recognize her own goodness. At these times when his heart felt most open, he was able to extend his prayers and genuinely include all beings in his circle of lovingkindness as well.

By the time the call came, late one night, that she was critically ill and certain to die within days, something had changed in Matt. He still wondered at first if this time it was really true or just another false alarm. But he felt a genuine willingness to be at her side when she needed him. Flying east to see her, probably for the last time, Matt resolved to let go of his old habits of pushing her away when he felt pulled on or stifled. He wanted to feel the same love for her face-to-face as he had during his lovingkindness meditations.

The Buddha taught that no other spiritual practice has the value of lovingkindness. He said, "Lovingkindness, which is freedom of the heart, absorbs them all; it glows, it shines, it blazes forth." As we practice sending wishes for happiness and peace to ourselves and to others, we touch the beauty and purity of our true nature. The practice of seeing goodness awakens lovingkindness, and the practice of lovingkindness enables us to move through life more awake to the goodness within and around us.

A LOVING AND GENTLE HEART: THE RADIANCE OF OUR TRUE NATURE

In a simple and profound teaching, the Dalai Lama states: "One of my fundamental beliefs is that . . . the basic human nature is gentleness." He goes on to say that he can see this clearly without needing "to resort to the doctrine of Buddha-nature."

> For example, if we look at the pattern of our existence from an early age until our death, we see the way in which we are so fundamentally nurtured by affection. . . . In addition, when we ourselves have affectionate feelings, we see how it naturally affects us from within. Not only that, but also being affectionate and being more wholesome in our behavior and thought seems to be much more suited to the physical structure of our body in terms of its effect on our health and physical well-being. . . . It must also be noted how the contrary seems to be destructive to health. For these reasons I think that we can infer that our fundamental human nature is one of gentleness.

This simple "proof" of our inherent nature is one we have all experienced in our own lives. When we love, we feel good and most truly who we are. As we come home to our Buddha nature our gentle heart becomes expansive and unconditional in its love. Matt's story is a good illustration.

When he arrived at the hospital, Matt found his mother in great pain. She was riddled with cancer and immobilized by a broken hip. For five days he sat by her side, holding her hand, witnessing the almost nonstop surges of pain, silently repeating his prayers of lovingkindness. On the fifth night, it hit him. This was it. His mother was really dying. She wasn't going to be with him much longer. As he gazed at her pale and emaciated face and listened to her labored breath, he saw, not the needy person trying to get something from him, not the frightened person demanding constant reassurance, but simply a being who wanted to be loved. She had been a widow for fifteen years. Who had really hugged her all this time? Who had held her, let her be vulnerable, let her feel embraced and loved? Now, outside all the roles and identities by which he had defined his mother, Matt saw the truth that all she had ever really wanted was to love and be loved.

Taking down the railing of her bed, Matt leaned over her and gently surrounded her small bony body with his arms. Feeling her frailness, he remembered how, when he was a child, she would so comfortingly touch his brow when he was sick. Deeper even than her longing to be loved was the essence of her heart; Matt felt she was the radiance of love itself. "May you be filled with lovingkindness," he whispered. "May you be peaceful, Mama. May you be free from this suffering."

With his face close to hers he told her over and over that he loved her, that he was with her, that love was here. He kissed her forehead, her whole being shone with the truth of her goodness. For several hours he held her, sometimes speaking softly to her, sometimes sobbing, always feeling the fragile thread of her precious life growing thinner. By the time he left, her breath seemed lighter and easier. She looked peaceful.

The next morning, Matt got a call from the hospital at 7 A.M. telling him his mother had passed away. Slowly he hung up the phone and sat unmoving on the edge of his bed. He knew that she had finally felt free to leave. She had been released into death with the blessing of uncomplicated, pure love. After a few minutes the tears came. Through his sobs Matt found himself repeating over and over, "Everybody just wants to be loved." That edge of resistance he had been living with all those years, the judgment and mistrust, had been replaced by a tender, gentle heart.

When Matt called me that night, he said his deepest prayer was to never forget that "everybody just wants to be loved." In the words of physician and author Rachel Naomi Remen, "One moment of unconditional love may call into question a lifetime of feeling unworthy and invalidate it." Matt had seen this power of love to heal. Crying, he said, "Now I know what my life work is about. I want to go around letting everyone know how lovable they are." Matt had found the goodness of love within him, a love that seeks the happiness of others.

Thich Nhat Hanh writes, "When you say something like [I love you] . . . with your whole being, not just with your mouth or your intellect, it can transform the world." Because we are interconnected, when we awaken love in ourselves and express it, our love changes the world around us. The hearts of those we touch are opened, and they in turn touch the hearts of others. Love is the basic nature, the goodness of all beings, waiting to manifest. Whether we offer love in silent prayer or aloud, we are helping love to flower in all beings everywhere. This expression of our deepest nature is the living power of lovingkindness—as the Buddha said, "it glows, it shines, it blazes forth."

LIVING IN LOVE

The Christian mystic Thomas Merton says, "Life is this simple. We are living in a world that is absolutely transparent and the divine is shining through it all the time. This is not just a nice story or a fable. This is true." To me, the divine is the loving awareness that is our source and essence. When we pay careful attention, we see every person as an expression of the love and goodness we cherish. Every being becomes the Beloved. Merton describes a profound moment when he realized this transfiguring truth:

> Then it was as if I suddenly saw the secret beauty of their hearts, the depth of their hearts where neither sin nor knowledge could reach, the core of reality, the person that each one is in the eyes of the divine. If only they could see themselves as they really are, if only we could see each other that way all the time, there would be no more need for war, for hatred, for greed, for cruelty. I suppose the big problem would be that we would fall down and worship each other.

When we see the secret beauty of anyone, including ourselves, we see past our judgment and fear into the core of who we truly are—not an entrapped self but the radiance of goodness.

As our trust in our basic goodness deepens, we are able to express our love and creativity more fully in the world. Rather than second-guessing ourselves, rather than being paralyzed by self-doubt, we can honor and respond to the promptings that arise from that goodness. In a similar way, when we trust the goodness in others, we become a mirror to help them trust themselves. The actions we take that arise out of lovingkindness are part of our path as a bodhisattva. When we are not consumed by blaming and turning on ourselves or others, we are free to cultivate our talents and gifts together, to contribute them to the world in service. We are free to love each other, and the whole of life, without holding back.

Guided Meditation: Cultivating a Forgiving Heart

While softening and opening our hearts cannot be willed, the following meditations nourish a willingness that makes forgiveness possible. They are based on the traditional Buddhist practices in which we first ask forgiveness from others, then offer forgiveness to ourselves and, finally, to those who have caused us injury.

Asking for Forgiveness

Sitting comfortably, close your eyes and allow yourself to become present and still. Rest your attention on the breath for a few moments, relaxing as you breathe in and relaxing as you breathe out.

Bring to mind a situation in which you have caused harm to another person. You might have intentionally hurt someone with insulting words or by hanging up the phone in a fit of anger. Or you might have caused pain unintentionally in the way you ended a romantic relationship, or by being preoccupied and not realizing your child needed some special attention. Maybe you feel you have been causing harm to someone over and over again through the years, violating him or her with your flare-ups of temper or lack of care. Take some moments to remember the circumstances that highlight how you have caused harm to another, and sense the feelings of hurt, disappointment or betrayal that person might have felt.

Now, holding this person in your awareness, begin asking for forgiveness. Mentally whisper his or her name and say, "I under-

stand the hurt you have felt and I ask your forgiveness now. Please forgive me." With a sincere heart, repeat several times your request for forgiveness. Then take some moments of silence and let yourself open to the possibility of being forgiven.

Forgiving Ourselves

Now bring to mind some aspect of yourself that feels unforgivable. Perhaps you can't forgive yourself for being a judgmental and controlling person, or for how you have hurt others. You might hate yourself for being cowardly, for not taking the risks that might make your life more fulfilling. You might not be able to forgive how you are ruining your life with an addictive behavior. You might feel disgust for your mental obsessions or feelings of jealousy. Sense what feels so bad about your unforgivable behavior, emotion or way of thinking. How does it make you feel about yourself? How does it prevent you from being happy? Allow yourself to feel the pain that makes you want to push away the addictive, insecure or judgmental part of yourself.

Now explore more deeply what is driving this unacceptable part of your being. If you have been addicted to food, nicotine or alcohol, what need are you trying to satisfy, what fear are you trying to soothe? When you are judging others, are you feeling fearful yourself? If you have wounded another person, did you act out of hurt and insecurity? Out of the need to feel power or safety? As you become aware of underlying wants and fears, allow yourself to feel them directly in your body, heart and mind.

Begin to offer a sincere message of forgiveness to whatever feelings, thoughts or behaviors you are rejecting. You might mentally whisper the words: "I see how I've caused myself suffering and I forgive myself now." Or you might simply offer yourself the words "Forgiven, forgiven." Meet whatever arises—fear or judgment, shame or grief—with the message of forgiveness. Allow the hurt to untangle in the openness of a forgiving heart.

As you practice you may feel as if you are going through the motions and are not actually capable of forgiving yourself. You might believe you don't deserve to be forgiven. You might be afraid that if you forgive yourself you'll just do the same thing again. Maybe you feel afraid that if you really open and forgive yourself, you'll come face-to-face with an intolerable truth about yourself. If these doubts and fears arise, acknowledge and accept them with compassion. Then say to yourself, "It is my intention to forgive myself when I am able." Your intention to forgive is the seed of forgiveness—this willingness will gradually relax and open your heart.

Forgiving Others

In the same way that each of us has hurt others, we each have been wounded in our relationships. Bring to mind an experience in which you were deeply disappointed or rejected, abused or betrayed. Without judging yourself, notice if you are still carrying feelings of anger and blame toward the person who hurt you. Have you shut this person out of your heart?

Recall with some detail the specific situation that most fully reminds you of how you were wounded. You might remember an angry look on a parent's face, harsh words from a friend, the moment of discovering that a trusted person had deceived you, your partner storming out of the house. Be aware of the feelings that arise, the grief or shame, anger or fear. With acceptance and gentleness, feel this pain as it expresses itself in your body, heart and mind.

Now look more closely at this other person and sense the fear, hurt or neediness that might have caused him or her to behave in a hurtful way. Experience this being as an imperfect human, vulnerable and real. Feeling this person's presence, mentally whisper his or her name and offer the message of forgiveness: "I feel the pain that has been caused and to the extent that I am ready, I forgive you now." Or if you are unable at this moment to offer forgiveness: "I feel the pain that has been caused, and it is my intention to forgive you." Remain connected with your own feelings of vulnerability, and repeat your message of forgiveness or intention for as long as you like.

You can practice forgiving informally throughout the day. When you realize you are judging yourself or another person harshly, you might pause and become aware of the thoughts and feelings of blaming. Take a few moments to connect with the wants or fears that are driving your judgment. Then begin extending, to your inner life or another, whatever message of forgiveness feels most natural. Be patient. With practice your intention to love fully will blossom into a forgiving heart.

Guided Meditation: Awakening Lovingkindness

Through the lovingkindness meditation we open our hearts to ourselves, to others and to all beings everywhere.

Sit in a way that allows you to be comfortable and relaxed. Scan through your body and let go of whatever tension you can. Loosen through the shoulders, soften the hands and relax the belly. Take a few moments to sense the image and feeling of a smile (see "Embracing Life with a Smile," page 91). Allow this to connect you with a spirit of gentleness and ease.

Now allow yourself to remember and open up to your basic goodness. You might bring to mind times you have been kind or generous. You might recall your natural desire to be happy and not to suffer. You might honor your essential wakefulness, honesty and love. If acknowledging your own goodness is difficult, then look at yourself through the eyes of someone who loves you. What does that person love about you? You might also bring to mind whoever to you embodies the Beloved—the Buddha, Kwan Yin, Divine Mother, Jesus, Shiva—and see yourself with this being's wise and loving eyes. When you have connected with a sense of your essential goodness, rest in a tender appreciation for a few moments.

Now with a silent whisper begin offering yourself lovingkindness through prayers of care. As you repeat each phrase, sense the meaning of the words and let them arise from the sincerity of your heart. Choose four or five phrases that are meaningful to you. They might include:

May I be filled with lovingkindness; may I be held in lovingkindness.

May I accept myself just as I am.
May I be happy.
May I touch great and natural peace.
May I know the natural joy of being alive.
May my heart and mind awaken; may I be free.

You might find that you begin to feel agitated as you offer yourself prayers of lovingkindness. The words might seem discordant and artificial if you are feeling down on yourself. Sometimes the exercise of offering yourself care only highlights how undeserving and bad you feel about yourself. Without judgment, include this reactivity in the meditation: "May this too be held in lovingkindness." Then resume offering the chosen phrases of care to yourself, remaining mindful and accepting of whatever thoughts or feelings may arise.

If you find that you are reciting the words mechanically during this or any part of the meditation, don't worry. As with the forgiveness practice, your heart has natural seasons of feeling open and closed. What most matters is your intention to awaken lovingkindness.

Now you can begin to open the circle of lovingkindness. Bring to mind someone who is dear to you. Reflect on this person's basic goodness, sensing what it is in particular that you love about him or her. Perhaps you love this person's capacity to love, their honesty or humor. You might remember that she wants to be happy and doesn't want to suffer. Be aware of his essence as good and wakeful and loving. In your heart feel your appreciation for this dear one and begin offering your prayer. You might draw from four or five phrases below or, if you prefer, create your own. As you silently whisper each phrase of lovingkindness, imagine how it might be for this person to experience the fruit of your blessing—the self-acceptance, peace, joy and freedom.

May you too be filled with lovingkindness; may you be held in lovingkindness.
May you feel my love now.
May you accept yourself just as you are.
May you be happy.
May you know great and natural peace.
May you know the natural joy of being alive.
May your heart and mind awaken; may you be free.

After offering your prayers for a loved one for several minutes, widen your circle of caring and awareness by bringing to mind a "neutral" person. This is someone you might see regularly but don't know well and don't have strong negative or positive feelings about. Reflect on this person's goodness by sensing how he or she also wants to be happy and doesn't want to suffer.

Sense this being's aliveness and essential caring about life. Using the phrases suggested above, or whatever other phrases you choose, offer lovingkindness to this person.

Now bring to mind someone with whom you have a difficult relationship—perhaps someone who evokes anger, fear or hurt. First take some moments to bring a kind attention to whatever arises in you as you reflect on this person. Hold your own feelings with lovingkindness. Then turning your attention to this person, try to see some aspect of his or her basic goodness. If it is difficult to perceive kindness or honesty, simply reflect on how this person wants to be happy and doesn't want to suffer. Sense this being's fundamental wakefulness, and remember that life matters to this person just as it does for you. Holding him or her in a gentle at-

tention, begin offering the phrases of lovingkindness that come most easily for you.

Next imagine that you are bringing together all those you have just prayed for—yourself, a dear one, a neutral person and a difficult person—and offer the prayers of lovingkindness for all at once. Sense your shared humanity, your vulnerability and your basic goodness. As you send prayers of care, hold yourself and these others in your heart, recognizing that you are all in this together.

Now allow your awareness to open out in all directions—in front of you, to either side, behind you, below you and above you. In this vast space, sense that your loving presence is holding all beings: the wild creatures that fly and swim and run across fields; the dogs and cats that live in our homes; the life-forms that are threatened with extinction; the trees and grasses and flowers; children everywhere; humans living in great poverty and those with great riches; those at war and those at peace; those who are dying and those who are newly born. Imagine that you can hold the earth, our mother, in your lap and include all life everywhere in your boundless heart. Aware of the joys and sorrows that all beings experience, again offer your prayers:

May all beings be filled with lovingkindness.
May all beings know great and natural peace.
May there be peace on earth, peace everywhere.
May all beings awaken; may all be free.

Repeat these phrases several times. Then allow yourself to rest in openness and silence, letting whatever arises in your heart and awareness be touched by lovingkindness.

You can weave the lovingkindness practice into your daily life. When you are with a loved one or with someone who elicits irritation or insecurity, you might pause, be aware of your heart and mentally whisper, "May you be happy." You might set the intention that you will reflect, each morning for a week, on the goodness of the people you live with. Then through the day whenever you remember, silently offer them prayers of lovingkindness. You might choose a person you see regularly toward whom you have neutral feelings, and for a week whenever you see him or her, silently offer your wishes for his or her well-being. Or you might choose a person whom you find difficult and daily offer him or her lovingkindness. As you do these practices, notice how your feelings change in relating to the people you are focusing on. Does their behavior change toward you?

Because the phrases and sequence of the formal practice can easily become mechanical, there are ways to keep your experience fresh and alive. In this spirit, you might experiment with the following:

—Select phrases that resonate in the moment.
—Whisper your prayer aloud.
—Say the name of the one to whom you are offering your prayer.
—Imagine you are holding in your heart those to whom you are sending lovingkindness, or placing your hand on their cheek with care.
—Imagine them feeling healed, loved and uplifted by your prayer.

Even a few moments of offering lovingkindness can reconnect you with the purity of your loving heart.

ELEVEN

AWAKENING TOGETHER: PRACTICING RADICAL ACCEPTANCE IN RELATIONSHIP

Stay together, friends.
Don't scatter and sleep.
Our friendship is made
Of being awake.
Rumi

I sought my god,
my god I could not see
I sought my soul,
my soul eluded me
I sought my brother
and found all three
Anonymous

In one of the legends of the Holy Grail, Parsifal, a young knight on a quest, wanders into a parched and devastated land where nothing grows. When he arrives at the capital of this wasteland, he finds the townspeople behaving as if everything were normal. They are not wondering, "What horror has befallen us?" or, "What can we do?" Rather, they are dull and mechanical, as if under a spell.

Parsifal is invited into the castle where, to his surprise, he discovers the king lying in bed, pale and dying. Like the land around him, the monarch's life is waning. Parsifal is full of questions, but because he had been told by an older knight that asking questions was improper for one of his stature, he keeps quiet. The next morning he leaves the castle to continue on his journey, but he hasn't gone far before he meets the sorceress Kundri on the road. When she hears that he hasn't asked the king about himself, she goes into a rage! How could he be so callous? He could have saved the king, the kingdom and himself by doing so.

Taking her words to heart, Parsifal returns to the wasteland and goes straight to the castle. Without even breaking his stride, he walks right up to where the king is lying on his couch. He kneels there and gently asks, "Oh, my lord, what aileth thee?" At that moment, the color comes back into the king's cheeks and he stands up, fully healed. Throughout the kingdom, everything comes to life. The people, newly awakened, talk with animation, laugh and sing together and move with a vigorous step. The crops begin to grow and the grass on the hills glows with the new green of spring.

When we feel cut off from others, as the king in this story was, our lives too can feel like a wasteland, empty of meaning, hollow and thin. We can neither awaken ourselves nor those around us from the trance of unworthiness. When into our wasteland comes someone who genuinely cares, we can come back to life in an instant. A friend of mine calls me from time to time when she has fallen into depression. She may have been feeling dull and empty for days or weeks, not knowing what ails her, disconnected from the pain of her sadness. Just my sincere question, "How are you?" opens the healing flood of tears.

When we're on a spiritual path, we might feel that to be freed from our emotional struggles is a matter of meditating or praying more. But no matter how much we meditate or pray, we still need others to help us dismantle the walls of our isolation and remind us of our belonging. Remembering that we are connected to others and our world is the essence of healing.

Anne, one of my meditation students, was four years old when her family moved to a new house across town. In the chaos of moving day, something happened that locked Anne inside herself for years. Anne had spent the morning playing in the basement as boxes were packed and carried out to her parents' cars. When she noticed that no one had come back for a while, she climbed up the stairs to find her mom. The cellar door was locked and the house was horribly still. Anne pounded and kicked at the door, shouting and wailing, and then huddled in a corner, silent and terrified. By the time her mother and father realized their error—each thought Anne was with the other—a couple of hours had passed.

As an adult Anne frequently found herself feeling very young and frightened. When she was home alone in her own apartment, she would sometimes find herself gripped by a grinding loneliness. Anne would try, as she learned in meditation classes, to hold the intense feelings of vulnerability with a kind presence. But inside she could hear the voice of a child screaming, "I don't want to be alone. I can't do this alone."

Because she was a meditator, when Anne came to me for spiritual counseling, she thought I would give her a meditation technique for handling her terror. To her surprise I emphasized instead how much of our spiritual healing and awakening happens with others. We are wounded in relationship, and we need to heal in relationship. For Anne, it was a relief to be told that the voice of the child crying out was not "unspiritual." She didn't have to be ashamed of needing others. Like Parsifal's king, a key to her awakening would be in feeling the genuine care and interest of others.

We are social beings—we eat, sleep, work, love, heal, fulfill ourselves and awaken with each other. Even when we are completely alone, we carry within us the sense of whom we belong with and our concerns about how others regard us. Feeling the care of others allows us, like the king, to awaken from trance and become whole. All of our relationships have the potential to nourish this flowering, whether they are with teachers, therapists, colleagues, family or friends. From a contemporary perspective, this is our sangha, and it encompasses the whole web of conscious relationships within which we heal and awaken. While some relationships will be mutually more healing and fulfilling than others, all can reveal our interconnectedness. When the two wings of Radical Acceptance, mindfulness and compassion, are present, our relationships with others become a sacred vessel for spiritual freedom.

CONSCIOUS RELATIONSHIP: THE HEART OF SPIRITUAL PRACTICE

In some adaptations of Buddhism in the West, the tendency has been to focus on individual meditation practices while leaving aside some of the interpersonal and social contexts in which they've been traditionally held. We seek protected and quiet spaces where we can sharpen the tools of awareness and learn how to become still, attentive and clear. While periods of solitude are a precious and vital part of spiritual practice, teachings that primarily emphasize silent meditation and a focus on one's inner life can lead to a basic misunderstanding. They may reinforce the misguided notion that we are on a grim and lonely path and that our spiritual goals can only be realized in a vacuum.

Tricycle magazine once printed a cartoon featuring an ad for a Buddhist personals column:

Tall, Dark, Handsome
Buddhist looking
For himself.

This can be seen as a clever commentary on how insular we can get when we interpret teachings to mean that we are on our own, meditating and working hard to free an encumbered self. Relationships with others matter, but they can seem incidental to our spiritual awakening.

If we consider our practice to be "spiritual" only when it takes place in the context of formal meditations, we are missing how critical daily relationships are to our awakening. We are avoiding the disturbing, exciting and confusing emotions that are whipped up in relationships. We are avoiding facing how easily the loving, peaceful person at a silent retreat can turn into an angry and hurtful person when in contact with another human being.

When I look back over my own years of spiritual practice, I see that my heart and mind have been most profoundly awakened in the context of deep human relationship—giving birth and raising a child, having my heart broken, helping and being helped, facing my fears of intimacy, struggling with a judgmental mind, trying to love more fully. Close relationships give rise to my most intense reactivity as well as to cherished experiences of connectedness.

I returned home from my first six-week vipassana retreat feeling happy, balanced and relaxed. Narayan's dad, Alex, had stayed at the house to take care of our son and I was excited to see both of them.

We spent the evening eating popcorn, chatting and catching up. The next morning I walked into my home office and found sitting on my desk the envelope with the mortgage payment I'd left for Alex to mail while I was away. Now it was late, and I'd be charged a fine. I called him up on the phone and started yelling at him about how I hadn't made any money for the last month and how I couldn't count on him . . . not even to get a letter into the mailbox. Clearly I was reacting to a buildup of old resentments, but my anger felt fresh and sharp.

He let me go on a bit before saying, "So this is what you learn at these Buddhist retreats?" His words could have been cutting but they weren't. Rather, I could hear the disappointment in his tone—he had been eager to witness the benefits of my extended practice, and yet we seemed to be caught in the same old routine. After I hung up the phone I felt immediate remorse. What good were my deep experiences of acceptance and peace if I could so easily lash out and fall back into old patterns? Alex's response—like the bells ringing at our meditation retreat—was a clear wake-up call. I was being called back to Radical Acceptance, back to meeting my arising feelings with mindfulness and care. My regret and sorrow reminded me that my relationships with others were right at the center of spiritual life.

The Buddha considered *sangha,* the community of monks and nuns following his teachings, to be one of the basic treasures on the spiritual path. His own relationship with Ananda, his loyal attendant and cousin, is an enduring example of spiritual love and friendship. Ananda, known among the sangha of monks and nuns for his kind and generous spirit, was selfless in taking care of the Buddha's personal needs. And the Buddha offered Ananda his attentive and loving guidance on the spiritual path. In fact, through their years together, Ananda's questions provided the Buddha with a kind of foil for clarifying his teachings. "Not so, Ananda . . ." is a familiar refrain in the scriptures, alerting us to the fact that we are about to receive a critical message. In one of his many questions, Ananda asks, "Is it not so that half of this holy life is good and noble friends, companionship with the good?" The Buddha responds (of course), "Not so, Ananda." Then he goes on, "It is the whole of this holy life, this friendship, companionship and association with the good." While the Buddha was not denying the value of solitary practice, he was certainly emphasizing the importance of mutual support in the awakening of our hearts and minds.

During his years of traveling and teaching, the Buddha introduced to his followers some principles for living harmoniously in community. His most basic ethical teaching was nonharming—to behave with reverence for all life. When someone in the sangha did behave in a way that caused injury, the Buddha advised that they seek to reconcile the conflict. He also made Right Speech—speaking what is true and helpful—one of the key practices on the eightfold path. In his book *Touching Peace,* Thich Nhat Hanh draws upon the Buddha's teachings to offer ways to handle situations when we've hurt others. The key elements are: taking responsibility for causing pain to another, listening deeply to understand the person's suffering, sincerely apologizing and renewing our resolve to act with compassion toward this person and all beings. Much like making amends in twelve-step programs, these simple yet powerful ways of paying attention and relating wisely with others open and free our heart.

After lashing out at Alex that morning, I called back and asked if he would come by the house for lunch so we could talk. When we sat down, I apologized immediately. We talked for a while, each naming what we were feeling. I told him how grateful I was that we could relate like this. We were doing together what I had been practicing for weeks in solitude: paying attention, weathering a storm and coming out the other side feeling more connected and awake.

In the safe container of our caring, we were also able to look toward how we might avoid such an interaction in the future. Alex acknowledged that he could follow through on what we agreed to. I admitted that I'd overreacted and resolved to pause and refrain from pouncing on him in anger. This was more than ten years ago, and looking back, it's clear that our progress on these fronts—albeit slow and imperfect—was possible because of our mutual acceptance. The deep spring of Radical Acceptance I had uncovered on retreat was flowing and alive in the midst of human relating.

To cover up the strong wants and fears we might feel in close relationships, we often hide behind our persona. We react to one another out of habit, instantaneously, lost in our patterns of defending, pretending, judging and distancing. In his book *Meditating Together, Speaking from Silence,* vipassana teacher Gregory Kramer offers a practice that can help us break such patterns of reaction right in the midst of communicating. He writes, "There is sitting meditation. There is walking meditation. Why not listening and speaking meditation? Isn't it sensible that one could practice mindfulness in relationship and so get better at it?"

Greg calls his interpersonal meditation practice *Insight Dialogue.* While engaged in conversation, instead of immediately responding when someone speaks, we pause for a moment, relax our body and mind and mindfully notice what we are experiencing. We might inquire, "What really wants attention?" and notice the feelings and thoughts that are arising. Are we judging or interpreting or commenting on what another person is saying? What sensations are we experiencing in our body? By pausing and paying attention we become acutely aware of our patterns of reaction.

Whether in a formal interpersonal meditation or in the midst of any of our daily interactions, this way of practicing Radical Acceptance with each other gives rise to more understanding and kindness in our relationships. When we practice pausing and deepening our attention, instead of being driven by unconscious wants and fears, we open up our options. We can choose to let go of our mental commentary and listen more deeply to another person's words and experience. We can choose to refrain from saying something that is intended to prove we are right. We can choose to name aloud feelings of vulnerability. We learn to listen deeply and speak with mindful presence, to speak what is helpful and true.

Awakening through conscious relationships is the heart of spiritual life. The fears and wants we experience in relating to others can either fuel our feelings of isolation and unworthiness or, if met with Radical Acceptance, become transfigured into compassion and lovingkindness. As I experienced with Alex, when I stopped reacting and we could speak together mindfully, both our hearts opened again.

Thich Nhat Hanh says: "In the West, the Buddha is the Sangha." Because of the extreme tendency in our culture to see ourselves as isolated individuals, a powerful and direct way for us to realize our Buddha nature is through our relationships with each other. As we devote ourselves to awakening through conscious relationships, we directly undo the conditioning that keeps us in the trance of separation.

THE CHALLENGE AND BLESSING OF VULNERABILITY

Anne had been working in her therapy sessions on the bind she felt caught in—fear of being alone but also fear of being with others, especially people she didn't know well. One day she came for her session, anxious and distressed, forced right up against one of her deepest fears. Anne greatly enjoyed singing, and for the past several years she had been part of a highly respected city choir. Now, the thirty-person choir was considering going on tour. A daylong retreat was scheduled for the following weekend to explore this possibility and make decisions about promotion and fund-raising. The prospect was terrifying. Anne had enjoyed being with others in the choir without feeling any real demands. It had become a safe space where she could keep to herself yet appreciate how her rich and resonate alto voice blended with the others. But going to a retreat and possibly on tour was different. She would have to interact with the others. And if she didn't, she knew she'd feel left out.

We talked about how she might handle fear if it came up at the retreat by pausing and offering it her care. Even in the midst of a conversation, she could try pausing long enough to relax a bit and recognize any feelings or stories that might be coming up. I told her that just listening and attending closely to what others might be experiencing could also help her feel more present, rather than caught up in her fear. I added, "You know, Anne, there's nothing wrong with saying aloud, 'I'm feeling anxious right now.' "

"To the whole group?!" Anne protested, with a nice edge of passion. I agreed that admitting to others how we feel isn't easy. And, of course, we need to pick our situations. But if we know that the people we're around are basically kind and well motivated, they would welcome someone being real. "It takes courage to tell the truth about how we feel, especially since we don't ever really know how it will be received," I said. "But opening ourselves can also be a gift to others . . . it invites them to do the same." Anne was still afraid when she left that day, but she had decided she would go to the retreat and do her best.

The morning of the retreat, the group became embroiled in a

heated discussion about whether the proposed tour might be too ambitious and costly. Anne's heart began pounding and her body trembling. She felt as if she were enclosed in a box that was steadily shrinking, and with each passing moment she felt increasingly suffocated and trapped. She decided she would leave at lunchtime. She could say she didn't feel well. It was true.

Anne looked at her watch. Still twenty minutes until lunch. Suddenly the memory of the cellar came vividly to mind. She was in a room of thirty people yet she felt completely isolated and desperate. Remembering the tools we had talked about, she tried to stay with her feelings, to send them kindness. But she was frozen in fear. She could hear the choir director in a frustrated tone reminding them that almost a half day was past and there still wasn't any consensus as to what to do. When he stopped Anne heard her own voice, small and faltering: "Would you mind . . . I need to say something." The room became immediately still and attentive. She swallowed and went on, "I'm not sure what is happening, but I'm really scared right now." That was it, she couldn't get any more words out. The tears began flowing and her body was shaking all over. The woman sitting next to her on the couch said, "Oh, sweetheart, it's okay," and came close, putting a comforting arm around Anne's shoulders. Anne folded into her and wept.

After a few minutes, she calmed down, and the woman holding her said gently, "You want to tell us what's going on?" Anne looked around. Everyone was watching her, but they didn't seem either shocked or disgusted. They looked patient, waiting for her. Even though her head was throbbing, she began to find words. She told them that this sometimes happened, that without much notice she could find herself feeling isolated and afraid. She only rarely let others see what was happening, but she didn't want to live like that anymore. Mostly she just needed them to know, so she wouldn't feel so horribly alone. As she saw their response, nodding heads, kind smiles, Anne's body began to relax.

Several people told Anne they respected her for being so brave. One woman in the group said she too had been feeling vulnerable and uncomfortable during the morning's exchange. It hadn't been nasty, but it wasn't friendly. The man sitting next to her agreed—he had expected that their retreat would be less businesslike, and more a chance to get to know each other better and maybe create something new together.

Listening to the others, Anne felt her coat of armor melting. The throbbing in her head was becoming a light pulse and her heart felt more at ease. For the next few hours, the group left behind their agenda and instead talked about the fears and challenges, joys and fulfillments of sharing music. By the time the day ended, doing the tour was no longer a question. Several people volunteered as support staff, and the group felt closer and more excited than anyone remembered. To Anne's surprise, instead of feeling scorned and rejected, she too felt closer to almost everyone. By sounding a note of human vulnerability, Anne had added a rich and poignant tone to the voice of her choir.

When we expose our own hurt or fear, we actually give others permission to be more authentic. Fortunately for Anne this is what happened. It's important to be sensitive to times when others, due to their own anger or confusion, might not be able to understand or respond in such an open way. In exposing vulnerability we are always taking a chance and sometimes might get hurt. What makes us willing is that the greater hurt, the real suffering, is in staying armored and isolated. While it takes courage to be vulnerable, the reward is sweet: We awaken compassion and genuine intimacy in our relationships with others.

THE GIFT OF RADICAL ACCEPTANCE

In one of his books, Anthony De Mello, a Jesuit priest, talks about an experience of Radical Acceptance that changed his life. He writes that he had been neurotic for years, "anxious and depressed and selfish." Like so many of us, he adopted one self-improvement project after another, and when nothing seemed to work, he was on the verge of despair. Part of what was so painful was that even his friends agreed that he needed to change and regularly urged him to become less self-absorbed.

His world stopped one day when a friend told him, "Don't change. I love you just as you are." Letting those words stream through his heart and mind felt like pure grace: "Don't change. Don't change. Don't change . . . I love you as you are." Paradoxically, it was only when he received permission not to, that he felt free to change. Father De Mello says he relaxed and opened to a feeling of aliveness that had been blocked off for years.

When others accept us exactly as we are, it does not mean they like everything we do. It does not mean that they will passively stand by if we are injuring ourselves or others. If we are lucky, our friends and family will jump in to intervene if we become alcoholic or start gambling away our paycheck. They will let us know when we have hurt their feelings. And if we are luckier still, they will make it clear that they continue to love us, that they accept the human confusion behind the hurtful ways we express our pain.

Loving acceptance combined with forthright honesty are the key components in what substance abuse professionals call an "intervention." My mother, Nancy Brach, who has worked for decades in the field of addiction recovery, describes an intervention as a session "in which carefully coached codependents confront their alcoholic or drug abuser in a loving, nonjudgmental manner." Even though the approach is confrontational, as she writes, "substance abuse professionals dropped the old adage that you must wait until your client is 'ready' before guiding him or her into a twelve-step recovery program. Too many addicts died before being 'ready' and their families were plenty 'ready' to kill them before being dragged further into the dregs."

When addiction is destroying the life of someone's family, friends and coworkers, they can arrange for such a session. A bed is booked in advance so the addict can (it is hoped) go directly from the session into a treatment program. One of my mother's favorite intervention stories is a good example of the power of Radical Acceptance. She writes:

> I didn't think Harry was ever going to make it to that reserved bed. His repeated bouts of bingeing already were showing in the small bright veins of his cheeks and eyes, in his extra watery weight; his behavior was grandiose and unpredictable, and he was about to lose his job.
>
> I worried about how the participants—his wife, two sons and elderly father—were going to manage being "loving and nonjudgmental" when each one was so furious with him. They were filled with grievances: the sons who couldn't bring friends home from school because their father was such a loose cannon; the wife who had lost a partner she could count on and who treated her with care; the father who never saw his only son. I feared they'd just curse him out, rather than communicate their caring.
>
> I was wrong. Harry came into that room and, he later told me, looked around at the faces of those he loved best in the whole world. They were all looking at him, all there for him. Something happened to the air in the room, he said, it seemed

to beat like a pulse. After he sank down in a chair, I suggested that Marge, his wife, begin the confrontation. But, instead of reciting his absences, his missed commitments, she just got up and kissed him. "Thank you for coming, Harry," she said. Then, to my surprise, each of the others, even the boys, got up and hugged him. It was hard to see what happened after that; all of us were in tears. When his family did go on to say what needed saying, Harry was listening. Afterward, he took the bed that had been saved for him. That was about fifteen years ago and, as far as I know, Harry is still attending his twelve-step meetings, and still aware of the courageous love—the acceptance and truth telling—that probably saved his life.

Witnessing the power of Radical Acceptance always amazes me. I have seen people, who for years had carried shameful secrets, join a twelve-step group or spiritual friends group (which I describe below) and feel immediately and profoundly relieved. Because they realize they are human, imperfect, and still lovable, they can breathe deeply and start fresh. I saw how, after several months of being held in a group's loving acceptance, one of my clients became capable of intimacy with her partner in a way that had seemed impossible. I've watched people shift careers and pursue work that truly inspires them just because they experienced acceptance. It is as if Radical Acceptance opens the door of our cage and invites us to move freely in our world.

WALKING THE PATH WITH SPIRITUAL FRIENDS

We use the word *friend* so casually that we forget its power and depth. Friendliness is one of the main translations of the Pali word *metta* or lovingkindness. The love and understanding of a friend, like a deep well of the purest water, refreshes the very source of our being. If all religions and great ideologies disappeared and our one pursuit was friendship—unconditional friendliness with each other, our inner life, all nature—ah, what a world!

Being with good friends helps us relax about our inner weather and stop regarding our painful emotions or confused behaviors as symptoms of spiritual backsliding. As we bring our vulnerability, insight and heart into conscious relationship, we realize we are all waking up together. In this environment of togetherness, deep healing becomes possible.

One of my meditation students, Karen, was struggling through a divorce from a man she had been married to for fifteen years, and they were embroiled in a nasty custody battle. Karen felt as if her life were falling apart, and that she was alone and isolated in her battle.

When Karen came to talk with me about how to handle her anger and self-doubt, I suggested she consider joining one of our meditation community's spiritual support groups. Called *kalyanna mitta* (in Pali, "spiritual friends"), these groups first emerged among students and teachers at Spirit Rock Meditation Center outside San Francisco. They so effectively filled a need that they soon popped up in Buddhist meditation communities around the country. Groups usually have about eight members and most meet every other week. A typical meeting starts with a period of silent meditation and opens into mindful dialogue. The topic might be the challenges of being spiritually awake in daily life, whether that means in work or intimate relationships, in facing an addiction or the fear of sickness and death. Sometimes the discussion revolves around deepening formal practice. Whatever the focus, the shared intention of group members is to speak and listen honestly, to be present and to communicate from the heart.

Karen was immediately interested and began attending kalyanna mitta (KM) meetings. There she was relieved to find she could talk about her feelings of rage, impotence and fear and not feel out of place or judged. She could even admit to ugly behaviors, ways she lost her temper and went into screaming fits when she felt criticized or misled by her ex-husband. The group's gentle acceptance helped Karen to trust that "this too" could be accepted as part of the path. Her out-of-control reactions didn't make her bad; they were not some nonspiritual derailment. Rather, the painful emotions were a call to deepen her attention and practice compassion.

As others within the group talked about confusing and messy parts of their lives, Karen could see she wasn't out of place. "I used to go to meditation gatherings and think that everyone else was so still and peaceful, like they were all realizing their Buddha nature or something. Meanwhile, I was the one neurotic person in the room caught in nonstop obsessing about my dramas." Now she was realizing that the moods and storms each might experience did not define them. Like the weather, these would change and pass. Furthermore, being with a group of spiritual friends helped her remember what she valued about herself—her empathy and humor and intuitive wisdom.

Belonging to this KM group changed how Karen related not only to herself but also to Richard, her ex-husband. Through their marriage, Karen had come to believe that her easily bruised feelings meant she was weak, that her need for affection and reassurance was a sign of basic insecurity. Yet after months of being in a KM group with others who shared their hurts and fears, she now knew nothing was "wrong" with her. Instead of feeling overwhelmed, crushed or furious each time she had to interact with Richard, she had developed a deeper confidence, a firmer center.

At one meeting Karen related an incident that happened several days earlier. She had been on the phone with Richard, discussing whether their oldest daughter, Melanie, should transfer to a private school. Richard made a nasty comment about how he hoped that her insecurities weren't rubbing off, causing their daughter's discontent at public school. Karen felt a hot surge of anger but didn't say anything. Instead she imagined the KM group, the now familiar and caring faces. She remembered feeling their acceptance and felt a huge wash of gratitude that she no longer needed to believe his story about her defects and limitations. Karen still felt annoyed and quickly ended the conversation, but she also felt excited and hopeful. By feeling supported and accepted, she had been able to step out of the old reactive dance with Richard.

Karen's growing self-trust served her well as she tried to help her daughter sort out which school might be best for her. Because she was more relaxed, she could listen openly to Melanie's concerns and fears, without feeling overwhelmed or inadequate. Together they met with her high school guidance counselor and visited the Quaker school her daughter wanted to attend. "The more I listened to Melanie, the more clearly I realized she was right about what she needed," Karen told me. "I knew this new school would be wonderful for her." When she next talked to Richard, he didn't even argue. "I guess he could get on board because I was on board—I had some confidence in myself." The acceptance Karen had received from her spiritual friends had taken root—her faith in herself was enabling her to relate to those around her with a growing balance and strength.

When Radical Acceptance blossoms in our relationships, it becomes a kind of spiritual re-parenting that enables us to trust the goodness and beauty of who we really are. Just as good parenting mirrors back to a child that they are lovable, when we understand and accept others, we affirm their intrinsic worth and belonging. To receive this kind of Radical Acceptance can transform our lives. By mirroring back to someone their goodness, we offer a priceless gift, and its blessings ripple out through a lifetime.

Rachael Naomi Remen writes, "When we recognize the spark of God in others, we blow on it with our attention and strengthen it. No matter how deeply it has been buried or for how long. . . . When we bless someone, we touch the unborn goodness in them and wish it well." The mirroring of inner beauty is the blessing any of us can give to each other. We only need to pause, see clearly who is before us and open wide our heart.

Some of our deepest awakenings happen through the intimate and loving connections that remind us most fully of who we are. Sufi teacher Idries Shah tells the story of a dervish who was so wise and beloved that every time he sat down at one of his favorite coffeehouses, he would be immediately surrounded by students and devotees. While he was humble and did not proclaim to be someone special, these very qualities were part of the vibrant aura that attracted his followers. The dervish was asked various questions about spiritual life, but the most frequent was personal: "How did you become so holy?" Invariably he would simply reply, "I know what is in the Koran."

This went on for quite a while until one day, after hearing this response, a rather arrogant newcomer challenged him. "Well, what is in the Koran?" he demanded. After regarding him kindly, the dervish responded, "In the Koran there are two pressed flowers, and a letter from my friend Abdullah."

Although scriptures guide us and practices focus and quiet us, as the dervish suggested, the living experience of love reveals our intrinsic wholeness and radiance. Our life is embedded in an interdependent field of being and when we are relating consciously—when, as Rumi says, "our friendship is made of being awake"—the suffering of our personal trance dissolves.

PAIN IS NOT PERSONAL

Michael Meade, renowned storyteller and teacher, tells about a healing ritual in Zambia. If a member of the tribe becomes ill—emotionally or physically—the belief is that an ancestor's tooth has lodged itself within the person and is responsible for the sickness. Because all members of the tribe are connected with each other, the suffering of one affects the others, and all become involved in healing. The tribe's healing ritual is based on the understanding that, as Meade relates, "The tooth will come out as the truth comes out." While the sick person must reveal the rage or hatred or lust he or she is experiencing, for the full truth to be revealed, each person in the tribe must express his or her own buried hurts and fears, anger and disappointment. As Meade describes it: "The release happens only when everything comes out, in the midst of dancing and singing and drumming. The whole village gets cleansed by the release of the tooth through the release of these difficult truths."

This ritual holds great wisdom. Unlike in our own culture where we consider illness or depression to be a personal liability or affliction, members of this tribe are not blamed or isolated in their suffering. Rather, suffering is a shared concern, a part of everyone's life. Pain does not belong to one individual. *Not taking pain personally is essential to Radical Acceptance.* As the Buddha taught, life's difficulties are not owned or caused by an individual—our changing states of body and mind are influenced by myriad variables. When we recognize this, remaining open and vulnerable and accepting with each other, we heal together.

Not taking our pain personally is a profound shift away from our habitual way of regarding our life. Even when we are trying not to judge ourselves, it is easy to assume that our jealous thoughts, our selfish tendencies, our compulsions and our often nonstop judging are a personal problem and sign of deficiency. But if we pay close attention to others, as Karen did in the KM group or as the Zambian tribe does, we see that we are not alone in our wants and fears. We also see that we share the same longing to be more loving and awake. Realizing the truth of belonging, that we are all suffering *and* awakening together on the path, is the most powerful antidote to personal feelings of unworthiness. When *my* fear or *my* shame becomes *our* shared suffering, Radical Acceptance flowers.

Habitual feelings of separation arise throughout life—this is simply part of our condition. When asked about how to deal with these persistent feelings of distance from each other, the Indian master Sri Nisargadatta gave this simple, beautiful advice: "Just let go of every thought except 'I am God . . . You are God.' " By relating to each other with Radical Acceptance, we affirm the truth of who we are. When, in friendship, we release all distancing thoughts and ideas, when we behold each other with clarity and love, we nourish the seeds of liberation.

Guided Reflection: Communicating with Awareness

The way we speak with and listen to others can communicate love or hate, acceptance or rejection. The Buddha described wise speech, the speech that expresses reverence for life, as speaking only what is true and what is helpful. Yet caught as we are in reacting to each other out of wanting and fear, how do we recognize what is true? How do we discern what is helpful? How do we speak and listen from our hearts?

The following meditative practices are guidelines for being mindful and openhearted in communicating with each other. They have been drawn from different sources and are used in varying combinations by kalyanna mitta and similar groups around the United States. You can practice them yourself whenever you are engaged in conversation, or you can use them as formal guidelines for interpersonal meditation where two or more people are gathered for the purpose of mindful dialogue.

Set your intention. *As a basic spiritual practice establish your intention to be present, honest and kind in relating to others in any circumstance. Remind yourself of your resolution at the start of each day, at the beginning of an interpersonal meditation or before any interaction with others.*

Let your body be an anchor. *Choose two or three touch points, places in your body where you can reawaken a sense of presence. These might be the sensations of breathing, the sensations in your shoulders, hands, stomach or feet. Return to them as often as possible when you are communicating with others. The more you practice staying aware of these touch points during* *your sitting practice and throughout the day, the more readily you'll sustain an embodied presence when you are with others.*

Listen from the heart. *While others are speaking, try to let go of your own thoughts and pay attention to what they are saying. This means letting go of your agenda for the conversation. Stay aware of the feelings and sensations that occur throughout your body and especially in the heart area. Be particularly aware of your mind wandering off into judgments. If you find yourself criticizing, analyzing or interpreting, meet these thoughts with mindfulness, let them go and return to receptive listening. This doesn't mean you are agreeing with whatever is being said, but rather you are honoring the other by offering your full presence and attention. Let your listening be wholehearted and deep, paying attention to the person's tone, pitch, volume and words. In addition to content, allow yourself to receive the mood and spirit of what another is expressing.*

Speak from the heart. *Try not to prepare and rehearse what you will say in advance, especially while another is speaking. Rather, in the present moment speak what feels true and meaningful. This might be a response to what you have just heard. Or as happens in meditative dialogue, it may not be necessary to respond. Rather, what you say arises from your immediate stream of experience. Speaking from the heart begins with inward listening. Speak slowly enough to stay mindfully connected with your body and heart.*

Pause, relax and attend. *During your interactions pause repeatedly. Pause briefly before and after you speak. Pause as you are speaking to reconnect with your body and feelings. Pause when another is done speaking, giving some space for what they have said to settle. With each pause relax your body and mind. Rest in openness, paying full attention to this moment's experience.*

After pausing you might deepen your attention by using inquiry to check in with your own heart and mind. Ask yourself, "What is true now? What am I feeling?" Deepen your awareness of the other by asking yourself, "What might this person be experiencing?" This inquiry is both active and receptive—you are intentionally asking and investigating, and also opening to whatever is arising. Use pause-relax-attend whenever you remember as a sacred pathway into presence.

Practice Radical Acceptance. *The effort to be present and awake with each other is very humbling. The given is that we will forget our intention, forget to connect with our body, forget to listen without thinking, forget not to rehearse, forget, forget, forget. Hold the whole process with Radical Acceptance, forgiving yourself and others again and again for being perfectly imperfect. When Radical Acceptance is a container for our relationships, genuine intimacy becomes possible.*

Training ourselves to be present with each other is a way to integrate mindfulness and lovingkindness into our daily life. In the moments when we communicate with honesty and kindness, we begin to dissolve the trance of separation. Instead of being driven by wanting or fear, we feel increasingly spontaneous and real. As much as any meditation, these practices allow us to discover, through relating wakefully with each other, the sweetness of our connectedness and belonging.

TWELVE

REALIZING OUR TRUE NATURE

O longing mind,
Dwell within the depth
Of your own pure nature.
Do not seek your home elsewhere . . .
Your naked awareness alone, O mind,
Is the inexhaustible abundance
For which you long so desperately.

Sri Ramakrishna

A legend from ancient India tells of a musk deer who, one fresh spring day, detected a mysterious and heavenly fragrance in the air. It hinted of peace, beauty and love, and like a whisper beckoned him onward. Compelled to find its source, he set out, determined to search the whole world over. He climbed forbidding and icy mountain peaks, padded through steamy jungles, trekked across endless desert sands. Wherever he went, the scent was there, faint yet always detectable. At the end of his life, exhausted from his relentless search, the deer collapsed. As he fell his horn pierced his belly, and suddenly the air was filled with the heavenly scent. As he lay dying, the musk deer realized that the fragrance had all along been emanating from within himself.

When we are trapped in the trance of feeling separate and unworthy, Buddha nature appears to be outside of us. Spiritual awakening, if it is even possible for this flawed self, seems to be far away, in another time or place. We might imagine that realization happened only in Asia, centuries ago, or only in monasteries, or to those who are far more devoted and disciplined than we are. Even if we follow their path we may be like the musk deer. We may spend our lives seeking something that is actually right inside us, and could be found if we would only stop and deepen our attention. But distracted, we spend our life on our way to somewhere else.

As we spiritually mature, our yearning to see truth and live with an open heart becomes more compelling than our reflex to avoid pain and chase after pleasure. We may feel mistreated and angry at our partner but we are willing to recognize our part, to see their pain, to forgive and keep loving. When we become lonely or sad, we are less inclined to dull the painful feelings with food, drugs or staying busy. We become increasingly aligned with our evolutionary destiny, which is to awaken into our natural wisdom and compassion.

Our true and original nature is described in Mahayana Buddhism as *prajnaparamita,* the heart of perfect wisdom. This perfection of wisdom is called the Mother of All Buddhas, "the one who shows the world [as it is]." She is called "the source of light . . . so that all fear and distress may be forsaken." When we are in touch with our true nature, we are completely free of the trance. No longer afraid or contracted, we know our deepest essence as the pure, wakeful awareness that beholds, with love, all of creation.

We may at times have a sudden and profound insight into our true nature. However, making ourselves at home in this truth, trusting it in our day-to-day living, usually depends upon a gradual unfolding. For this reason the process of realizing who we are is called a *path* of awakening. While a path implies getting somewhere else and different, in spiritual life the path opens us to the awareness and love that, as T. S. Eliot writes, is "here, now, always."

DOUBTING OUR BUDDHA NATURE

I was in the middle of a weeklong meditation retreat when our teacher posed a simple and profound question: "Do you really trust you are a Buddha?" My inner response was "Absolutely . . . sometimes." Countless times I had perceived my heart and mind awakening into freedom. In those moments, trust arose from a full-body realization that my original nature is pure awareness. When I was resting in that truth, I felt fully real and at home. Yet I knew that I also spent huge swaths of time each day believing I was a small self who was falling short and needed to be different in order to be okay.

Wishing to become more mindful of this persistent illusion of a small self, during the remainder of the retreat I periodically asked myself, "Who am I taking myself to be?" I was a meditator carried away by obsessive thinking and not trying hard enough. I was a woman wearing clothes that were too sexy and immodest for a Buddhist retreat. I was a judgmental person, running a constant commentary in my mind about how others appeared and behaved. I was a self-conscious yogi, wanting to impress my teacher during our interview. The question proved to be a very useful tool in revealing how fully and how often I slipped into the trance. I could see that whenever I took myself to be some version of a small self, I wasn't recognizing or trusting the wakeful presence that is my deepest nature. While not always intense, some feeling of fear and separation was always present.

In the aftermath of that retreat, my habit of mistrusting my true nature seemed even more extreme. One morning while Narayan was getting ready to leave for school, I was meditating in my bedroom. My mind was fairly quiet and still and rather than focusing attention, I was simply resting in awareness. As images, sounds and sensations arose and dissolved in the boundless space of mind, I perceived the beautiful freedom of not clinging to anything, and felt enormous tenderness for the world. The scent of Buddha nature was vibrant and immediate: I felt as wide-open as the sky, as wakeful as a radiant sun. There was nowhere to go; nothing was missing or outside of awareness.

In the midst of this sitting, there was a loud knock on the door and Narayan barged into my room. Apologetic and breathless, he asked me for a ride to school—he had run as fast and hard as he could but still missed the bus. My open shining universe suddenly collapsed into the roles and duties of being a mom. I agreed, threw on some jeans and we headed out the door. As we crept slowly through Washington's aggressive rush-hour traffic, I became increasingly edgy. When I asked him if he felt prepared for today's science quiz he mumbled, "Not exactly." Further questioning revealed that he had forgotten to take his lab notes home the prior day. I stopped myself from making my typical observations on how he organized his life, or from saying anything punitive. But inside, I could feel my gut tighten with irritation. When he made his habitual move for the radio, I muttered, "No way," and angrily pushed his hand away. Rap was just too much.

As I felt the grim set of my jaw and the tightness of my mind, I reminded myself that this too was another opportunity to practice mindfulness. But this reminder was only an abstraction. The concrete reality was I felt uptight and armored, a neurotic mother trapped in reactivity. The awareness I cherished and had so recently known as my true nature was a fragrance somewhere out there, distant and far away. It had nothing to do with the person making her way through the traffic.

When I returned home and pulled into my driveway, I turned off the car and just sat there. Sometimes the protective bubble of my car can be as good a space for touching the moment as the most sacred of meditation halls. At first I felt restless and had to resist the urge to dash inside and check my e-mail and phone messages. Instead I waited, feeling my body and sensing what most wanted attention. As I sat there, I could see the squirrels chasing each other around the trees in my side yard. My feelings were also chasing each other around, and I knew there was nothing to do but let them play out. In the hunch of my shoulders and the creeping sensations of fatigue, I recognized the feeling of failure.

I'd felt so peaceful and expansive just moments before my son had entered the room. How could I contract so suddenly, feel so inadequate, so irritated, so tight? I was falling short on all fronts—meditating, mothering, living life. This feeling of self-doubt was familiar. Would I ever be able to sustain a caring and open presence through life's daily ups and downs?

At the culminating moment of Gautama Buddha's awakening, he faced the enormous force of doubt. He had spent the night under the bodhi tree, responding with mindfulness and compassion to all the various challenges of Mara, the god of greed, hatred and delusion. As night was beginning to fade, Gautama knew that his heart and mind were awake, but he was not yet fully free. Mara then issued his final and most difficult challenge: By what right did Siddhartha aspire to Buddhahood? In other words, "Who do you think you are?" This voice of Mara is the one that urges us to turn against ourselves, to give up the path, convincing us that we are going nowhere.

In response to this challenge, Gautama reached down and touched the earth, calling on it to bear witness to his many lifetimes of compassion. In touching the earth, he was also touching the ground of wakeful presence—the heart of perfect wisdom from which all enlightened beings spring. He was calling on his true identity to dispel all the doubt that kept him from complete freedom. According to the legend, at the moment when he touched the ground, the earth trembled and the sky was filled with rumbling. Mara, seeing that he was facing not a man but the creative power of awareness itself, fearfully withdrew.

Sitting in my car that morning, I remembered to hold my chaos of feelings with Radical Acceptance. The tightness and hardness around my heart started to soften. Acknowledging and allowing the very immediate pain of self-doubt, I began to feel more real and awake. As the minutes passed, I felt myself returning to a caring and open awareness.

The squirrels had stopped their mad circling around the tree trunk and a light wind was moving through the leaves. Inside, I felt a growing sense of calm. Doubt was still there, but I was no longer taking myself to be a failing mother or inept meditator—it was more like the whisper of an uneasy, cautious self. As a way of continuing to free myself from any sense of contraction into "selfness," I asked myself, "Who is aware right now?" I was aware only of awareness: There was no "self" to locate. There was no entity that was failing, no self that was fearful and distraught, no foothold for self-doubt. While streams of sensations and emotions were moving through my body and mind, there was no one behind the scenes who possessed them or controlled them. I could find only the endless space of awareness—formless, open, knowing.

Just as the Buddha touched the earth in response to Mara's final challenge, when the voice of doubt afflicts us, we touch the ground by arriving, on the spot, in this moment. We touch the ground by directly connecting with the earth, the life of our bodies, our breath and our inner weather. We touch the ground by looking directly into the awareness that is the very source of our life. As we connect with what is right in front of us, we realize the true immensity of who we are.

SEEING BEYOND THE SELF AND LETTING GO INTO AWARENESS

When we sit down to meditate we begin with our immediate experience. As we offer a kind presence to the areas that are most calling for our attention, our body and mind begin to quiet. If we look closely we recognize that our sense of self begins to loosen. At this point there is a tendency to get caught up in a subtle but persistent contraction that still feels like "me." I am the "one who is calming down" or the "one guiding myself in meditating." This more diffuse and edgeless sense of self is what I call a "ghost" self. Some call it the observing witness or the self who is watching. Though less entrapping than an angry or fearful self, this ghost self is still a hanging on to an identity that prevents us from being free.

The Buddha taught that holding on to *anything,* including a sense of being the observer, obscures the full freedom of awareness. At these times, as I did in the driveway, we can pull the curtain on this faint aura of self-ness by asking, "Who is aware?" We might also ask, "What is aware?" or, "Who am I?" or, "Who is thinking?" We bring mindfulness to awareness itself. We *look into* awareness. By inquiring and then looking into awareness, we can cut through and dispel the deepest illusions of self that have held us separate and bound.

Jim had been attending my weekly meditation classes for eight months. He had approached me after class several times in frustration. Each time his mind quieted enough to look into awareness, he would end up sensing a witness self. When he asked, "Who is aware of this witnessing self?" the observing self would just pop up again. Worried that he wasn't "getting it," he came up again one night after class. I asked him to bring mindfulness to the sensations, images and mood of the witness self he perceived, and to tell me what he noticed. He said he saw a cloud of light behind him and heard his own voice saying, "This is me." I asked, "Who is aware of the light, the sound of a voice?" His response was immediate: "I am, of course!" He told me he felt irritated, as if someone—me, Buddhism—was challenging the self that he absolutely knew to be real. After some moments his annoyance turned to discouragement and Jim said flatly, "I don't know what I'm supposed to do. I'm confused, and this whole meditation makes me uncomfortable."

In looking into awareness, if we are anxious and trying to have a particular experience, our attention, rather than being unbiased and allowing, fixates on thoughts, sounds or sensations. Rather than recognizing and accepting the changing stream of phenomena, we feel compelled to grasp hold of something, anything. To try to orient ourselves, we take a mental snapshot of our experience and add a commentary. While we might initially look into awareness without ideas or expectations, within moments we are back into our conceptual mind trying to make sense of what is happening. The most basic way we do this is by holding on to the concept of a stable and enduring self. We try to secure our identity by nailing down our experience.

I encouraged Jim to explore how he might relax more fully while he practiced looking into awareness. I shared with him the instructions my Tibetan meditation teacher, Tsokney Rinpoche, gives for recognizing our true nature: "Look and see . . . Let go and be free." Rinpoche illustrates this by first holding his hands up about a foot in front of his face, palms facing outward. Our attention, like our palms turned outward, is always focusing on the movie of life—our outer as well as our inner world.

Turning his palms toward himself he demonstrates the act of looking directly into awareness—"Look and see." Releasing our focus on thoughts and other objects of experience, we look directly at who is looking. Then, with, "Let go, be free," Rinpoche's hands drift gently down to rest in his lap. When we look into our awareness and see what is true, we relax, completely letting go into that reality.

The following week Jim stayed after class and told me that, while sitting the evening before, he had touched an experience of deep realization. As had happened so many times before, after his mind quieted, he sensed the witness as a familiar sphere of brightness behind him. He became curious and asked, "Who is aware of this?" As he described it, "I could feel the tension in my mind wanting to locate 'me,' but the truth was, I couldn't find anything to land on. In that instant, before my mind came up with any explanation, I completely relaxed. That was it . . . there was nothing solid, nothing holding still. No self was there . . . the whole world was awareness."

In a classic Zen story, the disciple Hui-K'e asks his master, Bodhidharma, "Please help me to quiet my mind." Bodhidharma responds by saying, "Bring me your mind so that I can quiet it." After a long moment of silence Hui-K'e says, "But I can't find my mind!" "There," Bodhidharma replies with a smile. "I have now quieted your mind."

Like Hui-K'e, when we look within, there is no entity, no mind-substance, no self, no thing we can identify. There is just awareness—open empty awareness. We can't locate any center, nor can we find an edge to our experience. Unless we anchor ourselves again in thoughts, or grasp after desired sensations or feelings, we have nowhere to stand, no firm ground. This can be disconcerting, scary, incredibly mysterious. While there may be a profusion of activity—sounds, sensations, images—there is no thing to hold on to, no self behind the curtain managing things. This seeing of no thing is what the Tibetan teachers call "the supreme seeing."

But this emptiness, this "no-thingness," is not empty of life. Rather, empty awareness is full with presence, *alive with knowing.* The very nature of awareness is cognizance, a continuous knowing of the stream of experience. In this moment that you are reading, sounds are heard, vibration is felt, form and color are seen. This knowing happens instantaneously, spontaneously. Like a sunlit sky, awareness is radiant in cognizance and boundless enough to contain all life.

As Jim found, to recognize this pure awareness, we need to relax the veil of stories, thoughts, wants and fears that cover over our natural being. Sri Nisargadatta writes, "The real world is beyond our thoughts and ideas; we see it through the net of our desires divided into pleasure and pain, right and wrong, inner and outer. To see the universe as it is, you must step beyond the net. It is not hard to do so, *for the net is full of holes.*"

Our attention is always fixating on something—a flattering comment someone said, our plan for next Saturday, an image of our dirty kitchen, a rerun of an argument. Our reality is the thoughts and dramas we see in our mental movies. We step beyond the net by letting go of our stories and pursuits and turning toward awareness. This is like looking back at the projector and realizing it is actually light that is making the images look alive. We look back into the emptiness that is the creative source of all stories and emotions, into the formless fertile space that gives rise to all of existence. There, we "see the universe as it is."

Everything we can possibly see, hear, feel or imagine—this entire world—is a fantastic display, appearing and vanishing in awareness. When thoughts arise, where do they come from, where do they go to? As you explore looking into the space between thoughts, through the holes in the net, you are looking into awareness itself. You might sit quietly and simply listen for a few moments. Notice how sounds arise and dissolve back into formless awareness. Can you notice the beginnings of sounds, the ends of sounds? The spaces between? It is all happening in awareness, known by awareness.

To "Look and see . . . Let go and be free" is revolutionary and counterintuitive. Rather than trying to control or interpret our experience, we train to relax our grip. By wakefully letting go into what is right here, we are carried home into the mystery and beauty that is our deepest nature.

Lama Gendun Rinpoche writes:

> *Happiness cannot be found through great effort and will power,*
> *But is already there, in relaxation and letting-go.*
> *Don't strain yourself, there is nothing to do . . .*
> *Only our search for happiness prevents us from seeing it . . .*
> *Don't believe in the reality of good and bad experiences;*
> *They are like rainbows.*
>
> *Wanting to grasp the ungraspable, you exhaust yourself in vain.*
> *As soon as you relax this grasping, space is there*
> *—open, inviting, and comfortable.*
>
> *So, make use of it. All is yours already.*
> *Don't search any further . . .*
> *Nothing to do.*
> *Nothing to force,*
> *Nothing to want,*
> *—and everything happens by itself.*

The path of awakening is simply a process of wakeful, profound relaxing. We see what is here right now and we let go into life exactly as it is. How liberating!

With practice, recognizing our natural awareness takes less and less of an effort or sense of doing. Rather than climbing up a hill to get a view, we are learning the art of relaxing back and wakefully inhabiting the whole vista. We look back into awareness and then simply *let go into what is seen.* We become more at home in awareness than in any story of a self who is falling short or on our way somewhere else. We are at home because we have seen and experienced firsthand the vast and shining presence that is the very source of our being.

REALIZING OUR NATURE AS BOTH EMPTINESS AND LOVE

In Mahayana Buddhism, the open, wakeful emptiness of awareness is our absolute nature. Our original nature is changeless, unconditioned, timeless and pure. When we bring this awareness to the relative world of form, love awakens. We meet the ever-changing stream of life—this living, dying, breathing world—with accepting presence and our hearts invariably open. What our mind recognizes as empty awareness, our heart experiences as love.

Our being resides in both the unmanifest and the manifest, the absolute and the relative. This truth, embodied in the Heart Sutra, is considered the gem of Mahayana teachings. As the sutra says: "Form is emptiness, emptiness is also form. Emptiness is not other than form, form is not other than emptiness." The formless ocean of awareness gives rise to the varying and endless waves of life: emotions, trees, people, stars. Seeing that all of life springs from one awareness, we realize our connectedness and feel the fullness of love. In cherishing all living beings with compassion, we recognize the empty, wakeful awareness that is our common source.

Loving life and realizing our essence as formless awareness cannot be separated from each other. As a Japanese proverb expresses, "Seeing pure awareness without engaging lovingly with our life is a daydream. Living in this relative world without vision is a nightmare." We can be tempted, sometimes in pursuit of nonattachment, to distance ourselves from the messy wildness of our bodies and emotions, and from our relationships with each other. This pulling away leaves us in a disembodied daydream that is not grounded in awareness of our living world. On the other hand, if we immerse ourselves in the mental dramas and changing emotions of our lives without remembering the empty, wakeful awareness that is our original nature, we get lost in the nightmare of identifying as a separate, suffering self.

Sometimes our deepest realization of the interdependence of love and emptiness comes when we are facing the anguish of loss. A recent time where this was true for me was in losing my dog, who was one of my best friends. Her name was also Tara, and she was a black standard poodle. She was filled with good humor and play. I had the distinct sense that she was cheering me on during the steep uphills on our running route. As I lost speed she would start running circles around me. She meant no harm those few times when she dashed in front of me and sent me sprawling on the street. She was surprised, sorry, kind. Many of us know these friendships. They are quiet, often in the background. And yet they hold our life.

Tara got a brain tumor that took over six months to diagnose. She became lethargic and uncoordinated, but still followed me around, struggling gamely to be good company. When we realized the problem, I tried hard to save her life. She had her own shelf of medicines and patiently endured several months of radiation treatments. I was holding on tightly, hoping against the odds.

The treatment failed and her pain got worse. Because of the steroids, her fur started coming out in clumps. I'd wake up in the morning, and find her at the foot of my bed with yet another sore red patch of exposed skin. She'd still limply wag her tail or give me a soft, affectionate lick, but she didn't want to meet the day. I felt I had no choice but to end her life. I can so easily remember the trusting look in her eyes as I got her to step onto the steel platform in the vet's office. She was quiet and ready as he injected the chemicals that stopped her heart.

When my vet left me alone with Tara's body, I was flooded with the loss, sobbing with grief. I just kept stroking and kissing her dear head, feeling her presence and absence clashing and spinning through me at once. My dear friend was gone. She would never light up in seeing me, run with me, sleep warmly next to me again. Yet this aching loving bond was so here and alive! Holding her, hugging her, I could feel how this world of beloved forms plays out with relentless, commanding force. *Emptiness is form.* It felt like all that existed in the world were these tremendous waves washing through my utterly despondent self. I was deeply attached, losing, hurting, loving. There was nothing to do but include in awareness wave after wave of grief.

Yet as this heart-wrenching pain was happening, I also felt a soft presence, a compassionate "being with" my grief. These huge swellings of sadness were held in the space and kindness of awareness. When I asked who was aware, the stream of sore, aching, heavy sensations were appearing and unfolding in a vast and open awareness. As I let go into this wakeful openness, there was no self who owned the grieving and no friend to lose. I was seeing how this acutely vivid display was just happening, like the movement of the wind or the sudden darkening before a storm. *Form is emptiness.* There was only the tender field of awareness experiencing the arising and passing of life.

All of our emotions, perhaps grief especially—if met with Radical Acceptance—can carry us to the truth of the Heart Sutra. Poet David Whyte writes:

Those who will not slip beneath
the still surface on the well of grief

turning downward through its black water
to the place we cannot breathe

will never know the source from which we drink,
the secret water, cold and clear,

nor find in the darkness glimmering
the small round coins
thrown by those who wished for something else.

Our grief is the honest recognition that this cherished life is passing. No matter what we lose, we open to the ocean of grief because we are grieving all of this fleeting life. Yet our willingness to go into the black waters of loss reveals our source, the loving awareness that is deathless.

Radical Acceptance is the art of engaging fully in this world—wholeheartedly caring about the preciousness of life—while also resting in the formless awareness that allows this life to arise and pass away. There are times when the arising forms in our life will naturally be in the foreground of awareness. When Tara died, I would have been avoiding and postponing grief if I had not brought a full presence to the waves of pain moving through me. When we are filled with wanting, grief or fear, prematurely looking toward awareness may be a way of disengaging from the rugged rawness of our emotions.

Yet while we clearly need to embrace this life, we can't meet our experience with Radical Acceptance if we have forgotten the openness of formless awareness. In the moments of looking into awareness, I was seeing the changeless, timeless nature that was the essence of my dog, Tara, and is the empty essence of all beings everywhere. This was the source of those eyes that looked at me so warmly, the awareness that can never be lost, only forgotten.

THE PATHWAY HOME: STEPPING INTO UNCONDITIONAL PRESENCE

In one of the Jataka tales, mythical teaching stories based on the Buddha's previous lifetimes, the Buddha was a good merchant living in a small village in north India. One afternoon, while working in his shop, he glanced outside and saw a beautiful and luminous person walking across the town square. He was stunned. As he continued to watch, he felt his heart light up in celebration. Never in his life had he seen a human being so visibly radiating compassion. Never had he sensed the divine shining forth with such immanence.

The merchant knew immediately that he wanted to serve this being and give his life to awakening such love in his own heart. With great care he prepared a tray of ripe fruits and tea to offer as nourishment. He stepped out into the sunlit day, moving mindfully and joyfully toward the luminous one who seemed to stand awaiting him.

Suddenly, when the merchant was only halfway across the town square, the daylight suddenly turned to darkness. The ground quaked violently, and a gash in the earth appeared between him and the one he longed to serve. Lightning bolts ripped through the blackened skies, and he saw the glaring eyes and bloody mouths of horrifying demons. He was surrounded by the voices of Mara: "Go back! Turn around! It's too dangerous . . . you won't survive!" As crashing thunder shook the air the voices warned, "This way is not for you! Who do you think you are? Go back to your shop, to the life you know."

Terrified, the good merchant was about to turn around and flee for safety. But at that moment his heart swelled with a longing so great it could fill the entire universe. This desire for love and freedom was stronger than any voice of warning. With the image of the radiant being filling his mind, he took one step into the dark chaos of Mara. And then another and another. The demons disappeared, the brilliant light of day returned and the earth came together, healed and once again whole.

The merchant, trembling with aliveness, overflowing with love and gratitude, found himself standing right in front of the luminous figure. The great being embraced him, saying, "Well done, bodhisattva, well done. Walk on through all the fears and pain in this life. Walk on, following your heart and trusting in the power of awareness. Walk on, one step at a time, and you will know a freedom and peace beyond all imagining."

As he heard these words, the good merchant felt his entire being fill with light. Looking around, he saw this same divine presence shining through the ground and trees, the singing birds and every blade of grass. He and the great being and every part of this living world belonged to boundless, radiant presence.

No matter how thick are the clouds of fear, shame and confusion, we can, like the merchant, remember our longing to awaken compassion, our longing to be wise and free. Remembering what we cherish guides us to hold our fear and doubt with awareness. Moving in this way, moment by moment, we find what we long for.

When Mara appears, we can awaken by taking just one step—by touching the ground of this present moment with compassionate presence. During an angry exchange of words we take one step, feeling with awareness the rising pressure in our chest, the heat in our face. When our child has a high fever, we take a step by bringing awareness to our fear as we hold a cool cloth to his brow. When we're lost after dark in an unfamiliar city, we take a step by noticing with awareness the squeeze of anxiety as we turn yet another corner into an unknown street. This is the path—arriving over and over again in the moment with a kind awareness. All that matters on this path of awakening is taking one step at a time, being willing to show up for just this much, touching the ground just this moment.

The path of Radical Acceptance frees us from the voices of Mara that tell us we are separate and unworthy. Whenever we become fully present, we discover the natural wakefulness and care that is inherent within us. We come to understand, in a vivid and cellular way, who we really are. Rumi writes:

> *I am water. I am the thorn*
> *that catches someone's clothing . . .*
>
> *There's nothing to* believe.
> *Only when I quit believing in myself*
> *did I come into this beauty . . .*
>
> *Day and night I guarded the pearl of my soul.*
> *Now in this ocean of pearling currents,*
> *I've lost track of which was mine.*

When we live in awareness, we live in love. The loving awareness we cherish is not a distant fragrance, a treasure found only after an arduous journey. It is not a treasure that we have to fight for or protect. As the musk deer realized at his death, the beauty we long for is already here. By relaxing our stories of "who we are taking ourselves to be," by stepping wakefully into just this moment, we see that nothing is missing, nothing is outside this ocean of pearling currents.

Although we drift on the path and lose sight of our essential being, remembering what we love guides us back to sacred presence. *The Tibetan Book of the Dead* offers the deepest reassurance: "Remember these teachings, remember the clear light, the shining light of your own nature. No matter where or how far you wander, the light is only a split second, a half a breath, away. It is never too late to recognize the clear light of your pure awareness." We can trust the awareness and love that are our true home. When we get lost we need only pause, look at what is true, relax our heart and arrive again. This is the essence of Radical Acceptance.

Guided Meditation: Who Am I?

The fundamental question in most spiritual traditions is, who am I? The Tibetan Buddhist practice of *dzogchen* ("the great perfection") is direct training in how to realize our true nature. Before exploring the following version of dzogchen, it is best to take some time relaxing and quieting the mind. You might do a body scan (see p. 123) or vipassana meditation (see p. 46). While thoughts and emotions will naturally continue to arise during dzogchen, this practice is best initiated when emotions are not intense. An ideal setting to try this in is one where you can look directly at the open sky or at a view that is not distracting. It is also fine to look out a window, at a blank wall or at the open space of a room.

Sit comfortably in a way that allows you to feel both alert and relaxed. With your eyes open, rest your gaze on a point slightly above your line of sight. Soften your eyes so that your gaze is unfocused and you are also receiving images on the periphery of your vision. Relax the flesh around your eyes and let your brow be smooth.

Looking at the sky or imagining a clear blue sky, let your awareness mingle with that boundless space. Allow your mind to be wide-open—relaxed and spacious. Take some moments to listen to sounds, noticing how they are happening on their own. Rest in the awareness that includes even the most distant sounds.

In the same way that sounds are appearing and disappearing, allow sensations and emotions to arise and dissolve. Let your breath move easily, like a gentle breeze. Be aware of thoughts drifting through like passing clouds. Rest in an open and undis-

tracted awareness, noticing the changing display of sounds, sensations, feelings and thoughts.

When you realize your mind inevitably fixates on a particular thought—on a judgment or mental comment, an image or story—gently look into awareness to recognize the source of thinking. Inquire: "Who is thinking?" Or you might ask, "What is thinking?" or, "Who is aware right now?" Glance back into awareness with a light touch—simply taking a look to see who is thinking.

What do you notice? Is there any "thing" or "self" you perceive that is static, solid or enduring? Is there an entity that exists apart from the changing stream of feelings, sensations or thoughts? What actually do you see when you look into awareness? Is there any boundary or center to your experience? Are you aware of being aware? The entire net of thoughts, wants and fears is full of holes. As you look beyond it, you begin to see that all of life is arising from and dissolving into awareness.

Let go and relax fully into the sea of wakefulness. Let go and let be, allowing life to unfold naturally in awareness. Rest in nondoing, in undistracted awareness. When the mind fixates again on thoughts, look back into awareness, to see the source of thinking. And then let go and let be. With each instance of releasing the grip of thoughts, be sure to relax completely. Discover the freedom of wakefully relaxing, of letting life be, as it is. Look and see, let go and be free.

If sensations or emotions call your attention, look back into awareness in the same way, asking who is feeling hot or tired or afraid. However if they are in any way strong or compelling, instead of turning toward awareness, bring an accepting and kind attention directly to the experience. You might feel the grip of fear, for instance, and use the breath to reconnect with openness and tenderness. (See tonglen instructions on page 243.) When you are able again to relate to your experience with equanimity and compassion, resume the practice of dzogchen, resting in awareness.

Often in the wake of these strong emotions, it is common to find that the impression of a "ghost self" remains—a self who is holding the fear or hurt with compassion. If you sense this, inquire, "Who is being compassionate?" and look into awareness. Then let go into what is seen. Let go into selfless awareness, into emptiness suffused with compassion.

The natural arising of emotions is a profound opportunity to experience how the natural expression of awareness is love. Here the practice of dzogchen, looking into awareness and tonglen interweave.

It is important that we practice dzogchen in an easy and effortless way, not contracting the mind by striving to do it right. To avoid creating stress, it is best to limit practice to five- to ten-minute intervals. You might do short periods of formal practice a number of times a day. As an informal practice, take a few moments, whenever you remember, to look into awareness and see what is true. Then let go and let be.

ACKNOWLEDGMENTS

Writing *Radical Acceptance* has been one of the great lessons in how we don't own anything, much less a creative process. The kindness and intelligence and generosity of many dear ones have streamed together to birth this book.

I begin with Shoshana Alexander because her editorial midwifing and loving friendship supported me every step of the way. Shoshana helped me understand what I wanted to say and then guided me in how best to say it. A gifted writer and longtime dharma practitioner, she was one of the finest teachers I could have encountered in taking on this project.

From the first day I confided in Jack Kornfield that I wanted to write this book, he has offered steadfast support and encouragement. A wonderful mentor and friend, Jack's compassionate vision and confidence in me and this book have been an ongoing source of nourishment.

Heartfelt thanks to my Bantam editor, Toni Burbank, who is simply the best! It has been a rare privilege to have the guidance of one so skilled and so deep in her wisdom and humanity. My deepest gratitude to my agent, Anne Edelstein, for her brightness, good humor and warmth; for walking me through with such a reassuring, trustworthy hand. And my appreciation to my publicist, Anita Halton, for her steadiness and intelligence and belief in this book.

I have great appreciation for those who read the chapters at various stages in the book's unfolding and offered me feedback. Special thanks to Joseph Goldstein, my sister Darshan Brach, my brother Peter Brach, my parents Nancy and Bill Brach, my friends Tarn Singh, Carolyn Klamp, and Doug Klamp. And to Alice and Stephen Josephs, who read through the entire manuscript, giving so many hours of their bright minds and caring hearts. My everlasting gratitude to my sister Betsy Brach, who didn't read the chapters because she was so busy doing ten million other favors for me.

So many others have helped in so many ways. Thanks to Barbara Gates for her clarity and enthusiasm in helping to prepare my proposal; to Rebecca Cardozo, for such painstaking dedication in getting permissions; to Barbara Graham, who offered her editorial talent as well as her experience in the world of publishing to support me through these writing years. My gratitude also to Tim Kinney, who offered many hours of help with artistic design, and to Melanie Milgram, whose competence and warmth made working with Bantam smooth and easy. Sharon Salzberg took me under her wing in so many ways. She and her assistant, Gyano Gibson, both offered invaluable guidance and sisterly support. I honor the power of Focusing (www.focusing.org), and found with my focusing partner, Mary Hendrix, a beautiful blossoming of Radical Acceptance. And to each of my friends, too many to name, who helped me with creative consults, thank you.

I owe deep gratitude to my clients, to the Insight Meditation community of Washington, and to my global sangha of students and friends—I cherish feeling our togetherness on this sacred path. This book would not exist without your stories and inspiration. And to all my teachers, to all the compassionate Beings who have passed on the ancient truths and practices, I bow with love and gratitude.

Finally, it is my great good fortune to have family and friends who forgave my long absences and inattention, and continued through these last years to hold me with unconditional affection. To each of you, my deepest thanks. And to my dear friend, Alex, and beloved son, Narayan, bless you for being there always.

SOURCES AND PERMISSIONS

p.xi Rumi, Jalal Al-Din. "Out beyond ideas of wrongdoing and rightdoing," from THE ESSENTIAL RUMI by Coleman Barks. Copyright © 1995 by Coleman Barks. Reprinted by the permission of the author.

p.xx Berry, Wendell. "Do Not Be Ashamed," from THE SELECTED POEMS OF WENDELL BERRY by Wendell Berry. Copyright © 1998 by Wendell Berry. Reprinted by permission of Counterpoint Press, a member of Perseus Books, L.L.C.

p.24 Machado, Antonio. "Last night, as I was sleeping," from TIMES ALONE: SELECTED POEMS OF ANTONIO MACHADO, translated by Robert Bly. Copyright © 1983. Reprinted by permission of Wesleyan University Press.

p.36 Rumi, Jalal Al-Din. "Don't turn away," from THE ESSENTIAL RUMI by Coleman Barks. Copyright © 1995 by Coleman Barks. Reprinted by the permission of the author.

p.49 "Enough," from WHERE MANY RIVERS MEET by David Whyte. Copyright © 1990 by David Whyte. Used by permission of the author and Many Rivers Press.

p.73 Rumi, Jalal Al-Din. "This being human is a guest house," from THE ESSENTIAL RUMI by Coleman Barks. Copyright © 1995 by Coleman Barks. Reprinted by the permission of the author.

p.85 Brown, Ed. Pillsbury Biscuits story, excerpt from *Shambhala Sun* magazine, Copyright © July 1994. Permission granted by *Shambhala Sun*.

p.98 Excerpt from DIAMOND HEART: BOOK THREE—BEING AND THE MEANING OF LIFE by A. H. Almaas, © 1990 by A. Hameed Ali. Reprinted by arrangement with Shambhala Publications, Inc., Boston, www.shambhala.com.

p.121 Keyes, Roger. "Hokusai Says." Reprinted by permission of the author.

p.128 Rumi, Jalal Al-Din. "The urgent way lovers want each other" from THE ESSENTIAL RUMI by Coleman Barks. Copyright © 1995 by Coleman Barks. Reprinted by the permission of the author.

p.155 "A strange passion is moving in my head," from LOVE POEMS OF RUMI by Deepak Chopra, M.D., copyright © 1998 by Deepak Chopra, M.D. Used by permission of Harmony Books, a division of Random House, Inc.

p.193 "Tenth Elegy," from THE SELECTED POETRY OF RAINER MARIA RILKE by Rainer Maria Rilke, translated by Stephen Mitchell, copyright © 1982 by Stephen Mitchell. Used by permission of Random House, Inc.

p.198 Rumi, Jalal Al-Din. "God created the child, that is, your wanting," from THE ESSENTIAL RUMI by Coleman Barks. Copyright © 1995 by Coleman Barks. Reprinted by the permission of the author.

p.194 "Fourth Elegy," from THE SELECTED POETRY OF RAINER MARIA RILKE by Rainer Maria Rilke, translated by Stephen Mitchell, copyright © 1982 by Stephen Mitchell. Used by permission of Random House, Inc.

p.209 "Ich bete wieder, du Erlauchter/ I am praying again," from RILKE'S BOOK OF HOURS: LOVE POEMS TO GOD by Rainer Maria Rilke, translated by Anita Barrows and Joanna Macy, copyright © 1996 by Anita Barrows and Joanna Macy. Used by permission of Riverhead Books, an imprint of Penguin Putnam Inc.

p.212 "Absolutely Clear," from THE SUBJECT TONIGHT IS LOVE, by Daniel Ladinsky. Copyright © 1996 by Daniel Ladinsky. Reprinted by permission of the author.

p.215 "A Potted Plant," from THE SUBJECT TONIGHT IS LOVE, by Daniel Ladinsky. Copyright © 1996 by Daniel Ladinsky. Reprinted by permission of the author.

p.221 "Ich lebe mein Leben /I live my life in widening," from RILKE'S BOOK OF HOURS: LOVE POEMS TO GOD by Rainer Maria Rilke, translated by Anita Barrows and Joanna Macy, copyright © 1996 by Anita Barrows and Joanna Macy. Used by permission of Riverhead Books, an imprint of Penguin Putnam Inc.

p.233 Excerpt from "Kindness," from THE WORDS UNDER THE WORDS: SELECTED POEMS by Naomi Shihab Nye, copyright © 1995. Reprinted with the permission of Far Corner Books.

p.239 "It Happens All the Time in Heaven," from THE SUBJECT TONIGHT IS LOVE, by Daniel Ladinsky. Copyright © 1996 by Daniel Ladinsky. Reprinted by permission of the author.

p.240 Lawless, Gary. "When the animals come to us." From EARTH PRAYERS FROM AROUND THE WORLD, 365 PRAYERS, POEMS, AND INVOCATIONS FOR HONORING THE EARTH, Copyright © 1991 by Elizabeth Roberts and Elias Amidon. Reprinted by permission of the author.

p.256 "We sense that there is some sort of spirit," from THE KABIR BOOK by Robert Bly. Copyright © 1971, 1977 by Robert Bly. © 1977 by the Seventies Press. Reprinted by permission of the Beacon Press, Boston.

p.265 Excerpt from THE COCKTAIL PARTY, copyright 1950 by T. S. Eliot and renewed by Esme Valerie Eliot, reprinted by permission of Harcourt, Inc. and of Faber and Faber Ltd. (UK).

p.283 Rumi, Jalal Al-Din. "Stay together, friends," from THE ESSENTIAL RUMI by Coleman Barks. Copyright © 1995 by Coleman Barks. Reprinted by the permission of the author.

p.321 "Well of Grief," from WHERE MANY RIVERS MEET by David Whyte. Copyright © 1990 by David Whyte. Used by permission of the author and Many Rivers Press.

p.324 Rumi, Jalal Al-Din. "I am water. I am the thorn," from THE ESSENTIAL RUMI by Coleman Barks. Copyright © 1995 by Coleman Barks. Reprinted by the permission of the author.

PHOTO: JONATHAN FOUST

ABOUT THE AUTHOR

TARA BRACH, PH.D., is a clinical psychologist, lecturer and workshop leader, as well as the founder and senior teacher of the Insight Meditation Community of Washington. She has been practicing meditation since 1975 and leads Buddhist meditation retreats at centers throughout North America. She is also a cofounder of the Washington Buddhist Peace Fellowship. Tara lives in Maryland, with her son, Narayan, their standard poodle, and two cats.

For more information about Tara Brach's tapes and her teaching schedule, please contact:

Insight Meditation Community of Washington
P.O. Box 18143
Washington, D.C. 20036

Or visit:
www.imcw.org